The Reenchantment of Science

SUNY SERIES IN
CONSTRUCTIVE POSTMODERN THOUGHT
DAVID RAY GRIFFIN, EDITOR

THE

REENCHANTMENT
OF
SCIENCE

Postmodern Proposals

DAVID RAY GRIFFIN, *Editor*

STATE UNIVERSITY OF NEW YORK PRESS

Published by
State University of New York Press, Albany

For information, address State University of New York
Press, State University Plaza, Albany, N.Y., 12246

Library of Congress Cataloging in Publication Data

The Reenchantment of science : postmodern proposals / edited by David
Ray Griffin.
p.   cm. — (SUNY series in constructive postmodern thought)
Includes index.
Contents: The cosmic creation story / Brian Swimme — Postmodern
science and a postmodern world / David Bohm — The postmodern
challenge to biology / Charles Birch — The laws of nature as habits
/ Rupert Sheldrake — Religious world modeling and postmodern
science / Frederick Ferré — Ecology, science, and religion / John
B. Cobb, Jr. — The postmodern heresy—consciousness as causal /
Willis W. Harman — Parapsychology and postmodern science / Stanley
Krippner — Of minds and molecules / David Ray Griffin.
ISBN 0-88706-784-0.   ISBN 0-88706-785-9 (pbk.)
1. Science—Philosophy. 2. Science—Social aspects. 3. Religion
and science—1946- I. Griffin, David Ray, 1939- . II. Series.
Q175.R3919 1988   87-30692
501–dc19   CIP

10 9 8 7 6 5 4 3 2 1

for Ann

CONTENTS

INTRODUCTION TO SUNY SERIES IN CONSTRUCTIVE POSTMODERN THOUGHT

The rapid spread of the term *postmodern* in recent years witnesses to a growing dissatisfaction with modernity and to an increasing sense that the modern age not only had a beginning but can have an end as well. Whereas the word *modern* was almost always used until quite recently as a word of praise and as a synonym for *contemporary*, a growing sense is now evidenced that we can and should leave modernity behind—in fact, that we *must* if we are to avoid destroying ourselves and most of the life on our planet.

Modernity, rather than being regarded as the norm for human society toward which all history has been aiming and into which all societies should be ushered—forcibly if necessary—is instead increasingly seen as an aberration. A new respect for the wisdom of traditional societies is growing as we realize that they have endured for thousands of years and that, by contrast, the existence of modern society for even another century seems doubtful. Likewise, *modernism* as a worldview is less and less seen as The Final Truth, in comparison with which all divergent worldviews are automatically regarded as "superstitious." The modern worldview is increasingly relativized to the status of one among many, useful for some purposes, inadequate for others.

Although there have been antimodern movements before, beginning perhaps near the outset of the nineteenth century with the Romanticists and the Luddites, the rapidity with which the term *postmodern* has become widespread in our time suggests that the antimodern sentiment is more extensive and intense than before, and also that it includes the sense that modernity can be successfully overcome only by going beyond it, not by attempt-

ix

ing to return to a premodern form of existence. Insofar as a common element is found in the various ways in which the term is used, *postmodernism* refers to a diffuse sentiment rather than to any common set of doctrines— the sentiment that humanity can and must go beyond the modern.

Beyond connoting this sentiment, the term *postmodern* is used in a confusing variety of ways, some of them contradictory to others. In artistic and literary circles, for example, postmodernism shares in this general sentiment but also involves a specific reaction against "modernism" in the narrow sense of a movement in artistic-literary circles in the late nineteenth and early twentieth centuries. Postmodern architecture is very different from postmodern literary criticism. In some circles, the term *postmodern* is used in reference to that potpourri of ideas and systems sometimes called *new age metaphysics*, although many of these ideas and systems are more premodern than postmodern. Even in philosophical and theological circles, the term *postmodern* refers to two quite different positions, one of which is reflected in this series. Each position seeks to transcend both *modernism* in the sense of the worldview that has developed out of the seventeenth-century Galilean-Cartesian-Baconian-Newtonian science, and *modernity* in the sense of the world order that both conditioned and was conditioned by this worldview. But the two positions seek to transcend the modern in different ways.

Closely related to literary–artistic postmodernism is a philosophical postmodernism inspired variously by pragmatism, physicalism, Ludwig Wittgenstein, Martin Heidegger, and Jacques Derrida and other recent French thinkers. By the use of terms that arise out of particular segments of this movement, it can be called *deconstructive* or *eliminative postmodernism*. It overcomes the modern worldview through an anti-worldview: it deconstructs or eliminates the ingredients necessary for a worldview, such as God, self, purpose, meaning, a real world, and truth as correspondence. While motivated in some cases by the ethical concern to forestall totalitarian systems, this type of postmodern thought issues in relativism, even nihilism. It could also be called *ultramodernism*, in that its eliminations result from carrying modern premises to their logical conclusions.

The postmodernism of this series can, by contrast, be called *constructive* or *revisionary*. It seeks to overcome the modern worldview not by eliminating the possibility of worldviews as such, but by constructing a postmodern worldview through a revision of modern premises and traditional concepts. This constructive or revisionary postmodernism involves a new unity of scientific, ethical, aesthetic, and religious intuitions. It rejects not science as such but only that scientism in which the data of the modern natural sciences are alone allowed to contribute to the construction of our worldview.

The constructive activity of this type of postmodern thought is not limited to a revised worldview; it is equally concerned with a postmodern world that will support and be supported by the new worldview. A postmodern world will involve postmodern persons, with a postmodern spirituality, on the one hand, and a postmodern society, ultimately a post-modern global order, on the other. Going beyond the modern world will involve transcending its individualism, anthropocentrism, patriarchy, mechanization, economism, consumerism, nationalism, and militarism. Constructive postmodern thought provides support for the ecology, peace, feminist and other emancipatory movements of our time, while stressing that the inclusive emancipation must be from modernity itself. The term *postmodern*, however, by contrast with *premodern*, emphasizes that the modern world has produced unparalleled advances that must not be lost in a general revulsion against its negative features.

From the point of view of deconstructive postmodernists, this con-structive postmodernism is still hopelessly wedded to outdated concepts, because it wishes to salvage a positive meaning not only for the notions of the human self, historical meaning, and truth as correspondence, which were central to modernity, but also for premodern notions of a divine reality, cosmic meaning, and an enchanted nature. From the point of view of its advocates, however, this revisionary postmodernism is not only more ade-quate to our experience but also more genuinely postmodern. It does not simply carry the premises of modernity through to their logical conclusions, but criticizes and revises those premises. Through its return to organicism and its acceptance of nonsensory perception, it opens itself to the recovery of truths and values from various forms of premodern thought and practice that had been dogmatically rejected by modernity. This constructive, revis-ionary postmodernism involves a creative synthesis of modern and pre-modern truths and values.

This series does not seek to create a movement so much as to help shape and support an already existing movement convinced that modern-ity can and must be transcended. But those antimodern movements which arose in the past failed to deflect or even retard the onslaught of modern-ity. What reasons can we have to expect the current movement to be more successful? First, the previous antimodern movements were primarily calls to return to a premodern form of life and thought rather than calls to ad-vance, and the human spirit does not rally to calls to turn back. Second, the previous antimodern movements either rejected modern science, reduced it to a description of mere appearances, or assumed its adequacy in princi-ple; therefore, they could base their calls only on the negative social and spiritual effects of modernity. The current movement draws on natural science itself as a witness against the adequacy of the modern worldview. In the third place, the present movement has even more evidence than did previous movements of the ways in which modernity and its worldview *are* socially and spiritually destructive. The fourth and probably most decisive difference is that the present movement is based on the awareness that *the continuation of modernity threatens the very survival of life on our planet*. This awareness, combined with the growing knowledge of the interdependence of the modern worldview and the militarism, nuclearism, and ecological devastation of the modern world, is providing an unprecedented impetus for people to see the evidence for a postmodern worldview and to envisage postmodern ways of relating to each other, the rest of nature, and the cosmos as a whole. For these reasons, the failure of the previous antimodern movements says little about the possible success of the current movement.

Advocates of this movement do not hold the naively utopian belief that the success of this movement would bring about a global society of universal and lasting peace, harmony, and happiness, in which all spiritual problems, social conflicts, ecological destruction, and hard choices would vanish. There is, after all, surely a deep truth in the testimony of the world's religions to the presence of a transcultural proclivity to evil deep within the human heart, which no new paradigm, combined with a new economic order, new child-rearing practices, or any other social arrangements, will suddenly eliminate. Furthermore, it has correctly been said that "life is robbery": a strong element of competition is inherent within finite existence, which no social-political-economic-ecological order can overcome. These two truths, especially when contemplated together, should caution us against unrealistic hopes.

However, no such appeal to "universal constants" should reconcile us to the present order, as if this order were thereby uniquely legitimated. The human proclivity to evil in general, and to conflictual competition and ecological destruction in particular, can be greatly exacerbated or greatly mitigated by a world order and its worldview. Modernity exacerbates it about as much as imaginable. We can therefore envision, without being naively utopian, a far better world order, with a far less dangerous trajectory, than the one we now have.

This series, making no pretense of neutrality, is dedicated to the success of this movement toward a postmodern world.

David Ray Griffin
Series Editor

PREFACE

The postmodern world this series advocates involves a new science, a new spirituality, and a new society.

The full flowering of each of these dimensions will presuppose, and be presupposed by, the others. A reenchanted, liberating science will be fully developed only by people with a postmodern spirituality, in which the dualisms that have made modern science such an ambiguous phenomenon have been transcended, and only in a society organized for the good of the planet as a whole. Likewise, relational, ecological, planetary, postpatriarchal spirituality will only become dominant in the context of a postmodern society and with the support of a postmodern science. Finally, no possibility exists for the emergence of a society in which individualism, nationalism, militarism, anthropocentrism, and androcentrism have been transcended apart from the widespread acceptance of a postmodern science and the emergence of a postmodern spirituality.

This mutual interdependence of science, spirituality, and social order does not, however, make change necessarily an all-or-nothing affair. Because of the capacity of the human spirit partially to transcend the given conditions in imagination and sensibility, a postmodern science and spirituality can be considerably developed in a social order that is still overwhelmingly modern. And, although most attempts to develop an alternative form of community have proved short-lived in the context of a larger social order in which modern ideology and values are incessantly promulgated, a postmodern society can to some extent be *envisaged*. In other words, because theory can outstrip practice, and individual and communal spirituality can transcend that of the larger social order, the mutual interdependence of science, spirituality, and social order is not absolute. New developments can occur at different rates in the three dimensions. For example, whereas a new science presupposes a new spirituality and a new society, these latter may at first be realized not in the habits of the psychophysical organisms and the body politic, but only in the imagination of an individual or small community.

Whereas the partial autonomy of science, spirituality, and society makes this series possible, their interdependence makes the first two volumes presuppose each other. Volume 1, which deals with science, is presupposed by Volume 2, which focuses on spirituality and society, because those new visions of spirituality and society build importantly upon the new type of science which is emerging. But the first volume presupposes the second equally, because the new science is being developed in part out of the new spirituality and the hunger for a new social order which are emerging. Accordingly, although I did attempt to make the introduction to Volume 1 somewhat foundational for the series (as shown by its excessive length), I would encourage those readers for whom spirituality and social order are more immediate concerns to begin with Volume 2, entitled *Spirituality and Society: Postmodern Visions.*

The essays by Brian Swimme, Charles Birch, Willis Harman, and Stanley Krippner were prepared for a conference, "Toward a Postmodern World," held in Santa Barbara, California, in January 1987 and sponsored by the Center for a Postmodern World and the Center for Process Studies. (These centers are described in the "Notes on Contributors and Centers.") Neither these essays, nor those by David Bohm, Rupert Sheldrake, and John Cobb, have been previously published. Bohm's is based on a lecture he gave for the Center for a Postmodern World in March 1984, while Cobb's was originally delivered in April 1982 at a conference on ecology and religion at Hendrix College in Conway, Arkansas, which was cosponsored by the Marshall T. Steel Center of that college; the Meadowcreek Project at Fox, Arkansas; and the Center for Process Studies. Sheldrake's essay was solicited in 1986 for a then only vaguely conceived volume. Frederick Ferré's essay, "Religious World Modeling and Postmodern Science," was originally published in the *Journal of Religion*, Volume 62, number 2, July 1982 (1982 by the University of Chicago, ISSN 0022–4189), and is reprinted here with the permission of the author and the publisher in slightly edited form. My own essay was previously published under the title, "Of Minds and Molecules: Medicine in a Psychosomatic Universe," in Marcus P. Ford, ed., *A Process Theory of Medicine: Interdisciplinary Essays* (Lewiston, N.Y.: Edwin Mellen Press, 1987), and is reprinted here with the permission of the editor and the publisher in slightly edited form.

This volume is dedicated to my wife, Ann Jaqua, who suggested the title, and who provided much good advice with regard to the introductions. I also received helpful advice on both introductions from several of the contributors, especially John Cobb, Stanley Krippner, and Brian Swimme, and from several members of the Center for a Postmodern World in Santa Barbara, for which I am most grateful. I wish to express special thanks to the secretaries at the School of Theology at Claremont, especially Geneva Villegas and Leslie Brown, who spent far more hours than I could have staring at the screen of a computer—one of those modern contraptions without which life would now seem impossible. For the time off to begin this series,

I am indebted to the Trustees and President Richard C. Cain of the School of Theology at Claremont, and to Nancy Howell, through whose efficiency and assumption of extra burdens I have been freed from my usual responsibilities at the Center for Process Studies for one year. Finally, this series has only become a reality because of the enthusiasm of William Eastman of the State University of New York Press, with whom it is a delight to work.

1

INTRODUCTION: THE REENCHANTMENT OF SCIENCE

David Ray Griffin

At the root of modernity and its discontents lies what Max Weber called "the disenchantment of the world." This disenchanted worldview has been both a result and a presupposition of modern science and has almost unanimously been assumed to be a result and a presupposition of science as such. What is distinctive about "modern" philosophy, theology, and art is that they revolve around numerous strategies for maintaining moral, religious, and aesthetic sensitivities while accepting the disenchanted worldview of modernity as adequate for science. These strategies have involved either rejecting modern science, ignoring it, supplementing it with talk of human values, or reducing its status to that of mere appearance. The postmodern approach to disenchantment involves a reenchantment of science itself. The essays herein reflect some of the dimensions that would be involved in a reenchanted science. This introduction positions these essays by showing how they imply a reversal of the modern disenchantment of science and nature and how this reversal fits within the larger contemporary reassessment of natural science.

1

The first section explains the relationship between the mechanistic philosophy underlying modern science and the process of disenchantment. The second section shows the way a variety of recent developments in the philosophy, sociology, psychology, and history of science, as well as science itself, are converging to undermine the modern basis for disenchantment. The third section explains some of the central ideas of the postmodern organismic philosophy which underlies most of the essays in this volume.

I. MODERN SCIENCE AND THE DISENCHANTMENT OF THE WORLD

In disenchanting nature, the modern science of nature led to its own disenchantment. This happened because the mechanistic, disenchanted philosophy of nature, which was originally part of a dualistic and theistic vision of reality as a whole, eventually led to the disenchantment of the whole world. This first section spells out this development.

What does the "disenchantment of nature" mean? Most fundamentally, it means the denial to nature of all subjectivity, all experience, all feeling. Because of this denial, nature is disqualified—it is denied all qualities that are not thinkable apart from experience.

These qualities are legion. Without experience, no aims or purposes can exist in natural entities, no creativity in the sense of self-determination or final causation. With no final causation toward some ideal possibility, no role exists for ideals, possibilities, norms, or values to play: causation is strictly a matter of efficient causation from the past. With no self-determination aimed at the realization of ideals, no value can be achieved. With no experience, even unconscious feeling, there can be no value received: the causal interactions between natural things or events involve no sharing of values. Hence, no intrinsic value can exist within nature, no value of natural things for themselves. Also, unlike the way our experience is internally affected, even constituted in part, by its relations with its environment, material particles can have no internal relations. Along with no internalization of other natural things, no internalization of divinity can occur. Friedrich Schiller, who spoke of the disenchantment of nature a century before Weber, used the term *Entgotterung*, which literally means the dedivinization of nature. Deity, for the founders of the modern worldview, such as Descartes, Boyle, and Newton, was in no way immanent in the world; it was a being wholly external to the world who imposed motion and laws upon it from without. The laws of nature were, hence, not at all analogous to sociological laws which reflect the habits of the members of human society. A further and in fact central feature of the disenchantment of nature was the denial of action at a distance. Weber's term for disenchantment was *Entzauberung*, which literally means "taking the magic out." It was at the heart of the mechanistic vision to deny that natural things had any hidden ("occult") powers to attract other things (a denial that made the phenomena of magnetism and gravitation very difficult to explain).[1] In these ways, nature was bereft of all qualities with which the human spirit could feel a sense of kinship and of anything from which it could derive norms. Human life was rendered both alien and autonomous.

Whereas this disenchantment of nature was originally carried out (by Galileo, Descartes, Boyle, and Newton & Company) in the framework of a dualistic supernaturalism in which the soul and a personal deity were assigned explanatory functions and hence causal power, the successes of the objectifying, mechanistic, reductionistic approach in physics soon led to the conviction that it should be applied to all of reality. God was at first stripped of all causal power beyond that of the original creation of the world; later thinkers turned this deism into complete atheism. The human soul or mind was at first said to be "epiphenomenal," which meant that it was real but only as an effect, not as a cause; later thinkers, believing nature should have no idle wheels, denied that it was a distinct entity at all, declaring it to be simply one of the brain's emergent properties. In those ways, the "animistic" viewpoint, which attributes causality to personal forces, was completely rejected. All "downward causation" from personal to impersonal processes was eliminated; the reductionistic program of explaining everything in terms of elementary impersonal processes was fully accepted. The world as a whole was thus disenchanted. This disenchanted view means that experience plays no real role not only in "the natural world" but in the world as a whole. Hence, no role exists in the universe for purposes, values, ideals, possibilities, and qualities, and there is no freedom, creativity, temporality, or divinity. There are no norms, not even truth, and everything is ultimately meaningless.

The ironic conclusion is that modern science, in disenchanting nature, began a trajectory that ended by disenchanting science itself. If all human life is meaningless, then science, as one of its activities, must share in this meaninglessness. For some time, many held that science at least gives us the truth, even if a bleak one. Much recent thought, however, has concluded that science does not even give us that. The disenchantment is complete.

The main point to emphasize is that modern thinkers have assumed that this disenchantment of the world is *required by science itself*. A few examples: just as Darwin felt that any "caprice" in the world would make science impossible, so that both divine and free human activity had to be eliminated from our worldview,[2] so Michael Ghiselin, a contemporary Darwinian, says that to deny the ideal of predictive determinism by affirming teleological causation "is to opt out of science altogether."[3] Jacques Monod says:

> The cornerstone of the scientific method is the postulate that nature is objective. In other words, the *systematic* denial that 'true' knowledge can be got at by interpreting phenomena in terms of final causes—

that is to say, of 'purpose'. . . . [T]he postulate of objectivity is consubstantial with science. . . . There is no way to be rid of it, even tentatively or in a limited area, without departing from the domain of science itself.[4]

While recognizing that the objectivist view of the world outrages our values and forces us to live in an alien world, Monod nevertheless insists that we must adopt it, because all "animist" views, which make us feel at home in nature by attributing purpose to it, are "fundamentally *hostile* to science."[5]

"So-called purposive behavior," said behaviorist psychologist Clark Hull, is to be regarded as a secondary, epiphenomenal reality, derivative from "more elementary objective primary principles."[6] Likewise, B. F. Skinner argues that psychology must follow physics and biology in rejecting "personified causes," and that to be "natural" is to be completely determined by one's environment. From the viewpoint of "the science of behavior," says Skinner, the notion of the "autonomous," which "initiates, originates and creates," is the notion of the "miraculous." He adds: "A scientific analysis of behavior dispossesses autonomous man and turns the control he has been said to exert over to the environment."[7] Whereas this statement suggests that determinism is a *result* of the application of the scientific approach, Skinner had earlier revealed that it is a *presupposition*: "We cannot apply the methods of science to a subject matter which is assumed to move about capriciously. . . . The hypothesis that man is not free is essential to the application of scientific method to the study of human behavior."[8]

While Hull and Skinner come from a previous generation, and advocated a behaviorist psychology which is now widely rejected, William Uttal is a contemporary psychobiologist. He says that reductionism, according to which all the activities of the mind are reducible to the most elementary levels of organization of matter, is "the foundation upon which the entire science of psychobiology is built." To introduce any definition of consciousness that goes beyond the operations used in surgery and the behavioral laboratory would mean "a total collapse into prescientific modes of thought."[9]

The idea that science requires a reductionistic account, and rules out all downward causation from personal causes and all action at a distance, is illustrated by the treatment of apparent parapsychological phenomena by physicist John Taylor. After studying several people who he had come to believe had the psychokinetic power to bend metal without touching it, he published a book entitled *Superminds*, complete with supporting photographs. [10] However, after deciding later that no explanation was to be found for psychokinetic effects within the scientific worldview, he wrote a second book called *Science and the Supernatural* in which he declared that no such events can occur. Although he still believed that there was good evidence for psychokinetic events, and admitted that he could not explain how the particular events he had witnessed could have been faked, he concluded that all such reports must be due to hallucination, trickery, credulity, the fear of death, and the like. "Such an explanation is the only one which seems to fit in with a scientific view of the world."[11] The reasoning behind this conclusion was as follows: First, scientific explanation can only be in materialistic terms; if anything, such as the human mind, could not be explained in quantitative, materialistic terms, then the scientist would have to choose between silence and irrationality.[12] Second, according to "the scientific viewpoint," all explanation must be in terms of the four forces of physics. Third, none of these forces can explain psychokinesis. Therefore, he says, we must believe that no genuine psychokinesis occurs. Taylor concludes by castigating himself and other scientists for having seriously investigated "phenomena which their scientific education should indicate are impossible."[13]

This idea that the very nature of science rules out the scientific study of anything not understandable in materialistic terms has in our century probably been more prevalent in fields other than physics. James Alcock, a social psychologist, says that a "spiritual science," which parapsychology is sometimes said to be, is a contradiction in terms. "How can a science of the spirit exist, given that science is by its very nature materialistic?"[14]

Besides ruling out purpose, freedom, personal causation, and any non-materialistic interactions from the scientific account of nature, the dominant viewpoint has even eliminated temporality. Ilya Prigogine regards the fact that modern science has been nontemporal as the root of the cleavage between the "two cultures" (C. P. Snow) of science and the humanities.[15] This elimination of temporality has been supported by many twentieth-century physicists, including Albert Einstein, who said: "For us believing physicists, the distinction between past, present and future is only an illusion, even if a stubborn one."[16] A contemporary physicist, P. C. W. Davies, spells out the implied dualism between objective nature and subjectivity:

> The notion that time flows in a one-way fashion is a property of our consciousness. It is a subjective phenomenon and is a property that simply cannot be demonstrated in the natural world. This is an incontrovertible lesson from modern science. . . . A flowing time belongs to our mind, not to nature.[17]

A well-read physician, citing several physicists who endorse this view, says that we must assimilate it, in spite of the fact that it is an affront to common sense, because "we cannot ignore what modern physical science has revealed to us about the nature of time."[18]

As stated earlier, the final disenchantment of modern science is its conclusion that its own discoveries prove the meaninglessness of the whole universe, which must include the scientists and their science. Near the end of his popular book, *The First Three Minutes*, physicist Steven Weinberg says, "The more the universe seems comprehensible, the more it also seems pointless."[19]

I momentarily interrupt the recital of evidence to respond to a counter-argument that is probably growing in the mind of many readers. This is the argument that it is not the job of the scientist *qua* scientist to deal with the true nature of time and matter in themselves and with the question whether the universe is meaningful. These are the tasks, it could be argued, for metaphysicians and theologians, or for poets, whom Shelley called the "unacknowledged legislators of mankind." Hence, according to this argument, no need exists for a postmodern science; it is only necessary to point out the inherent limitations of science so that people will look elsewhere for answers to these larger questions. The problem with this solution is that the ideal of an "inherently limited science" does not work in practice. Science is inherently not only realistic, trying to describe the way things really are, but also imperialistic, bent on providing the only genuine description. The word *science*, after all, means *knowledge*; what is not vouchsafed by "science" is not considered knowledge in our culture. The cultural effect of modern science has been to make scientists the only "acknowledged legislators" of humankind, because its worldview has ruled out the possibility that metaphysics, theology, or poetry would have anything to add. Unless science itself is seen as giving a different answer, the disenchantment of the world will continue. With this brief apologia, I return to the topic.

Not only scientists themselves but also many philosophers have supported the view that science necessarily disenchants the world, proving that experience and those qualities that presuppose it are inoperative. D. M. Armstrong says that we have "general scientific grounds for thinking that man is nothing but a physical mechanism," that "mental states are, in fact, nothing but physical states of the central nervous system," so that we should be able to "give a complete account of man in purely physico-chemical terms."[20] In his 1956 preface to *The Modern Temper,* originally published in 1929, Joseph Wood Krutch summarized the book's thesis (with which he had later come to disagree):

> The universe revealed by science, especially the sciences of biology and psychology, is one in which the human spirit cannot find a comfortable home. That spirit breathes freely only in a universe where what philosophers call Value Judgements are of supreme importance. It needs to believe, for instance, that right and wrong are real, that Love is more than a biological function, that the human mind is capable of reason rather than merely of rationalization, and that it has the power to will and to choose instead of being compelled merely to react in the fashion predetermined by its conditioning. *Since science has proved that none of these beliefs is more than a delusion*, mankind will be compelled either to surrender what we call its humanity by ad-

justing to the real world or to live some kind of tragic existence in a universe alien to the deepest needs of its nature."[21]

Better known is the following purple passage from "A Free Man's Worship," in which Bertrand Russell summarizes "the world which Science presents for our belief":

> That Man is the product of causes which had no prevision of the end they were achieving; that his origin, his growth, his hopes and fears, his loves and beliefs, are but the outcome of accidental collocations of atoms; . . . that all the labours of the ages, all the devotion, all the inspiration, all the noonday brightness of human genius, are destined to extinction in the vast death of the solar system . . . —all these things, if not quite beyond dispute, are yet so nearly certain, that no philosophy which rejects them can hope to stand.[22]

The modern consensus then, as reflected in the preceding quotations, has been that science and disenchantment go hand in hand. On the one hand, it is assumed, science can only be applied to that which has already been disenchanted, which means deanimated.[23] To deanimate is to remove all anima or soul, in Plato's sense of a self-moving thing which determines itself, at least partly, in terms of its desire to realize particular values. On the other hand, it is assumed that the application of the scientific method to anything confirms the truth of the disenchanted view of it, that it can be adequately understood in purely impersonal terms, as embodying no creativity, no self-determination in terms of values or norms, and nothing that could be considered divine.

The only way to prevent the disenchantment of the universe as a whole, on this view, is to draw a line, usually between the human being as purposive agent and the rest of nature, above which the scientific method is said to be inapplicable. But any such essential dualism is undermined by several things: the fact that human behavior, including human experience, is subject to a great extent to causal analysis; the idea that we, like all other species, are products of the evolutionary process; the difficulty of understanding how a human mind, which operates in terms of reasons, purposes, or final causes, could interact with bodily parts operating strictly in terms of mechanistic causes; and the general pressure toward a unified approach to knowledge. Accordingly, the attempt to prevent total disenchantment by means of an essential dualism—between mind and matter, understanding and explanation, hermeneutics and science—[24] is difficult to maintain intellectually. Whereas all people live in terms of the conviction that they are more than behaviorism, sociobiology, and psychobiology allow, and may feel that the totally disenchanted approach to human beings is inappropriate, it has been extremely difficult to state these convictions and feelings in an intellectually defensible way. Besides thereby seeming to leave no alternative beyond antihumanitarianism or a humanitarianism based on an arbitrary choice, modern science also seems to alienate us from our bodies and from nature in general. Because it has disenchanted the world, many people have become disenchanted with science.

Others, however, have distinguished between *modern science*, which disenchants, and *science as such*, which may be open to reenchantment.

II. REVERSING DISENCHANTMENT: THE CONVERGING REASONS

During the twentieth century, while the disenchanting march of modernity has continued in most areas, a countermovement has been occurring in the philosophy, history, sociology, and psychology of science and in the sciences themselves. This movement, which has acquired great momentum in the latter half of the century, has cut the tie between science and disenchantment, thereby opening the way for the reenchantment of science. (While it might be thought improper to speak of the *re*enchantment of science on the assumption that science has from the beginning been disenchanted, there is now much evidence, some of which is presented in Section B and the works cited in its notes, that the dominant form of science throughout most of the sixteenth and seventeenth centuries *was* enchanted.)

There are four major reasons why the seemingly necessary connection between science and disenchantment is being broken: a new view of the nature of science, a new view of the origin of modern science, new developments within science itself, and reflections on the mind-body problem.

A. A New View of the Nature of Science

The conviction is growing that science is not a value-free enterprise or, to put it more precisely, that values other than the purely intellectual value of truth for its own sake, and that factors other than rational and empirical ones, essentially shape the worldview of the scientific community. Of course, it has long been recognized that the scientific community is composed of human beings, so that the same types of distortion, projection, power plays, and other nonrational factors operate in it as in other communities. But it was assumed, as classically formulated by Robert Merton, that science as a social system, in which these nonrational factors operate, can be separated from science as a cognitive system, which is governed by logic and empirical facts.[25] Science as a cognitive system was thought to be essentially value-free, except for those values that are internal to science itself, i.e., its distinctive way of pursuing truth. But now it is widely held that this separation is not possible and that the social factors affect science essentially, not just superficially. Rather than standing as an impartial tribunal of truth, transcendent over the battle field of competing social forces, science is seen as one more interested participant, using its status to legitimate certain social, political, and economic forces and to delegitimate others. More than that, the scientific community's interest in its own social power relative to other professions and institutions is now seen to condition the picture of the world it sanctions as "scientific."[26]

As alluded to above, the old view, according to which science seeks truth and nothing but truth and alone gives us truth, has been replaced in some circles by the opposite view, according to which science neither gives nor seeks truth. This extreme view (which is sometimes called *postmodernism* and is briefly discussed in the introduction to the series) is based upon a confluence of several notions. The recognition of the way our interpretations and even perceptions are conditioned by language, by culture in general, by the dominant worldview of the time, by personal (including unconscious) interests, and by interests based on race, gender, and social class—this recognition has led many to the conclusion that a worldview is wholly a construction or a projection, not at all a reflection or discovery of the way things "really" are.[27] Even the concern for truth, the very meaning of *truth*, and the criteria for determining truth, are sometimes seen as purely context-dependent.[28] These reflections based on language, psychology, and the "sociology of knowledge" are buttressed by philosophical doubts about whether there is a "given" (as opposed to a constructed) element in perception and whether the notion of truth as correspondence between idea and external reality is even meaningful.[29] Some or all of these notions, combined with the recognition that modern science has both sought and achieved power over nature, lead easily to the suggestion that this power, not truth, is science's aim and its achievement. The worldview of science is "true" in the sense and only in the sense, according to this view, that it works, i.e., that it is successful in terms of this particular interest.[30] Hence, it is not "true" for those who have never had, or who have rejected, this interest; it can accordingly be ignored by them. Other worldviews, based on equally legitimate interests, are equally valid.

However, this extreme view is no more satisfactory than the naive objectivism which it replaced. First, the valid facts upon which this extreme view is based do not require this view. Second, the view is so extreme as to be self-refuting: if we are unable to know the truth about how things are, then the "facts" on which this view is based cannot be true.[31] Third, this extreme view cannot command consent, because we cannot help but believe that the scientific theories that led (say) to effective immunizations against various diseases correspond in some very strong way to the physiological realities.[32]

Rejection of this extreme view does not require a return to the dominant modern view. Recognition that the scientific community seeks truth is fully compatible with the recognition that the truths it seeks are selected according to various interests and prejudices. Recognition that science has discovered a wide range of truths is compatible with the conviction that a wide range of truths it has *not* discovered exists, and that its formulations of the truths it *has* discovered are one-sided, presenting only abstractions from the full truth. Recognition that there must be some truth to the "modern scientific worldview," which supports and is supported by the select truths of modern science, is fully compatible with the view that other world-views exist that, all things considered, correspond equally well or even better to the full nature of reality.[33] Hence, we do not have to deny that science is capable of discovering truths and that it sometimes does so in order to recognize the various ways and enormous degrees to which the worldview, the methods, and the results of the scientific community at any time and place are products of extrascientific interests and prejudices.[34] It is this recognition that is the main point. It is freeing many people from the assumption that the modern disenchanted worldview is either proved or presupposed by science as such.

B. A New View of the Origin of Modern Science

The formal points in the previous section have been fleshed out by historians and sociologists who have been reexamining the origins of modern science. Three major conclusions have reversed long-held assumptions. First, the atheistic, materialistic worldview of today does not have behind it the authority of the seventeenth-century founders of modern science, such as Galileo, Mersenne, Descartes, Boyle, and Newton.[35] Their mechanistic view of nature was incorporated within a supernaturalistic and dualistic framework that was by no means incidental to them. Second, even this partially mechanistic view, in which (nonhuman) nature was viewed mechanistically, was not the context presupposed by many of the discoveries usually considered to lie at the root of modern science. Harvey was an Aristotelian, and Copernicus, Gilbert, and Newton thought in terms of a "magical" worldview, in which attraction at a distance was central. If good science has been done apart from mechanistic assumptions, they can hardly now be said to be requisite for good science.[36] Third, the mechanistic view of nature was adopted less for empirical than for theological, sociological, and political reasons. This third point, about the influence of extrascientific interests upon the modern scientific worldview, is a complex issue; a brief summary of a few of the illustrations provided by historians will have to suffice here.

One theological interest behind mechanism was the conviction, especially by Robert Boyle, that the divine excellency required that God be wholly transcendent, wholly external to nature, and that there be no self-movement in nature which could be taken to be divine.[37] The mechanistic view of nature was also used, for example by Boyle and Newton, to argue for the existence of God: if nature was devoid of self-motion, there had to be a supernatural being to have put it into motion and also to have imposed laws of motion upon it. Newton also argued that the mechanistic materialistic conception of matter, according to which it has no hidden powers and acts only by contact, shows the need for a cosmic spiritual being to explain the mutual attraction of bodies (gravitation) and the cohesiveness of atoms in solid bodies.[38] The mechanistic picture of the human body was used by Descartes, Boyle, and Locke to support the doctrine of an immortal soul: if the mortal, material body is composed of parts devoid of the power of self-motion, obviously something in us is different in kind from matter.[39] The defense of miracles was one of the main motives for mechanism. The Hermetic, Cabalistic, and Neoplatonic philosophies, by allowing influence at a distance as a natural phenomenon, could be used to deny that the miracles reported in the Bible and in the lives of Christian saints were supernaturally caused, meaning that they would therefore not prove the unique truth of Christianity.[40] Mersenne, Gassendi, Descartes, Boyle, and the Royal Society used the mechanistic philosophy to prove that action at a distance was *not* naturally possible, so that when extraordinary events occurred (which no one doubted) they had to be considered genuinely miraculous.[41]

These motives for mechanism were not simply theological but were equally sociological, in that they defended the Church's authority and thereby the State at a time when they were under attack. The Church's authority depended importantly upon the idea of rewards and especially punishments after death, which was thought to require a supernatural God and an immortal soul. This idea was considered essential for the preservation of the sociopolitical order against those who were seeking a wider distribution of material goods and political enfranchisement.[42] Of particular significance was the authority of the Biblical passage stating that rulers are appointed by God and should be obeyed (not overthrown!).

There were yet other sociological motives for advocating the "new mechanical philosophy" as part of an extreme dualism between the soul and nature and between God and the world. In opposing pantheistic or panentheistic worldviews in which God was immediately present to and in all things, the Royal Society distinguished itself clearly from those other philosophies which, also based on "natural magic" (i.e., mathematics), had been used to support "leveling" social movements which had opposed hierarchical views of society and of the Church.[43] It also, by eliminating all feeling as well as divinity and creativity from nature, was intended (e.g., by Descartes and Boyle) to sanction the uninhibited exploitation of nature for human ends, such as mining and vivisection.[44]

Another extrascientific influence, whether it be considered sociological or psychodynamic, was the desire to develop a "masculine" science of nature in contrast with the "feminine" or "hermaphrodite" science of the alchemists and other Hermeticists. In this masculine science, domination over nature replaced harmonious cooperation as the goal; dispassionate objectivity replaced the union of head and heart as the proper stance of the scientist, who therefore needed no personal transformation; and nature, understood as feminine, was emptied of all spirit and feeling, and especially all divinity.[45]

This complete dualism between God and the human soul as subjects, on the one hand, and nature as a realm of pure objectivity, with no inherent values, on the other, also provided a neat division of territory between theology and politics on the one hand, and natural science on the other. The implicit pledge by science to be value-neutral and not to deal with theological matters (except perhaps to give indirect support) removed any reason for the State and the Church to take offense at science's conclusions and hence any reason for it to interfere in its activities.[46]

Later, when secularization had proceeded to the point where there was little reason to fear ecclesiastical censure and when the leading members of the scientific community were no longer committed to supernatural Christianity and the Church's social authority, dualism could be turned into materialism, with the result that the scientific community would no longer have to share authority to establish truth with any other community.[47] It would be reductionistic to follow some sociologists in explaining the materialistic worldview entirely in terms of a bid for social power and prestige; after all, there *were* genuine intellectual problems, such as the problem of evil and the mind-body problem. But it would be falsely idealistic to ignore or discount this motive altogether.[48]

Because of studies revealing these influences, a conviction is growing that good science does not presuppose mechanism and that the mechanistic view of nature was adopted more for theological and sociological than for empirical reasons. A representative statement is provided by Jerome Ravetz:

> The 'scientific revolution' itself becomes comprehensible if we see it as a campaign for a reform of ideas *about* science, introduced quite suddenly, injected into a continuous process of technical progress *within* science . . . . [S]cientific revolution was primarily and essentially about metaphysics; and the various technical studies were largely conceived and received as corroborating statements of a challenging world-view. This consisted essentially of two Great Denials: the restriction of ordinary faculties such as sympathy and intelligence to humans and to a remote Deity; and the relegation of extra-ordinary faculties to the realms of the nonexistent or insignificant. . . . The great historical myth of this philosophy is that it was the necessary and sufficient cause of the great scientific progress of the seventeenth century. This was a central point in its propaganda, for itself at the time and in histories ever since. Yet the results of historical enquiry, some old and some new, contradict this claim.[49]

This new view has done much to undermine the modern conviction that a necessary connection exists between science and disenchantment (referred to in the above quotation as the "two Great Denials").

It should perhaps be stressed that an *enchanted science* is a wholly different thing from a *sacred science*; in fact, the decline of the latter is necessary for the reemergence of the former. A *sacred science* , as described in Sandra Harding's helpful discussion, is one whose method, worldview, and central facts are thought to be immune from social influences so that science itself is not to be understood in the same terms as it recommends that all other social activities are understood. That is, while science promotes the view that all (other) social practices are best understood in terms of influences from the environment, it maintains that the "development of science alone is to be understood through the stories scientists and a scientific culture tell about themselves." She asks rhetorically: "To what other 'community of natives' would we give the final word about the causes, consequences, and social meanings of their own beliefs and institutions?" We must, she says, be "willing to try to see the favored intellectual structures and practices of science as cultural artifacts rather than as sacred commandments handed down to humanity at the birth of modern science."[50] Since modern science has disenchanted the world and thereby itself, this desacralization of science, the progress of which we have traced in this and the previous sections, is a necessary condition for the reenchantment of the world and of science itself.

C. Recent Developments in Science

The move away from the mechanistic, deterministic, reductionistic worldview associated with modern science has been based not only on formal reflections upon the nature of modern science but also on substantive developments within science itself.

Many discussions of this topic focus primarily, if not exclusively, upon quantum physics, seeing it as not only destroying the Cartesian-Newtonian worldview but as also suggesting a new worldview—or a return to an old one, usually a mystical worldview, perhaps Taoist or Buddhist. However, the dominant interpretation of quantum physics, the Copenhagen interpretation, is limited to rules of calculation to predict the content of observations.[51] In other words, it is a nonrealist, phenomenalist interpretation, in which the attempt to describe what is really going on in the world of subatomic entities, independently of human measurement, is eschewed. Most popular accounts of the implications of quantum physics for our worldview neglect this fundamental point. The phenomenalist descriptions are presented as if they tell us something deep about the nature of reality.

A recent interpretation of the significance of quantum physics for the worldview of the founders of quantum theory themselves presents a more sophisticated account. Rejecting the notion that a direct connection exists between quantum theory and mysticism, Ken Wilber argues that quantum theory did nevertheless promote mysticism, but only indirectly. That is, as these physicists became aware that physical theory gave them only shadows and symbols of reality, rather than reality itself, they became freed from the materialistic worldview and hence open to taking their own conscious experience as real and revelatory.[52]

But, regardless of the way the dominant interpretation of quantum physics did in fact loosen the grip of the mechanistic worldview, it does not provide us with the basis for a new worldview. The question remains whether quantum physics, under a different interpretation, might say something more directly helpful about the nature of reality.

There are some physicists, such as David Bohm and Henry Stapp, who have sought to develop a realistic (nonphenomenalist) account of the quantum realm. Bohm has thereby been led to distinguish between the "explicate" order, upon which physics thus far has focused, and the "implicate" order, which a more complete physics would describe.[53] In this implicate order, enduring things are not separate from each other, as they appear to be in the explicate order, but are mutually enfolded in each other. Each electron, for example, in some sense enfolds in itself the universe as a whole and hence all its other parts. Accordingly, internal relatedness to other things which we directly experience in our conscious experience is generalized analogically all the way down to the simplest individuals. As Bohm points out in his essay in this volume, in overcoming the dualism between mind and matter this view implies the transcendence of the modern separation between facts and values, truth and virtue. Henry Stapp likewise regards each event as a process of enfoldment: each event enfolds previous events within itself.[54]

This view, that the events of nature are internally constituted by their appropriations from other things, is the central theme of those who are suggesting that the mechanistic paradigm in science be replaced by an ecological one—a view represented in this volume by Charles Birch, John Cobb, and Frederick Ferré. The term *ecological* most readily suggests biology. But it is important to all of these thinkers that internal relations are characteristic not only of living beings but also of the most elementary physical units. For one thing, only when this view prevails will the current drive to make mechanistic explanations ultimate even in the science of ecology be overcome.

Because internal relatedness is a necessary feature of subjects, the attribution of internal relations to individuals at all levels is one condition for overcoming an ultimate dualism between subjects and objects; *completely* overcoming dualism would involve the attribution of other essential features of subjects, such as feeling, memory, and aim or decision, at least in embryonic form, all the way down. Birch refers to Donald Griffin, who is one of several scientists calling for the scientific study of animals to go beyond behaviorism by speaking of subjective experience. Although "thinking" may occur only in the higher animals, Griffin suggests, the notions of memory and internal imaging seem necessary to understand the behavior of bats and even bees.[55] Whereas bats and bees are very complex, highly evolved organisms, bacteria are unicellular microorganisms, the simplest form of life, which evidently emerged about four billion years ago, according to the most recent discoveries. Daniel Koshland and his colleagues have provided evidence of rudimentary forms of both "memory" and "decision" in bacteria.[56] Going even further down, there is reason now to believe that DNA and RNA macromolecules are not simply passive entities which change as their parts are changed, but that they are active organisms which actively transpose their parts.[57] Going even further, it has been suggested that the Pauli Principle provides reason to think of an atom as a self-regulating whole.[58]

Against the ontological reductionism of the materialistic worldview, according to which all causation runs sideways and upward, from parts to parts and from parts to the whole (with all apparent wholes really being aggregates), there are now developments in science stressing "downward causation," from the whole to the parts. One of the most striking developments is evidence that the genes, which neo-Darwinism considers necessarily impervious to influence from the organism as a purposive whole, are in fact influenced by the organism.[59]

This recognition of downward causation from mind to body is aided if materialism and dualism are transcended. Those positions made it inconceivable that subjective purposes, feelings, decisions, and the like could influence the body. But if bodily cells and their components themselves have subjective experience, then downward causation from mind to body is no longer counterintuitive and the recognition of downward as well as upward causation between other levels will be easier. Willis Harman's essay in this volume[60] speaks to this issue especially with regard to "psychosomatic effects," as does my own.

More inclusive forms of downward causation would be involved in assertions of the influence of the planet as a living organism, and of the universe as a whole, on their parts. Something like the former could be suggested by the "Gaia hypotheses" of J. E. Lovelock and Lynn Margulis.[61] The latter is involved in David Bohm's view that every natural unit, as an act of enfoldment, in some sense enfolds the activity of the universe as a whole within it. Because the universe as an active whole can be regarded as divine,[62] Bohm in effect is suggesting that postmodern science, in speaking of the implicate order, would include reference to divine activity. He is thus reversing the dedivinization of nature bemoaned by Schiller.

The organismic view also overcomes the modern (and premodern) view that, for the world at its most fundamental level, temporality, in the sense of an irreversible distinction between past and future, is unreal. The notion that each electronic or protonic event enfolds past events within itself makes reversibility no more conceivable at the subatomic than at the human level.[63] According to Brian Swimme in this volume, we should, instead of regarding the historical evolution of the cosmos as an epiphenomenal development on the surface of the immutable laws of physics, see these laws themselves as products of a temporal development. Accordingly, physics no longer disenchants our stories; physics itself provides us with a new story which can become a common, unifying story underneath our more particular stories. Rupert Sheldrake in this volume, agreeing with Swimme that the laws of physics should not be considered changeless, suggests further that they be conceived as habits that have evolved and that continue to evolve. The laws of nature hence become sociological laws, an idea that reduces further the modern dualism between humanity and nature. Rather than seeing mechanisms as fundamental and organisms as derivative phenomena to be explained mechanistically, Sheldrake suggests the opposite: mechanistic phenomena represent the extreme possibility of habit formation on the part of organisms. Sheldrake here restates a major theme of organismic scientists, represented in the essays by Bohm, Birch, and Ferré as well, that while a mechanistic starting point cannot account for genuine organisms, an organismic starting point can account for all the mechanistic phenomena evident in the world

Sheldrake's original contribution is his hypothesis about the way such habits could be formed. This hypothesis of morphic resonance, which attributes a cumulative power to the repetition of a similar form, depends not only upon the irreversibility of time, but also upon influence at a distance, that is, over both temporal and spatial gaps. He is thereby bringing back, in a postmodern form, one of the notions that early modern thought most vigorously opposed (see Note 1 and the above-cited quotation from Jerome Ravetz). That Sheldrake's proposal was condemned by a representative of the modern scientific establishment even prior to its testing is no surprise.[64]

The issue of action at a distance is, of course, central to the controversies about parapsychology. Numerous treatments show that the main difficulty with parapsychological claims, probably even more fundamental than the problem of repeatability, is the fact that "paranormal claims seem to clash with our twentieth-century presuppositions about reality."[65] And, as concluded by a recent reexamination of C. D. Broad's "basic limiting principles" which paranormal claims seem to violate, the crucial principle is that "any event that is said to cause another event (the second event being referred to as an 'effect') must be related to the effect through some causal chain."[66] This principle is violated by telepathy, clairvoyance, and psychokinesis (and precognition, which also violates the principle that the cause must precede the effect temporally). The author concluded that "the absence of a specifiable and recognizably causal chain seems to constitute a difficult, if not insurmountable, objection to our giving a coherent account of what it means to make such a claim."[67] C. D. Broad himself had suggested that, if there are any well-established facts that are exceptions to these principles, the good thinker "will want to revise his fundamental concepts and basic limiting principles in such a way as to include the old and new facts in a single coherent system."[68] As we saw earlier, the notion that a "causal chain" of contiguous events or things must exist between a cause and an effect at a distance is part and parcel of the mechanistic worldview and is based on the assumption that the constituents of the world are bits of matter, analogous to billiard balls or parts of a machine, which can only affect each other by contact. But if the basic units of the world are less like cogs or billiard balls than like moments of experience, which enfold influences from previous moments of experience into themselves, that all influence must come from contiguous events is no longer intuitively self-evident. Hence, in line with their nonmechanistic, organismic views of nature, Bohm and Stapp in physics and Sheldrake in biology point to evidence of nonlocal effects.[69] In this context, the claims of parapsychologists, such as those reported by Stanley Krippner herein, need not be rejected *a priori*, on the grounds that they clash with the rest of our worldview. In fact, Bohm, Sheldrake, and Stapp (as did Whitehead before them) all suggest that events exert two forms of influence on the future, one form on contiguous events, another on noncontiguous ones.[70] They use this nonlocal causation, in which what is normally called *physical energy* is not involved, to explain phenomena that seem inexplicable in terms of causation through chains of contiguous events alone.

These recent developments in the scientific community, some of which are reflected herein, are reversing the disenchantment of science and its worldview. They are carrying forward what Floyd Matson described in 1964 as "the affirmative countermovement in postmodern science."[71]

D. Reflections on the Relation between Mind and Matter

The main philosophical reason for rejecting the mechanistic, nonanimistic view of nature is that that view makes the relation between mind and matter problematic. Four aspects of this problem can be distinguished: the traditional mind-body problem, the problem of mind as the Great Exception, the problem of emergence, and the problem of where to draw the line.

This mind-body problem is due to the conjunction of a directly known fact, an apparent fact, and an inference. The *directly known fact* is that we have, or are, a mind, in the sense of a stream of experiences. As Descartes stressed, if there is one thing I cannot doubt, it is that I am experiencing. The *apparent fact* is that the mind and the body seem to interact; that is, the mind seems to be affected by the body and seems to affect it in return. The *inference* is that the human body is composed of things that are devoid of experience. The resulting problem is: How is it understandable that these two totally unlike things appear to interact? The problem is intensified once we realize that the dualism between nonexperiencing and experiencing things entails a *set* of absolute contrasts, so that the question becomes: How can the impenetrably spatial relate to the nonspatial, the nontemporal to the temporal, the mechanistically caused to the purposively acting, the idea-less to the idea-filled, the purely factual to the value-laden, the externally locomotive to the internally becoming?

Because the founders and early defenders of the dualistic[72] worldview were supernaturalistic theists, they did not find the problem insurmountable. Although they differed in details (with Descartes speaking of an ethereal pineal gland, Malebranche of occasionalism, Leibniz of preestablished harmony or parallelism), they all agreed in essence with Thomas Reid, who simply said that God, being omnipotent, can cause mind and matter to interact, even if such interaction is inconceivable to us.[73] These thinkers thereby illustrated Whitehead's complaint about supernaturalists: having a God who can rise superior to metaphysical difficulties, they did not rethink their metaphysical principles but simply invoked God to prevent those principles from collapsing.[74]

However, as this appeal to God has become unacceptable, dualists are left with no answer. They either ignore the problem or regard it as a mystery we simply must accept. For example, at one time Karl Popper said: "What we want is to understand how such nonphysical things as *purposes, deliberations, plans, decisions, theories, tensions*, and *values* can play a part in bringing about physical changes in the physical world."[75] At a later time, however, he evidently decided that no such understanding was possible. He still confessed to belief in a "ghost in a machine," but dismissed the question of their interacting with the lame comment that "complete understanding, like complete knowledge, is unlikely to be achieved."[76] Materialists use this admitted unintelligibility of dualistic interaction as the basis for equating mind and brain.

The second problem raised against dualism by some materialists is the implausibility of the idea that everything in the universe except human experience can be understood in physicalistic terms. This is the problem of the human mind as the Great Exception. J. C. C. Smart says: "That everything should be explicable in terms of physics . . . except the occurrence of sensations seems to me to be frankly unbelievable."[77] This problem is lessened somewhat when dualists extend experience to all animals having central nervous systems, as do many dualists; it is lessened even more if experience is attributed all the way down to the lowest forms of life.

However, this solution simply raises the problem of interaction in a new form, resulting in a third problem, the problem of emergence. Whether the ontological gap is located between the human mind and its body or between an experiencing cell and its insentient atoms, the communication across the gap is equally unintelligible. As Smart states: "How could a nonphysical property or entity suddenly arise in the course of animal evolution? . . . What sort of chemical process could lead to the springing into existence of something nonphysical? No enzyme can catalyze the production of a spook!"[78]

A fourth problem for dualists, if they try to solve the first two by extending experience below the human mind, is just *where* to draw the absolute line between sentient and insentient things. Drawing the line with Descartes between the human soul and the rest of nature, so that dogs are simply barking machines, was never very plausible, and it became less so with the theory of evolution. But drawing an absolute line anywhere else seems arbitrary, especially in an evolutionary context. Some vitalists have drawn an absolute line between living and nonliving matter, but the once-clear line between living and nonliving has become vague. Is the cell living and sentient, while its remarkable DNA and RNA macromolecules are insentient mechanisms? Is the bacterium a sentient organism, while the virus is not? Any such line seems arbitrary. For example, while agreeing that crystals and DNA molecules show signs of memory, and that even atoms and elementary particles have "propensities," Karl Popper refuses to attribute experience any further down than to single-celled animals.[79] The reason Popper cannot attribute experience to atoms and electrons is clear; it is that he, being a modern man, shares "with old-fashioned materialists the view that . . . solid material bodies are the paradigms of reality."[80]

Given that modern starting point, the only way to avoid the insoluble problems of dualism is to affirm total materialism. Materialists avoid the problem of mind-body dualism by affirming identism, the doctrine that mind and brain are identical. J. C. C. Smart, not being able to believe that experience is "made of ghost stuff," says that it is "composed of brain stuff." In other words: "Sensations are nothing over and above brain processes."[81] In D. M. Armstrong's words, "mental states are in fact nothing but physical states of the central nervous system."[82]

Materialism has even more problems than does dualism, because it shares most of the problems of dualism and then adds some of its own. To begin with the problems it shares with dualism: First, it has not really escaped the problem of emergence which it levels against dualism. The identist's claim is that conscious experience is a quality that has "emerged" in the evolutionary process analogously to the way in which other properties have emerged, such as saltiness, wetness, and furriness. Just as saltiness emerged out of a particular configuration of things none of which were by themselves salty, so experience has arisen out of a particular configuration of things (neurons) none of which by themselves had experience. In spite of the initial analogical plausibility of this argument, it hinges on a "category mistake." All the other emergent properties (saltiness, etc.) are properties of things *as they appear* to us from without, i.e., to our conscious sensory perception. *But conscious experience itself is not a property of things as they appear to us from without; it is what we are in and for ourselves.* The suggestion that an analogy exists between the other examples of emergent properties and the alleged emergence of sentience out of insentient things confuses two entirely different matters under a single category.[83] All the other examples involve the emergence of one more characteristic of things as they appear to others; *only* in the case of experience is the alleged new property a feature of what the thing is for itself. Surely the question of whether an individual is something for itself is categorically different from the question of what it is for others. Once this is seen, that materialism has the same problem of unintelligibility as does dualism is evident. It equally involves the claim that a thing that is something for itself emerged out of things that are mere objects for others. The fact that the thing in question is called a distinct mind by dualists and a brain by materialists is a secondary matter; an absolutely unique type of causal relation is still being posited. Things that are nothing for themselves are said to causally produce a thing (a brain) that is metaphysically unique in being not only an object for others, but a subject for itself.

Most materialistic identists also share with dualists the implausible idea that experiencing things constitute a Great Exception. For example, after suggesting that mind is strictly identical with matter, so that there is "only one reality which is represented in two different conceptual systems," i.e., physics and phenomenological psychology, Herbert Feigl makes clear that he does not intend panpsychism: "nothing in the least like a psyche is ascribed to lifeless matter." Rather, whereas the language of physics applies everywhere, the language of psychology is applicable "only to an extremely small part of the world."[84]

The materialist identist also shares the dualist's problem of where to draw the line between things that can be described in physical terms alone, and those to which psychological terms are appropriate. Drawing a line is equally arbitrary whether or not the things with experience are thought to be distinct actualities.

Some identists seek to overcome these problems by denying that psychological language need be used at all, even for our own experience. All language about pains, colors, intentions, emotions and the like would be eliminated. One would talk entirely in physicalistic terms, for example, by talking in terms of certain neuron firings instead of anger, in terms of other neuron firings instead of pain, etc.[85] This so-called eliminative materialism shows the desperate straights to which the mechanistic view of nature can lead.

Besides the problems that identism shares with dualism, it has several of its own. One is that, while claiming to be empirical, it denies the full reality of the directly known in the name of the inferred. That is, the one thing we know from inside, so that we know what it is *in itself*, is our own conscious experience. As almost all modern philosophers have insisted, we do not directly know what objects of sensory perception are in themselves, but only how they appear to us. The idea that these objects are *mere* objects, mere matter, can only be the result of metaphysical speculation. And yet materialists, on the basis of the speculative inference that the human body is composed of "matter" which is *in itself devoid of experience*, deny that our directly known conscious experience can be a distinct actual thing on the grounds that that hypothesis requires interaction between experiencing and nonexperiencing things.

A second problem unique to materialism is that, in denying the distinction between the mind and the brain, it gives up the hypothesis that had provided the materialistic or mechanistic view of nature its *prima facie* plausibility in the first place. That is, the mechanistic view entailed a distinction between so-called *primary* qualities, which were really attributes of physical things, and *secondary* and *tertiary* qualities, which were only in the mind, although they might falsely appear to be in nature. Hence, nature consisted solely of quantitative factors, locomotion, and mechanistic causation; all color and smells, all pain and pleasure, all good and evil, and all purposes and self-motion, resided solely in the mind. By having two types of actual things, dualism could deny that these nonphysical qualities exist in nature without making the counterintuitive assertion that they are wholly unreal. But in materialistic identism the modern worldview has lost its mind and must thereby deny that most of the qualities that are immediately experienced are real. They are illusions created by an illusion.

The materialistic denial that experience plays a causal role in the world also creates a problem of understanding how experience, and then conscious experience, ever emerged. Within an evolutionary framework, especially the neo-Darwinian one presupposed by materialists, the emergence and stabilization of a new property only can be explained in terms of its enhancement of the chances for survival. But the point of materialistic identism is to deny that experience exerts causal power on the physical world; experience is a concomitant of some physical processes that would by hypothesis interact with the rest of the world in the same way if they were devoid of experience.[86] Hence, by this view, experience cannot enhance an organism's chances of survival. The materialist therefore has no evolutionary explanation as to why any of the things in the world should have experience of any sort, let alone conscious and self-conscious experience.

Adding further to the difficulties of materialistic identism is the fact that, in rejecting the dualism between mind and body, it necessitates a dualism between theory and practice. Whereas dualism said that the mind was the one thing with the power of self-motion, a large part of the motivation for the materialistic denial of nonmaterial mind is to deny that there is any part of the world that is not subject to the deterministic, reductionistic method of modern science. But we all, including the avowed materialists among us, live in practice as if we and other people were partly free from total determination from beyond ourselves. The resulting dualism between theory and practice is at least as vicious as that between mind and matter.

In summary, both dualism and materialism are unintelligible. But if the modern premise that the elementary units of nature are insentient is accepted, dualism and materialism are the only options. This fact suggests that the premise that lies behind the modern disenchantment of the world is false.

Accordingly, a strong philosophical argument converges with recent developments in the philosophy, sociology, and history of science, and in science itself, to undermine the basis for the modern disenchantment of the world.

III. POSTMODERN ORGANICISM AND THE UNITY OF SCIENCE

The postmodern organicism represented in this series has been inspired primarily by the scientist-turned-philosopher Alfred North Whitehead. Various features of this viewpoint are explained or employed in the essays herein (those by Birch, Cobb, Ferré, and me, and to some extent Bohm, Sheldrake, and Swimme),[87] and in future volumes. However, it is necessary here, without trying to summarize the whole position, to indicate briefly how it relates to the question of the unity of science, with a focus on the question of causation. I will do this in terms of a contrast of "paradigms," understood as the basic worldviews presupposed by communities of scientists.

This postmodern organicism can be considered a synthesis of the Aristotelian, Galilean (both forms), and Hermetic paradigms. Aristotelian organicism had a unified science by attributing purposive or final causation to everything, most notoriously saying that a falling stone seeks a state of rest. The Galilean paradigm, in its first form, distinguished absolutely between two types of primary beings: (1) those that exercised purposive or final causation; and (2) those that did not and could consequently be understood completely in terms of receiving and transmitting efficient causation. At first, limiting the beings in the first category to human minds was customary, but that limitation is neither necessary to the dualistic paradigm nor very credible. Many Galilean dualists have accordingly, as mentioned in the previous section, extended final causation further down the animal kingdom: those who are termed *vitalists* see it as arising with the first form of life. Wherever the line was drawn, the drawing of a line between two ontologically different types of primary beings split science into two parts. One science spoke only of efficient causes; the other science (psychology) spoke in terms of final causes or purposes. The second form of the Galilean paradigm tried to restore unity to science by abolishing an internalistic psychology of final causes. Psychology, under the name of *behaviorism*, was transformed into an attempt to describe and explain human and other animal behavior solely in terms of efficient causes and other externalistic terms. *Eliminative materialism*, mentioned earlier, is the extreme version of this way to achieve unity.

Postmodern organicism holds that all primary individuals are organisms who exercise at least some iota of purposive causation. But it does not hold that all visible objects, such as stones and planets, are primary individuals or even analogous to primary individuals. Rather, it distinguishes between two ways in which primary organisms can be organized: (1) as a compound individual,[88] in which an all-inclusive subject emerges; and (2) as a nonindividuated object, in which no unifying subjectivity is found. Animals belong to the first class; stones to the second. In other words, there is no ontological dualism, but there is an organizational duality which takes account of the important and obvious distinction that the dualists rightly refused to relinquish. Hence, there are (1) things whose behavior can only be understood in terms of both efficient causes and their own purposive response to these causes, and (2) things whose behavior can be understood, for most purposes, without any reference to purposive or final causation. In this sense, there is a duality within science.

However, the qualification *for most purposes* is important. Whereas the Galilean paradigm maintained that a nonteleological explanation of material things could be adequate for all purposes, including a complete understanding, at least in principle, the postmodern paradigm contends that any explanation devoid of purposive causation will necessarily abstract from concrete facts. *Fully* to understand even the interaction between two billiard balls requires reference to purposive reactions—not indeed of the balls as aggregates, but of their constituents. Because the study of nonindividual objects as well as that of primary individuals and compound individuals requires, at least ultimately, reference to final as well as efficient causes, there is a unity of science.

The relation between final and efficient causation in Whiteheadian postmodern organicism is different from their relation in any previous form of thought, even from other forms of panexperientialism (often called panpsychism), although it was anticipated in Buddhist thought. Other forms of thought that have attributed experience to all individuals, such as that of Gottfried Leibniz and Teilhard de Chardin, have assumed the ultimate constituents of the world to be enduring individuals. An individual was physical from without to others, but was conscious or mental from within, for itself. From without, it interacted with other enduring individuals in terms of efficient causation; from within, it lived in terms of purposes or final causation. Given this picture, relating efficient and final causation to each other was difficult. The common view has been that they do not relate, but simply run along parallel to each other. However, as discussed above in relation to materialistic identism, this parallelism raises serious problems. If experience or mentality makes no difference to an individual's interactions with its environment, how can we explain why the higher forms of experience have evolved? And without appeal to a supernatural coordinator, how can we explain the parallelism between inner and outer; e.g., why should my brain's signal to my hand to lift a glass follow right after my mental decision to have a drink, if my decision in no way *causes* the appropriate neurons in the brain to fire?

However, if the ultimate individuals of the world are momentary events, rather than enduring individuals, a positive relation can exist between efficient and final causation. Efficient causation still applies to the exterior of an individual and final causation to the interior. But because an enduring individual, such as a proton, neuron, or human psyche, is a temporal *society* of momentary events, exterior and interior oscillate and feed into each other rather than running parallel. Each momentary event in an enduring individual originates through the inrush of efficient causation from the past world, i.e., from previous events, including the previous events that were members of the same enduring individual. The momentary subject then makes a self-determining response to these causal influences; this is the moment of final causation, as the event aims at achieving a synthesis for itself and for influencing the future. This final causation is in no way unrelated to efficient causation; it is a purposive response to the efficient causes on the event. When this moment of subjective final causation is over, the event becomes an object which exerts efficient causation on future events. Exactly what efficient causation it exerts is a function both of the efficient causes upon it *and* of its own final causation. Hence, the efficient causes of the world do not run along as if there were no mentality with its final causation. An event does not necessarily simply transmit to others what it received; it may do this, but it also may deflect and transform the energy it receives to some degree or another, before passing it on. (*We* do this to the greatest degree when we return good for evil.)

To say that the categories of both final and efficient causation must be employed for the study of all actual beings does *not* imply that the two categories will be *equally* relevant for all beings. Indeed, as already indicated, an appeal to final causation is irrelevant for almost all purposes when studying nonindividuated objects, such as rocks, stars, and computers.[89] Even with regard to individuals, the importance of final or purposive causation will vary enormously. In primary individuals, such as photons and electrons (or quarks, if such there be), final causation is minimal. For the most part, the behavior of these individuals is understandable in terms of efficient causes alone. They mainly just conform to what they have received and pass it on to the future in a predictable way. But not completely: behind the epistemic "indeterminacy" of quantum physics lies a germ of ontic self-determinacy. The importance of self-determination or final causation increases in compound individuals, especially in those normally called *living*. It becomes increasingly important as the study focuses upon more complex, highly evolved animals; all the evidence suggests that final causation is the most important, on our planet, in determining the experience and behavior of human beings. The importance of efficient causes, i.e., of influence from the past, does not diminish as one moves toward the higher individuals; indeed, in a sense higher beings are influenced by *more* past events than are lower ones. But the totality of efficient causes from the past becomes less and less explanatory of experience and behavior, and the individual's own present self-determination in terms of desired ends becomes more explanatory.

From this perspective we can understand why a mechanistic, reductionistic approach has been so spectacularly successful in certain areas and so unsuccessful in others. The modern Galilean paradigm was based on the study of nonindividuated objects, such as stellar masses and steel balls, which exercise *no final causation* either in determining their own behavior or that of their elementary parts. Absolute predictability and reduction is possible in principle. This paradigm was next applied to very low-grade individuals, in which the final causation is *negligible* for most purposes except to the most refined observation. With this refinement, the absolute predictability of behavior broke down with the most elementary individuals; the ideal of predictability could be salvaged only by making it statistical and applying it to large numbers of individuals. With low-grade forms of life, and in particular with their inherited characteristics and certain abstract features of their behavior, Galilean science has still been very successful, but not completely. Certain features of even low-grade life seemed intractable to this approach, just those features which led to the rise of vitalism. This paradigm has been even less successful with rats than with bacteria. At this level, various problems are virtually ignored, because little chance of success is apparent, and scientists are interested in applying their method where the chances for success are most promising. Finally, the method has been less successful yet with humans than with rats. The record of success at this level is so miserable that many scientists and philosophers of science refuse to think of the so-called social or human sciences, such as psychology, sociology, economics, and political science, as sciences at all. This pattern of success and failure of the Galilean paradigm fits exactly what the postmodern paradigm predicts. As one leaves nonindividuated objects for individuals, and as one deals with increasingly higher individuals, final causation becomes increasingly important, and regularity and hence predictability become increasingly less possible. Hence, nothing but confusion and unrealistic expectations can result from continuing to regard physics as the paradigmatic science.[90]

This framework can explain why it has been even less possible to discover regularities and attain repeatability in parapsychology than in certain aspects of ordinary psychology. Although every event (by hypothesis) exerts influence directly upon remote as well as spatially and temporally contiguous events, its influence on contiguous events is much more powerful. Hence, the effects of the kind of influence that is exerted upon remote events indirectly *via* a chain of contiguous events will be much more regular and hence predictable than the effects of the kind of influence that is exerted on remote events directly, without the intervening chain. Accordingly, because sensory perception arises from a chain of contiguous events (photons and neuron firings in vision) connecting the remote object with the psyche, the sensory perception of external objects is much more regular and reliable, hence predictable, than any extrasensory perception of them. Likewise, because effects produced in the external world by the psyche by means of the body are mediated by a chain of contiguous causes, whose reliability, like that of the sensory system, has been perfected over billions of years of evolution, such effects are much more reliable than any psychokinetic effects produced by the direct influence of the psyche upon outer objects without the body's mediation. Additionally, although *unconscious* extrasensory perception and *subtle* and *diffused* psychokinetic action occur continually (by hypothesis), the power to produce *conscious* extrasensory perception and *conspicuous* psychokinetic effects *on specific objects* is—at least for the majority of human beings most of the time—evidently lodged in an unconscious level of experience, which by definition is not under conscious control. Given these assumptions, the fact that parapsychology has attained little repeatability with conspicuous psychokinetic effects and conscious extrasensory perception is what should be expected.[91] In this way, the element of truth in the Hermetic paradigm is coordinated with the elements of truth from the Aristotelian and Galilean paradigms.

What then is science—what constitutes its unity? The anarchistic or relativistic view that "anything goes," that there is no such thing as a scientific method, is surely too strong. But it serves a useful function, as indeed it was intended,[92] to shake us free from parochial limitations on what counts as science. A description of science for a postmodern world must be much looser than the modern descriptions (which were really *pre*scriptions).

Any activity properly called *science* and any conclusions properly called *scientific* must, first, be based on an overriding concern to discover truth.[93] Other concerns will of course play a role, but the concern for truth must be overriding, or the activity and its results would better called by another name, such as *ideology*, or *propaganda*, or *politics*.[94] Second, science involves demonstration. More particularly, it involves testing hypotheses through data or experiences that are in some sense repeatable and hence open to confirmation or refutation by peers. In sum, science involves the attempt to establish truth through demonstrations open to experiential replication. What is left out of this account of science are limitations (1) to any particular domain, (2) any particular type of repeatability and demonstration, or (3) any particular contingent beliefs.

(1) Science is not restricted to the domain of things assumed to be wholly physical, operating in terms of efficient causes alone, or even to the physical aspects of things, understood as the aspects knowable to sensory perception or instruments designed to magnify the senses.[95] As the impossibility of behaviorism in human and even animal psychology has shown, science must refer to experience and purposes to comprehend (and even to predict) animal behavior. Although we cannot *see* the purposes motivating our fellow humans or other animals, assuming that such purposes play a causal role is not unscientific, if this hypothesis can be publically demonstrated to account for the observable behavior better than the opposite hypothesis. And, once it is explicitly recognized that science *can* deal with subjectivity, there is no reason in principle for it to limit itself to the objective or physical side of other things, if there is good reason to suspect that an experiencing side exercising final causation exists. At the very least, even if we cannot imagine very concretely what the experience of a bacterium or a DNA molecule would be like, we need not try to account for its observable behavior on the metaphysical assumption that it has no experience and hence no purposes.

Just as the need for experiential replication by peers does not limit science to the physical or objective side of actual things, it does not even limit it to the realm of actuality. Mathematics deals with relationships among ideal entities, and is able to achieve great consensus; geometry was for Descartes of course the paradigmatic science. Therefore, the fact that logic, aesthetics, and ethics deal with ideal entities does not, in itself, exclude them from the realm of science.

Furthermore, the domain of scientific study should not be thought to be limited to regularities, or law-like behavior. There is no reason why the discussion of the origin of laws should not belong to science. If the laws of nature are reconceived as habits, the question of how the habits originated should not be declared off-limits.[96] In fact, we should follow Bohm in replacing the language of "laws" with the more inclusive notion of "orders," for the reasons Evelyn Fox Keller has suggested: the notion of "laws of nature" retains the connotation of theological imposition, which is no longer appropriate but continues to sanction unidirectional, hierarchical explanations; it makes the simplicity of classical physics the ideal, so that the study of more complex orders is regarded as "softer" and less fully scientific; and it implies that nature is dead and "obedient" rather than generative and resourceful.[97]

(2) While science requires repeatable experiential demonstration, it does not require one particular type of demonstration, such as the laboratory experiment. As Patrick Grim says:

> Field studies, expeditions, and the appearances of comets have played a major role in the history of science. Contemporary reliance on mathematics reflects a willingness to accept a priori deductive as well as inductive demonstration. And there are times when the course of science quite properly shifts on the basis of what appear to be almost purely philosophical arguments.[98]

In regard to Grim's last example, I have suggested above that the philosophical difficulties with both dualism and materialistic identism provide a good reason for the scientific community to reconsider the metaphysical-scientific hypothesis that the ultimate constituents of nature are entirely devoid of experience and purpose. More generally, the bias toward the laboratory experiment in the philosophy of science has philosophically reflected the materialistic, nonecological assumption that things are essentially independent of their environments, so that the scientist abstracts from nothing essential in (say) removing cells from the human body or animals from a jungle to study them in a laboratory; it reflects the reductionistic assumption that all complex things are really no more self-determining than the elementary parts in isolation, so that they should be subject to the same kind of strong laboratory repeatability;[99] it reflects the assumption that the main purpose of science is to predict and control repeatable phenomena; and it reflects the assumption that the domain of science is limited to the actual, especially the physical. Recognizing the wide domain of science means recognizing the necessity and hence appropriateness of diverse types of demonstrations, and the artificiality of holding up one type as the ideal.

(3) Besides not being limited to one domain or one type of demonstration, the scientific pursuit of truth is not tied to any set of contingent beliefs, meaning beliefs that are not inevitably presupposed by human practice, including thought, itself. Science is, therefore, not limited to any particular type of explanation. [100] For example, science is not tied to the belief that the elementary units of nature are devoid of sentience, instrinsic value, and internal relations, that time does not exist for these units, that the laws of nature for these units are eternal, that all natural phenomena result from the (currently four) forces rooted in these elementary units, that accordingly all causation is upward and that freedom and purposive or teleological causation are illusory, [101] that ideal entities other than mathematical forms play no role in nature, that there is no influence at a distance, [102] that the universe as a whole is not an organism which influences its parts, or that the universe and its evolution have no inherent meaning.

However, the fact that science as such is not permanently wedded to these contingent beliefs that reigned during the modern period does not mean that there are *no* beliefs that science as such must presuppose. If beliefs exist that are presupposed by human practice, including human thought, as such, then scientific practice and thought must presuppose them. Any theories that verbally deny them should therefore be eschewed on this ground alone. Although any such beliefs would transcend perspectivalism, because they by hypothesis would be common to all people, regardless of their worldview, the questions of whether there are any such beliefs, and if so what they are, are matters not for pontification from some supposedly neutral point of view, because no human point of view is neutral, but for proposals to be subjected to ongoing public discussion among those with diverse worldviews. [103]

To illustrate the types of beliefs intended and to show that they are not limited to innocuous, noncontroversial issues, I propose five principles as candidates. The first three principles relate to the crucial issue of causality. First, every event is causally influenced by other events. This principle rules out, for example, the idea that the universe arose out of absolute nothingness or out of pure possibility. [104] Second, neither human experience nor anything analogous to it is wholly determined by external events; rather, every genuine individual is partially self-determining. Incidentally, these first two principles, taken together, provide the basis for a scientific understanding of the activity of scientists themselves in terms of a combination of external and internal causes, which is increasingly seen to be necessary. [105]

Third, every event that exerts causal influence upon another event precedes that event temporally. (Self-determination or self-causation does not fall under this principle, because in it the same event is both cause and effect.) This principle rules out the notion of particles "going backwards in time," the notion of "backward causation," and any notion of "precognition" interpreted to mean that an event affected the knower before it happened or to mean that temporal relations are ultimately unreal.[106]

The final two principles proffered deal with science's concern for truth. These are the traditional principles of correspondence and noncontradiction, which are recovered in a postmodern context.

The idea that truth is a correspondence between statements and objective reality has been subject to a great deal of criticism. Much of this criticism is based upon confusion, inasmuch as the critics, often while verbally rejecting positivism, still presuppose the positivistic equation of the meaning of a statement with the means of its verification. The correspondence notion of truth properly refers only to the *meaning* of "truth," which is not even identical with the question of knowledge, let alone with the question of the justification of knowledge-claims. Much of the rejection of the relevance of the correspondence notion of truth has conflated truth with knowledge and then assumed that there could be no knowledge, in the sense of justified true belief, in the absence of adequate evidence to defend the knowledge-claim. [107]

However, much of the criticism of the notion of truth as correspondence is valid, especially in relation to naively realistic ideas of a one-to-one correspondence between statements and objective facts. For one thing, our ideas about physical objects, insofar as they are based primarily upon visual and tactile perception, surely involve enormous simplifications, constructions, and distortions of the realities existing independently of our perception. For another, language is inherently vague and, in any case, cannot as such "correspond" in the sense of being similar to nonlinguistic entities. Language aside, the way in which an idea can correspond to a physical object is not self-evident, because an idea can only be similar to another idea. Even many conceptions of truth as the correspondence between one's ideas and the ideas in another mind are held in falsely naive ways, insofar as it is assumed that achieving truth, in the sense of absolute correspondence, is possible. Many critics go on from these valid starting points to argue that the meaning of a statement is exhausted by its relation to other statements, so that language constitutes a closed system, or in some other way argue that our statements can in no meaningful sense correspond to any nonlinguistic entities. Science, in this extreme view, is a linguistic system disconnected from any larger world.

Postmodern organicism rejects this view of language. While language as such does not correspond to anything other than language, it expresses and evokes modes of apprehending nonlinguistic reality that can more or less accurately correspond to features of that reality.[108] Hence, science can lead to ways of thinking about the world that can increasingly approximate to patterns and structures genuinely characteristic of nature.

The other traditional principle involved in science's concern for truth is the principle of noncontradiction. It says that if two statements contradict each other, both cannot be true. This principle has also been subject to much valid criticism. Certainly two statements that appear to contradict each other may not in reality when one or both are more deeply understood. This can be because language is vague and elusive, because various levels of meaning exist, and/or because seemingly contradictory assertions may apply to diverse features of the referent or to different stages of its development. There are yet other objections to simple-minded applications of the principle of noncontradiction. But after all necessary subtleties and qualifications have been added, the principle remains valid and is necessarily presupposed even in attempts to refute it. Accordingly, science must aim for coherence between all its propositions and between its propositions and all those that are inevitably presupposed in human practice and thought in general. (Obtaining such coherence is indeed the primary method of checking for correspondence.)

All of these principles are in harmony with postmodern organicism. Indeed, they are not epistemically neutral principles but ones that are, especially in regard to their exact formulation, suggested by postmodern organicism. However, the claim is made that they are, in fact, implicit in human practice, including human thought (although not, of course, in the content of all the theories produced by human thought). If this claim is sustained through widespread conversation, then this set of beliefs (along with any others that could prove their universality in the same way) should be considered to belong to science as such.[109]

CONCLUSION: A NEW COLLABORATION

To summarize: Whereas modern science has led to the disenchantment of the world and itself, a number of factors today are converging toward a postmodern organicism in which science and the world are reenchanted. Besides providing a basis for overcoming the distinctive problems of modernity that are due primarily to disenchantment, this postmodern organicism gives science a better basis than it has heretofore had for understanding its own unity.

This volume can be seen as a first step in carrying out the effort called for by Stephen Toulmin in his important book, *The Return to Cosmology: Postmodern Science and the Theology of Nature*. By a return to cosmology, Toulmin means a return to the attempt to think about the universe as a *cosmos*, "a single integrated system united by universal principles," which portrays "all things in the world—human, natural, and divine—as related together in an orderly way."[110] The trajectory begun in the seventeenth century led to a disciplinary specialization in which natural science became separated from the "natural theology" of which it had originally been a part. The only recognized facts about the universe as a whole were reached by aggregating the facts from the various disciplines, as it was nobody's task to integrate those facts into a transdisciplinary cosmology. The modern dictum became: "What Science hath put asunder let no mere Theologian seek to join together again!"[111] One reason Toulmin's book is important is that he had previously been an influential representative of that modern viewpoint.[112]

Toulmin now calls for a new dialogue among scientists, philosophers, and theologians. [113] His statement of hope for this dialogue refers implicitly to overcoming disenchantment: "Cosmology . . . need not remain forever a source of disappointment or disillusion."[114] He suggests that developments in postmodern science allow us again to *feel* at home in the universe and also point to how we should behave if we are to *be* at home in it. [115] The formal conditions for such a postmodern cosmology, in which our understandings of humanity and nature are integrated with practice in view, include reinserting humanity and, in fact, life as a whole, back into nature, and regarding our fellow creatures not merely as means to our ends but as ends in themselves.[116] The essays herein represent a first step in the collaborative, postmodern dialogue for which Toulmin calls.[117]

NOTES

1. Because of this purpose, and because the contributors can speak for themselves herein, I have (for the most part) not drawn upon their previous writings in preparing this introduction, even though in some cases I could have done so heavily. For example, Frederick Ferré's *Shaping the Future: Resources for the Postmodern World* (New York & San Francisco: Harper & Row, 1976) discusses many of the themes central to this introduction. The books of the other contributors most germane to this volume are mentioned in the "Notes on Contributors and Centers." (I do, however, refer to ideas of David Bohm and Rupert Sheldrake, because they provide especially apt illustrations of certain features of postmodern science.)

2. Mary Hesse points out that the rejection of action-at-a-distance in favor of action-by-contact explanations was based on the replacement of all organismic and psychological explanations by mechanical ones (*Forces and Fields: The Concept of Action at a Distance in the History of Physics* [Totowa, N. J.: Littlefield, Adams & Co, 1965], 98, 291). Richard Westfall makes clear how central was the change:

> the mechanical philosophy also banished . . . attractions of any kind. No scorn was too great to heap upon such a notion. From one end of the century to another, the idea of attractions, the action of one body upon another with which is not in contact, was anathema. . . . An attraction was an occult virtue, and 'occult virtue' was the mechanical philosophy's ultimate term of opprobrium.

Westfall reports that Christiaan Huygens wrote that he did not care whether Newton was a Cartesian "as long as he doesn't serve us up conjectures such as attractions"

("The Influence of Alchemy on Newton," Marsha P. Hanen, Margaret J. Osler, and Robert G. Weyant, eds., *Science, Pseudo-Science and Society* [Waterloo, Ontario: Wilfrid Laurier University Press, 1980], 145–70, esp. 147, 150). Brian Easlea has provided convincing evidence that the desire to rule out the possibility of attraction at a distance was, in fact, the main motivation behind the mechanical philosophy and its denial of all hidden qualities within matter; see his *Witch Hunting, Magic and the New Philosophy: An Introduction to Debates of the Scientific Revolution 1450–1750* (Atlantic Highlands, N. J.: Humanities Press, 1980), esp. 93–95, 108–15, 121, 132, 135.

3. Neal C. Gillespie, *Charles Darwin and the Problem of Creation* (Chicago: University of Chicago Press, 1979), 55–56, 120, 139–40.

4. Michael Ghiselin, *The Economy of Nature and the Evolution of Sex* (Berkeley: University of California Press, 1974), x, 13.

5. Jacques Monod, *Chance and Necessity: An Essay on the Natural Philosophy of Modern Biology* (New York: Vintage Books, 1972), 21.

6. *Ibid.*, 172–73, 171.

7. Clark Hull, *Principles of Behavior: An Introduction to Behavior Theory* (New York: Appleton-Century, 1943), 29.

8. B. F. Skinner, *Beyond Freedom and Dignity* (New York: Vintage Books, 1972), 12, 191, 196.

9. B. F. Skinner, *Science and Human Behavior* (New York: Free Press, 1965), 6, 447.

10. William R. Uttal, *The Psychobiology of Mind* (Hillsdale, N. J.: L. Erlbaum Associates, 1978), 9, 10, 27, 52–53.

11. John G. Taylor, *Superminds* (London: Macmillan, 1975).

12. John G. Taylor, *Science and the Supernatural* (London: Panther Books, 1981), 6, 69, 108, 164.

13. *Ibid.*, 25–30, 83, 165–69. The issue here is not whether Taylor's original evidence was solid (which many parapsychologists doubt), but only that the modern worldview by itself led him to deny his own data.

14. James A. Alcock, "Parapsychology as a 'Spiritual' Science," Paul Kurtz, ed., *A Skeptic's Handbook of Parapsychology* (Buffalo, N. Y.: Prometheus Books, 1985), 537–65, esp. 562. Interestingly enough, Alcock makes his claim even though he realizes that a nonmaterialistic science is advocated by John Eccles, a Nobel prize-winner, and Karl Popper, the most influential philosopher of science of the twentieth century (558). Also, he repeats the conventional idea that "the path of science . . . [was] laid down upon the foundation of materialism," even though he had reviewed recent writings of Eugene Klaaren, Martin Rudwick, and others who show that this was not true, especially for Isaac Newton (562, 555).

15. Ilya Prigogine and Isabelle Stengers, *Order Out of Chaos: Man's New Dialogue with Nature* (New York: Bantam Books, 1984), xxvii.

16. Einstein's statement, which occurred in a letter, is cited in Banesh Hoffman (with Helen Dukas), *Albert Einstein: Creator and Rebel* (New York: Viking Press, 1972), 258.

17. P. C. W. Davies, *The Physics of Time Asymmetry* (Berkeley: University of California Press, 1976), 151.

18. Larry Dossey, *Space, Time and Medicine* (Boulder, Co.: Shambhala, 1982), 152, 153. Many people, rightly assuming that linear time has been a central feature of modernity, especially in the notions of *progress* and *evolution*, have wrongly assumed that the assertion of the ultimate unreality of time, vouchsafed by physics, would be a postmodern idea, liberating us from one of the shackles of modernity. The truth is that Western (as well as most Eastern) thought has generally held temporality to be unreal for the ultimate form of being, be it Plato's ideas (in one side of his thought), Aristotle's unmoved mover, the God of classical theists such as Augustine, Maimonides, and Thomas Aquinas, or the ultimate particles of modern physics. Although temporality has been central for Western thought and experience, especially in the modern period, it has seldom, as Stephen Toulmin and June Goodfield have shown (*The Discovery of Time* [New York: Harper & Row, 1965]), been considered to be fundamental, in the sense of real for the most real type of existent. Twentieth-century physics, in speaking of the ultimate unreality of time (largely through the influence of the interpretation given to relativity theory by Einstein with his Spinozistic leanings), has thereby not introduced a new idea but simply revitalized an old one. For further discussion, see the introduction to David Ray Griffin, ed., *Physics and the Ultimate Significance of Time: Bohm, Prigogine, and Process Philosophy* (Albany: State University of New York Press, 1986).

19. Steven Weinberg, *The First Three Minutes: A Modern View of the Origin of the Universe* (New York: Basic Books, 1977), 154.

20. D. M. Armstrong, "The Nature of Mind," C. V. Borst, ed., *The Mind-Brain Identity Theory* (London: MacMillan, 1979), 75, 67.

21. Joseph Wood Krutch, *The Modern Temper: A Study and a Confession* (New York: Harcourt, Brace & World [A Harvest Book], 1956), xi; emphasis added. By 1956, Krutch had decided that, of the two options noted in that final sentence, "Social Engineering rather than Existentialist resignation [has become] the dominant religion of today" (xiii). Krutch himself had in the meantime come to reject the view, which he still regarded as "the most prevalent educated opinion," that "there is no escaping the scientific demonstration that religion, morality, and the human being's power to make free choices are merely figments of the imagination" (xii). He no longer believed that "the mechanistic, materialistic, and deterministic conclusions of science do have to be accepted as fact and hence as the premises upon which any philosophy of life or any estimate of man and his future must be based" (xiii). His reasons for this change of mind were set forth in *The Measure of Man: On Freedom, Human Values, Survival and the Modern Temper* (Indianapolis, Ind.: Bobbs-Merrill, 1953), which is in harmony with the present volume, while not going as far and of course not having the advantage of the historical and scientific evidence that has appeared in the intervening decades.

22. Robert E. Egner and Lester E. Dennon, eds., *The Basic Writings of Bertrand Russell 1903–1959* (New York: Simon & Schuster, 1961), 67.

23. Krutch says of modern individuals: "It is easy for . . . all of us to believe that a man may be 'the product of' any one of a number of external 'forces'. . . . The one thing which we find it hard to believe is that what he might be 'the product of' is himself." And Krutch gives one of the reasons why: "The idea that [the realm of the subjective] might be autonomous and creative suggests the possibility that the methods which were working everywhere else might not work there. Concern with it was unscientific and therefore unintelligent" (*The Measure of Man,* 254, 117).

24. For a discussion and critique of Hans-Georg Gadamer's methodological dualism between hermeneutics and science, see Joel C. Weinsheimer, *Gadamer's Hermeneutics: A Reading of Truth and Method* (New Haven, Conn.: Yale University Press, 1985), 1–41; on Jürgen Habermas's views, see Richard J. Bernstein, ed., *Habermas and Modernity* (Cambridge, Mass.: MIT Press, 1985), especially the essays by Martin Jay, Thomas McCarthy, and Albrecht Wellmer.

25. Among Robert Merton's writings, see *The Sociology of Science: Theoretical and Empirical Investigations,* Norman W. Storer, ed. (Chicago: University of Chicago Press, 1973); "Priorities in Scientific Discovery: A Chapter in the Sociology of Science," *American Sociological Review* 22 (1957), 635–59; and "Sociology of Science: An Episodic Memoir," R. Merton and J. Gaston, eds., *The Sociology of Science in Europe* (Carbondale: Southern Illinois University Press, 1977), 71–109. For a discussion of the point, see M. D. King, "Reason, Tradition and the Progressiveness of Science," Gary Gutting, ed., *Paradigms and Revolutions: Appraisals and Applications of Thomas Kuhn's Philosophy of Science* (Notre Dame, Ind.: University of Notre Dame Press, 1980), 97–116, esp. 97–100.

26. See Paul K. Feyerabend, *Against Method: Outline of an Anarchistic Theory of Knowledge* (London: Verso, 1975), esp. 302–04; Steven Lukes, "On the Social Determination of Truth," chap. 7 of his *Essays in Social Theory* (New York: Columbia University Press, 1977); Martin Rudwick, "Senses of the Natural World and Senses of God: Another Look at the Historical Relation of Science and Religion," Arthur Peacocke, ed., *The Sciences and Theology in the Twentieth Century* (Notre Dame, Ind.: University of Notre Dame Press, 1981), 241–61; J. R. Ravetz, "The Varieties of Scientific Experience," *ibid.,* 197–206; Margaret J. Osler, "Apocryphal Knowledge: The Misuse of Science," Marsha P. Hanen, Margaret J. Osler, & Robert G. Weyant, eds., *Science, Pseudo-Science and Society;* Margaret C. Jacob, *The Newtonians and the English Revolution 1689–1720* (Ithaca, N. Y.: Cornell University Press, 1976), 173–74; John C. Greene, *Science, Ideology, and World View: Essays in the History of Evolution Ideas* (Berkeley: University of California Press, 1981); Stephen Jay Gould, *The Mismeasure of Man* (New York: W. W. Norton, 1981); Sandra G. Harding, *The Science Question in Feminism* (Ithaca, N. Y.: Cornell University Press, 1986).

27. Jane Flax, articulating a feminist postmodernism in the relativistic sense, says: "Perhaps 'reality' can have 'a' structure only from the falsely universalizing perspective of the master. That is, only to the extent that one person or group can dominate the whole, can 'reality' appear to be governed by one set of rules or be constituted by one privileged set of social relations." "Gender as a Social Problem: In and For Feminist Theory," *American Studies/Amerika Studien,* 1986, 17; quoted by Sandra Harding, *The Science Question in Feminism,* 26–27.

28. See Paul K. Feyerabend, *Against Method*, 208, and *Science in a Free Society* (London: NLB, 1978), 20, 27, 38, 40; Richard Rorty, *Philosophy and the Mirror of Nature* (Princeton:, N. J.: Princeton University Press, 1979), 174, 190–91, and *Consequences of Pragmatism* (Minneapolis: University of Minnesota Press, 1982), 204.

29. In the "Postscript" Thomas Kuhn added in the second edition of *The Structure of Scientific Revolutions* (Chicago: University of Chicago Press, 1970), he rejected the charge that his position was irrationalist. Nevertheless, he expressed the opinion that there is "no theory-independent way to reconstruct phrases like 'really there,' " and that "the notion of a match between the ontology of a theory and its 'real' counterpart in nature now seems to me illusive in principle" (206). For an extreme statement of this position, see Richard Rorty, *Philosophy and the Mirror of Nature*, 10, 176–79; *Consequences of Pragmatism*, xvi, xvii, xxv, xxvi, 106, 164, 192, 202.

30. Rorty, *Consequences of Pragmatism*, xvii, xxiv, xliii, xlvi, 140, 191–92.

31. Sandra Harding's important book *The Science Question in Feminism* largely revolves around this issue. Whereas one strand in feminist thinking about science advocates a "successor science," which would be a feminist and therefore degendered science (104, 122), another strand, often coexisting in the same thinkers, suggests that the very rigor and objectivity required by science is androcentric, sometimes adding relativistic postmodernism's denial of any preideological experience of reality. Harding, summarizing with approval some ideas of Donna Haraway's "In the Beginning Was the Word: The Genesis of Biological Theory" (*Signs* 6/3 [1981], 469–81), points out the tension involved "when feminists appeal to scientific 'facts' to refute sexist claims to provide scientific 'facts,' while simultaneously denying the possibility of perceiving any reality 'out there' apart from socially constructed languages and belief systems." Harding asks rhetorically: "How can we appeal to our own scientific research in support of alternative explanations of the natural and social world that are 'less false' or 'closer to the truth,' and at the same time question the grounds for taking scientific facts and their explanations to be the reasonable end of justificatory arguments?" (138). In pointing to the tension in some feminists who have accepted relativistic postmodernism, Harding is, in effect, bringing out the central contradiction within this form of postmodernism in general.

32. Evelyn Fox Keller, a mathematical biophysicist who has become a historian and philosopher of science, joins other feminists in adding a masculinist bias to the list of extrascientific influences on modern science (see note 45). Nevertheless, she rejects the "increasingly radical critique that fails to account for the effectiveness of science." She seeks a position between that position and one "that draws confidence from that effectiveness to maintain a traditional, and essentially unchanged, philosophy of science" (*Reflections on Gender and Science* [New Haven, Conn.: Yale University Press, 1985], 6). Colin A. Russell, in *Science and Social Change 1700–1900* (London: Macmillan, 1983), also seeks a position between the two extremes that science is " 'nothing but' a social phenomenon" and the "older view that science operates quite independently of social constraints" (4). His model "posits a cognitive content for science that is susceptible to cultural influences of all kinds while still being conformable to nature" (8). As an illustration of this context-transcending correspondence to nature, he says: "An inverse cube law, instead of

an inverse square law, for gravitational attraction, is . . . inconceivable in any social context" (7). Frederick Suppe, in an "Afterword" to the second edition of *The Structure of Scientific Theories* (Urbana: University of Illinois Press, 1977, 617–730), provides a critical review of recent thinking in the philosophy of science, and an account of *historical realism*, which he regards as the emerging consensus, and which steers a middle course between the old positivism and the extreme sociological views (652, 705). According to this view, "an adequate philosophy of science must embrace a 'hard-nosed' metaphysical and epistemological realism wherein how the world *is* plays a decisive role in the epistemic efforts and achievements of science," and "an adequate epistemology of science must involve a correspondence notion of truth" (649, 723).

33. I believe that this position reflects the intention of Paul Feyerabend better than the extreme position, which many of his statements suggest (such as those on the pages cited in note 28), that we cannot speak of scientific or other ideas as corresponding to reality at all. For example, he suggests that "Aristotelian science, taken as a whole, may have been more adequate than its highly abstract successors" (*Against Method*, 61, 17). Feyerabend's reputation as an extremist is due in large part to his advocacy of an "anarchistic" theory of knowledge; but he clearly says that he intends his anarchism only as a medicine, not as an epistemology and philosophy of science (*Science in a Free Society*, 127). What he has consistently opposed is the notion that the (modern) scientific method, as the successor to The One True Religion, gives us "the one true method" (*Against Method*, 216–18).

34. Sandra Harding points out that "scientific theories whose conceptual schemes contain oppressive political metaphors can nevertheless extend our understanding of the regularities of nature and their underlying causal tendencies" (*The Science Question in Feminism*, 239).

35. This point is by itself very important because, in Sandra Harding's words,

> reasoning based on the vast majority of assumptions that make up 'the scientific world view' . . . is now closer to folk thought than to rational, critical thinking . . . . Most of the beliefs of the average or even extraordinary Western scientist or intellectual are grounded in the 'authority of the ancients' rather than in critical individual evidence gathering (*The Science Question in Feminism*, 184–85).

36. The thesis of Hugh Kearney's *Science and Change 1500–1700* (New York: McGraw-Hill Book Co., 1971) is that "there were, during this period, at least three approaches to nature which may be broadly termed 'scientific' in the sense that they all produced discoveries which have been incorporated within the modern scientific tradition" (22–23).

37. Eugene Klaaren, *Religious Origins of Modern Science: Belief in Creation in Seventeenth-Century Thought* (Grand Rapids, Mich.: William B. Eerdmans, 1977), 98–99, 149. Klaaren's book is an illuminating study of Boyle's thought, with considerable discussion also of Newton's. See also Brian Easlea, *Witch Hunting, Magic and the New Philosophy*, 112, 138.

38. Klaaren, 173–77; Alexandre Koyré, *From the Closed World to the Infinite Universe* (Baltimore, Md.: The Johns Hopkins Press, 1968), 178–84, 210–13.

39. James R. Jacob, *Robert Boyle and the English Revolution* (New York: Franklin, Burt Publishers, 1978), 172. Brian Easlea, *Witch Hunting, Magic and the New Philosophy*, 113, 234–35.

40. Brian Easlea, *ibid.*, 94–95, 109, 132, 135.

41. Easlea, *ibid.*, 108–15, 138, 158, 210; James R. Jacob, *Robert Boyle and the English Revolution*, 161–76; Robert Lenoble, *Mersenne ou la naissance de méchanisme* (Paris: Librairie Philosophique J. Vrin, 1943), 133, 157–58, 210, 375, 381.

42. Easlea, *Witch Hunting, Magic and the New Philosophy*, 100–07, 113, 125, 130, 135, 137, 233.

43. Margaret C. Jacob, *The Newtonians and the English Revolution 1689–1720*, 237–42, 248; Frances Yates, *The Rosicrucian Enlightenment* (Boulder, Co.: Shambhala, 1978), 189–91, 226–28; Morris Berman, *The Reenchantment of the World* (Ithaca, N. Y.: Cornell University Press, 1981), 124–26.

44. Easlea, *Witch Hunting, Magic and the New Philosophy, 110, 139, 144;* Carolyn Merchant, *The Death of Nature: Women, Ecology and the Scientific Revolution* (San Francisco: Harper & Row, 1980), 164, 170, 193, 195, 227–32, 279; Morris Berman, *The Reenchantment of the World*, 126. In criticizing the "vulgar" notion of nature, which sees it as having life and power, Boyle said: "The veneration, wherewith men are imbued for that they call nature, has been a discouraging impediment to the empire of man over the inferior creatures of God" (*The Notion of Nature*, Vol. IV of *The Works of the Honorable Robert Boyle* [London, 1944], 363).

45. For this paragraph, I am indebted to Carolyn Merchant, *The Death of Nature*, 149, 156, 165, 168 and *passim*; Brian Easlea, *Witch Hunting, Magic and the New Philosophy*, 43, 89–90, 141, 221, 241–52; and especially Evelyn Fox Keller, *Reflections on Gender and Science*, chap. 3.

46. Sandra Harding summarizes an argument of W. Van den Daele about modern science's separation of fact and value: After the restoration of the monarchy in 1660 following the tumultuous period of the Puritan Revolution, during which science was closely allied with religion and with movements for social reform, science paid for royal support and protection by "the abandonment of the social reform goals which had motivated much of the new science in the first place . . . . The claim that science is value-neutral was not arrived at through experimental observation . . . ; it was instead a statement of intent, designed to ensure the practice of science a niche in society rather than the emancipatory reform of that society" (*The Science Question in Feminism*, 222, 224).

47. Colin A. Russell in *Science and Social Change 1700–1900* has suggested that the hostile relation that developed between science and religion in England in the late nineteenth century had less to do with the threat of scientific facts to theology and organized religion than with the question of "wherein was to lie the cultural leadership of the new generation of intellectuals." Remarking on the cultural control hitherto exerted by the Church, Russell continues: "The aim of the secularizing scientists was therefore to displace the ecclesiastical hegemony with a scientific one . . . . [S]cience was being used as an ideological weapon to advance the interests of the community that it founded" (258). The agent of this secularization was "Vic-

torian Scientific Naturalism—the view that nature's activity can be interpreted without recourse to God, spirits, etc . . . " (256). In reference to J. W. Draper's *History of the Conflict Between Religion and Science* (1875) and A. D. White's *The History of the Warfare of Science with Theology in Christendom* (1895), Russell says: "Such Whiggish historiography would not be acceptable today, but it served well the cause of triumphalist science. Indeed one is not too far from the mark to assert that the conflict thesis . . . is an artifact of Victorian social ambition" (258).

48. As shown in note 32, this *both-and* approach is shared by Colin Russell.

49. J. R. Ravetz, "The Varieties of Scientific Experience," 200–01.

50. Sandra Harding, *The Science Question in Feminism*, 38, 212, 39.

51. Henry P. Stapp, "Einstein Time and Process Time," David Ray Griffin, ed., *Physics and the Ultimate Significance of Time: Bohm, Prigogine, and Process Philosophy*, 264–70, esp. 264.

52. "Introduction: Of Shadows and Symbols," Ken Wilber, ed., *Quantum Questions: Mystical Writings of the World's Great Physicists* (Boston: Shambhala, 1984), 3–29, esp. 1–11.

53. David Bohm, "The Implicate Order: A New Order for Physics," Dean Fowler, ed., *Process Studies* 8/2 (Summer 1978), 73–102; *Wholeness and the Implicate Order* (London: Routledge & Kegan Paul, 1980); "Hidden Variables and the Implicate Order," *Zygon* 20/2 (June 1985), 111–24; "Time, the Implicate Order and Pre-Space," David Ray Griffin, ed., *Physics and the Ultimate Significance of Time: Bohm, Prigogine, and Process Philosophy*, 177–208.

54. Henry P. Stapp, "Einstein Time and Process Time"; "Whiteheadian Approach to Quantum Theory and the Generalized Bell's Theorem," *Foundations of Physics* 9/1–2 (1979), 1–25.

55. Donald R. Griffin, *The Question of Animal Awareness: Evolutionary Continuity of Mental Experience* (New York: Rockefeller University Press, 14, 23.

56. A. Goldbeter and D. E. Koshland, Jr., "Simple Molecular Model for Sensing and Adaptation Based on Receptor Modification with Application to Bacterial Chemotaxis," *Journal of Molecular Biology* 161/3 (1982), 395–416; Jess Stock, Greg Kersulis, and Daniel E. Koshland, Jr., "Neither Methylating nor Demethylating Enzymes are Required for Bacterial Chemotaxis," *Cell* 42/2 (1985), 683–90.

57. John H. Campbell, "Autonomy in Evolution," R. Milkman, ed., *Perspectives on Evolution* (Sunderland, Mass.: Sinauer Assoc., 1982), 190–200, and "An Organizational Interpretation of Evolution," David J. Depew and Bruce H. Weber, eds., *Evolution at a Crossroads: The New Biology and the New Philosophy of Science* (Cambridge, Mass.: MIT Press, 1985), 133–68; see also the discussion by Depew and Weber, xiv, 248. The lonely pioneer in the study of "transposons" was Barbara McClintock; see Evelyn Fox Keller, *A Feeling for the Organism: The Life and Work of Barbara McClintock* (New York: Freeman, 1983).

58. Ian Barbour, *Issues in Science and Religion* (Englewood Cliffs, N. J.: Prentice-Hall, 1966), 295–99, 333.

59. John H. Campbell, "An Organizational Interpretation of Evolution," 134–35.

60. As Harman points out in a note, his position is different from that of the other essays in this volume, in that his is more monistic, the others more pluralistic. All agree that creative experience is the ultimate reality; but Harman's monism gives causal primacy to conscious experience as a unitary whole, while the more pluralistic authors locate all causality in individual embodiments of creative experience. The pluralists do not deny an all-inclusive unity of creative experience, but the localized experiences are also regarded as fully actual, not mere appearances of the all-inclusive experience. What both positions share is the denial of what Whitehead has called "vacuous actuality," meaning actuality not constituted by experience. Hence, while we welcome Roger Sperry's stress on downward causation from conscious experience to the body, we cannot rest content with his own philosophical account of it, in which he explicitly rejects the idea that "every individual entity in the universe is held to possess consciousness or psychic properties of some sort"; see Roger Sperry, "Mental Phenomena as Causal Determinants in Brain Functions," *Process Studies* 5/4 (1975), 247–56, esp. 248.

61. J. E. Lovelock and Lynn Margulis, "Atmospheric Homeostasis by and for the Biosphere: The Gaia Hypothesis," *Tellus* 26/2 (1973); J. E. Lovelock, *Gaia: A New Look at Life on Earth* (Oxford: Oxford University Press, 1979); Lynn Margulis and Dorion Sagan, *Micro-Cosmos: Four Billion Years of Microbial Evolution* (New York: Summit Books, 1986). Neither Lovelock nor Margulis draws organismic conclusions from their hypothesis. Lovelock has distanced himself from the view that the planet as a whole is sentient and teleological, suggesting that all the phenomena can be interpreted cybernetically (*Gaia*, ix-x, 61–63), and Margulis has endorsed a fully mechanistic, reductionistic philosophy (*Micro-Cosmos*, 229, 256–75).

62. Bohm is reluctant to use the term *God* because of its supernaturalistic connotations. But he does think of the holomovement as holy, and as embodying intelligence and compassion; "Hidden Variables and the Implicate Order," 124; Reneé Weber, "The Enfolding-Unfolding Universe: A Conversation with David Bohm," Ken Wilber, ed., *The Holographic Paradigm and Other Paradoxes* (Boulder, Co.: Shambhala, 1982), 187–214, esp. 60–70.

63. I have dealt with this issue in the "Introduction" to *Physics and the Ultimate Significance of Time*, 10–15.

64. An editorial in a British journal (*Nature* 293 [September 24, 1981], 245–46) condemned Sheldrake's book, *A New Science as Life: The Hypothesis of Formative Causation* (London: Blond & Briggs, 1981), as an "infuriating tract" and "the best candidate for burning there has been for a long time." The editorial complained that the book was being hailed as an answer to materialistic science and was becoming "a point of reference for the motley crew of creationists, anti-reductionists, neo-Lamarckians and the rest." Calling the book "pseudo-science," it dismissed Sheldrake's claim that the hypothesis is testable, adding that "no self-respecting grant-making agency will take the proposals seriously." Of particular interest for the present discussion was the editor's statement that "finding a place for magic within scientific discussion . . . may have been part of the [author's] objective," and his apparent view that anti-reductionists and neo-Lamarckians are as far from the true faith as

creationists. This editorial evoked a number of critical responses from scientists, including Nobel prizewinning physicist Brian Josephson (*Nature* 293 [October 29, 1981], 594). In response to the editor's complaint that Sheldrake had not described the nature or origin of morphogenetic fields, Josephson said that the properties of heat, light, sound, electricity, and magnetism were investigated long before their natures were understood. The editor's stipulation that *all* aspects of a theory must be testable if it is to be called scientific would, Josephson added, bar general relativity, black holes, and many other concepts of modern science from the status of legitimate scientific ideas. Josephson closed by saying: "The fundamental weakness is failure to admit even the possibility that genuine physical facts may exist which lie outside the scope of current scientific descriptions. Indeed, a new kind of understanding of nature is now emerging, with concepts like implicate order and subject-dependent reality (and now maybe formative causation). These developments have not yet penetrated to the leading journals. One can only hope that editors will soon cease to obstruct this avenue of progress . . . ?"

65. Jane Duran, "Philosophical Difficulties with Paranormal Knowledge Claims," Patrick Grim, ed., *Philosophy of Science and the Occult* (Albany: State University of New York Press, 1982), 196–206, esp. 196. Paul Kurtz says that parapsychology's findings "contradict the general conceptual framework of scientific knowledge" (Paul Kurtz, ed., *A Skeptic's Handbook of Parapsychology* [Buffalo, N. Y.: Prometheus, 1985] 504). James Alcott, another critic, says that its constructs involve "drastic violations of the currently accepted laws of nature" (*ibid.*, 540). On this ground they insist that the evidence for parapsychological interactions would have to be more repeatable and undeniable than the evidence demanded by some other sciences (510, 540).

66. Jane Duran, 196; these limiting principles are taken from "The Relevance of Physical Research to Philosophy," C. D. Broad, *Religion, Philosophy and Psychical Research* (New York: Humanities Press, 1969), 7–26. Paul Kurtz, in referring to these principles, expresses the conventional, empircist view that they "have been built up from a mass of observations" (Paul Kurtz, ed., *A Skeptic's Handbook of Parapsychology,* 504). But we have learned that the denial of influence at a distance was based instead on *a priori*, originally theological, considerations.

67. Duran, 202.

68. Broad, 9, cited by Duran, 197.

69. David Bohm, "The Implicate Order: A New Order for Physics," 87–93; Henry Stapp, "Whiteheadian Approach to Quantum Theory and the Generalized Bell's Theorem"; Rupert Sheldrake, *A New Science of Life*, 93–96.

70. Bohm, *Wholeness and the Implicate Order*, 129, 186; Reneé Weber, "Conversations between Rupert Sheldrake, Reneé Weber, David Bohm," *ReVISION* 5/2 (Fall 1982), esp. 39, 44 (reprinted in Reneé Weber, ed., *Dialogues with Scientists and Sages: The Search for Unity* [London: Routledge & Kegan Paul, 1986]); Sheldrake, *A New Science of Life*, 95–96; Stapp, "Bell's Theorem and the Foundations of Quantum Physics," *American Journal of Physics* 53 (1985), 306–17; Alfred North Whitehead, *Process and Reality*, corrected edition, David Ray Griffin and Donald W. Sherburne, ed. (New York: Free Press, 1978), 308, and *Adventures of Ideas* (New York: Free Press, 1967), 248. For a comparison of Sheldrake and Whitehead on this

point, see my review of Sheldrake's book in *Process Studies* 12/1 (Spring 1982), 38–40.

71. Floyd W. Matson, *The Broken Image: Man, Science and Society* (1964; Garden City, N. Y.: Doubleday & Co., 1966), vi. In the light of Stephen Toulmin's crediting Frederick Ferré with having coined the term *postmodern science* (*The Return to Cosmology: Postmodern Science and the Theology of Nature* [Berkeley: University of California Press, 1982], 210), surely with reference to Ferré's 1976 book, *Shaping the Future: Resources for the Postmodern World* and his 1982 article reprinted herein, it is of pedantic historical interest to note that Matson had, unbeknownst to Ferré and Toulmin, spoken of postmodern science in 1964.

72. The term *dualism* is perhaps the most ambiguous, multivalent term in our language. It can refer, among other things, to a distinction between any of the following: (1) a natural and a supernatural world; (2) an actual and an ideal world; (3) time and eternity; (4) good and evil; (5) good and evil cosmic agents; (6) sentient and insentient things; (7) living and nonliving things; or (8) mind and body. Discussions about dualism often become unnecessarily charged because dualism in one sense is assumed to entail dualism in one or more of the other senses when it does not. In this discussion, dualism is always used, unless stated otherwise, to mean either (7) or (8) *in conjunction with* (6). As I stress in my essay herein, the term *dualism* should not be used for (8) alone, i.e., for the assertion that mind and body (or brain) are numerically distinct, rather than numerically identical, because this doctrine does not necessarily imply (6), i.e., the assertion that the mind is sentient while the brain and its components are insentient. Because the term *dualism* in this context inevitably connotes *Cartesian* dualism, with its problem of interaction, the term should not be used unless meaning (6) is also involved.

73. Thomas Reid, *Essays on the Intellectual Powers of Man* (Cambridge, Mass.: MIT Press, 1969), 96–97, 99, 110, 118, 123, 220, 240, 318.

74. Whitehead, *Process and Reality*, 343.

75. Karl R. Popper, *Of Clouds and Clocks* (St. Louis: Washington University Press, 1966), 15; emphasis his.

76. Karl R. Popper and John C. Eccles, *The Self and its Brain: An Argument for Interaction* (Heidelberg: Springer-Verlag, 1977), 16, 37, 105.

77. J. C. C. Smart, "Sensations and Brain Processes." C. V. Borst, ed., *The Mind-Brain Identity Theory* (London: Macmillan Ltd., 1979), 52–66, esp. 53–54.

78. J. C. C. Smart, "Materialism," C. V. Borst, ed., *ibid*, 159–70, esp. 165, 168–69.

79. Popper and Eccles, *The Self and its Brain*, 29–30.

80. *Ibid.*, 10.

81. Smart, "Sensations and Brain Processes," 63, 56.

82. D. M. Armstrong, "The Nature of Mind," C. V. Borst, ed., *The Mind-Brain Identity Theory*, 67–79, esp. 75.

83. As Thomas Nagel says, "much obscurity has been shed on the [mind-body] problem by faulty analogies between the mental-physical relation and rela-

tions between the physical and other objective aspects of reality" (*Mortal Questions* [Cambridge: Cambridge University Press, 1979], 202). He argues that it is unintelligible to speak of the emergence of experience, which is something *for* itself, out of things that are purely physical: "One cannot derive a *pour soi* from an *en soi* . . . . This gap is logically unbridgeable. If a bodiless god wanted to create a conscious being, he could not expect to do it by combining together in organic form a lot of particles with none but physical properties" (189; see also 166, 172, 182, 188).

84. Herbert Feigl, "Mind-Body, *Not* a Pseudoproblem;" Sydney Hook, ed., *Dimensions of Mind* (New York: New York University Press, 1960), 24–36, esp. 32, 33.

85. Richard Rorty, "Mind-Body Identity, Privacy and Categories;" *Review of Metaphysics* 19 (1965), 25–54; *Philosophy and the Mirror of Nature* (1979), 70–127. Rorty claims in his later "pragmatic" position no longer to espouse eliminative materialism, but it seems still to be presupposed.

86. D. E. Wooldridge, in *The Machinery of the Brain* (New York: McGraw-Hill, 1963), says:

No useful purpose has yet been established for the sense of awareness that illumines a small fraction of the mental activities of a few species of higher animals. It is not clear that the behavior of any individual or the course of world history would have been affected in any way if awareness were nonexistent (240).

87. On Harman, see note 60. On Bohm, see my "Bohm and Whitehead on Wholeness, Freedom, Causality, and Time;" John Cobb's "Bohm and Time;" and Bohm's "Reply to Comments of John Cobb and David Griffin" in Griffin, ed., *Physics and the Ultimate Significance of Time*, 127–76. On Sheldrake, see my review mentioned in note 70. Swimme is unconvinced of the appropriateness and helpfulness of the distinction between compound individuals and nonindividuated objects, developed below.

88. See Charles Hartshorne, "The Compound Individual;" Otis H. Lee, ed., *Philosophical Essays for Alfred North Whitehead* (New York: Longmans Green, 1936), 193–220.

89. Of course, to understand a computer one must take into acount final causation in the sense of the purpose for which it was made. But throughout this discussion the subject is internal, immanent final causation, not external, imposed final causation.

90. Sandra Harding supports this change, pointing out that physics, among other restrictions, "looks at either simple systems or simple aspects of complex systems;" so that it need not deal with the difficult question of intentional causality (*The Science Question in Feminism*, 44, 46).

91. For a development of the ideas in these two sentences, see the writings of psychiatrist Jule Eisenbud, whom philosopher Stephen Braude has called "parapsychology's premier living theoretician." Many of Eisenbud's essays have been collected in *Parapsychology and the Unconscious* (Berkeley, Calif.: North Atlantic Books, 1983), the "Preface" of which contains the accolade by Braude (7). For the various ideas, see 21, 22, 40, 72, 125, 167, 173, 183. On the resultant unlikelihood

of obtaining repeatable experiments in the ordinary sense, see 156–61. These points are also supported in Braude's own *The Limits of Influence: Psychokinesis and the Philosophy of Science* (London: Routledge & Kegan Paul, 1986), esp. 7–10, 23, 70, 278.

92. See the discussion of Feyerabend in note 33.

93. My discussion is this and the following paragraph is dependent upon Patrick Grim, *Philosophy of Science and the Occult*, 314–15; Ken Wilber, *Quantum Questions*, 13–14; and Nicholas Rescher, "The Unpredictability of Future Science," Robert S. Cohen and Larry Lauden, eds., *Physics, Philosophy and Psychoanalysis: Essays in Honor of Adolf Grünbaum* (Dordrecht: D. Reidel, 1983), 153–68.

94. It is often said that power and knowledge (or truth) have been the twin aims of modern science (e.g., Evelyn Fox Keller, *Reflections on Gender and Science*, 71). Of these twin aims, traditional descriptions spoke mainly of the quest for truth, while recent appraisals, whether condemnatory or positivistic, have seen the drive for power as the central aim. My position is that, while much of modern science has sought those truths that would provide power over nature (and sometimes thereby over other humans), it is not the quest for power that makes modern science "science" but the quest for truth (in the way specified in the second criterion), regardless of how limited these truths are and of the ulterior purposes for which they are sought. See also note 34.

95. Nicholas Rescher, "The Unpredictability of Future Science," 165, says: "Domain limitations purport to put entire sectors of fact wholly outside the effective range of scientific explanation, maintaining that an entire range of phenomena in nature defies scientific rationalization." See also Ken Wilber, *Quantum Questions*, 14.

96. This is one topic on which I disagree with Rupert Sheldrake, who wishes to exclude the topic of the origin of laws from science, assigning it instead to theology or metaphysics; see the final chapter of his *A New Science of Life*.

97. Evelyn Fox Keller, *Reflections on Gender and Science*, 131–36.

98. Patrick Grim, *Philosophy of Science and the Occult*, 315.

99. Jule Eisenbud (*Psi and Psychoanalysis* [New York: Grune & Stratton, 1970], 96) says that one particular kind of repeatability has given parts of physics such reliability that "few people (strangely) question its right to provide a model of 'reality.' " But, as he says, this kind of repeatability is only one of many considerations in authentication, not relevant for many questions in geology, meteorology, astronomy, biology, and much of psychology. Both Kurtz and Alcott (see notes 65 and 66 above) have claimed that parapsychological experiments, to be acceptable, would have to exemplify "strong" repeatability, meaning that, in Alcott's words, "any competent researcher following the prescribed procedure can obtain the reported effect" (540). But if the kind of phenomenon with which parapsychology is concerned is held to be an inherently elusive, not consciously controllable one, as Eisenbud and Stephen Braude hold (see note 91 above), this requirement for strong replicability amounts to a "Catch-22": parapsychologists could only prove that it exists by proving that it does not!

100. Nicholas Rescher ("The Unpredictability of Future Science," 163) says: "The contention that this or that explanatory resource is inherently unscientific should always be met with instant scorn. For the unscientific can only lie on the side of process and not that of product—on the side of *modes* of explanation and not its *mechanism*; of arguments rather than phenomena."

101. Rescher (*ibid.*, 166) says that "there is no reason why, in human affairs any more than in quantum theory, the boundaries of science should be so drawn as to exclude the unpredictable." Long ago, William James said that "the spirit and principles of Science are mere affairs of method; there is nothing in them that need hinder Science from dealing successfully with a world in which personal forces are the starting points of new effects" ("Presidential Address," *Proceedings of the Society for Psychical Research* 12 [1896–97], 2–10, esp. 10).

102. Rescher (*ibid.*, 169) says:

Not only can we never claim with confidence that the science of tomorrow will not resolve the issues that the science of today sees as intractable, but one can never be sure that the science of tomorrow will not endorse what the science of today rejects. This is why it is infinitely risky to speak of this or that explanatory resource (action at a distance, stochastic processes, mesmerism, etc.) as inherently unscientific. Even if X lies outside the range of science as we nowadays construe it, it by no means follows that X lies outside science as such.

103. If there are such common beliefs, their recognition by members of diverse linguistic communities is, while difficult, not impossible. Even though a given worldview will predispose its adherents to recognize some such beliefs while ignoring, distorting, or even verbally denying other such beliefs that are noticed by adherents of other worldviews, it is possible, when the search for truth through public demonstration is sincere, to recognize such beliefs through conversation and self-observation.

104. In spite of my agreement, expressed in prior notes, with Nicholas Rescher's formal ideas, I cannot accept his substantive idea that actualities could have emerged out of a realm of mere possibility. I do not see how we can abandon the notion that agency requires actuality, and hence the "hoary dogma," as Rescher calls it, that *ex nihilo nihil fit*. I have reviewed Rescher's *The Riddle of Existence: An Essay in Idealistic Metaphysics* (Lanham, Md.: University of America Press, 1985) in *Canadian Philosophical Reviews*, December, 1986, 531–32.

105. Sandra Harding points out that the one-sided attempts to explain science either from a purely externalist or a purely internalist approach lead to paradox. The externalist approach, which understands the development of science in terms of external causes alone, leads to a self-refuting relativism. "Why should changes in economic, technological, and political arrangements make the new ideas reflecting these arrangements better ideas? Why shouldn't we regard the externalist program itself as simply an epiphenomenon of nineteenth- and twentieth-century social relations destined to be replaced as history moves along?" (*The Science Question in Feminism*, 215). The internalist or intentionalist approach praises natural science for showing that all natural and social phenomena are to be explained in externalistic terms, then supports the truth of this idea by "defending an intentionalist approach

to explaining the development of science alone" (212). What we need is an approach that recognizes the two-way causal influences between ideas and social relations, and which thereby allow us both to understand how "social arrangements shape human consciousness" and "to retain the internalist assumption that not all beliefs are equally good" (209, 231, 214). On the recognition of the need for this both-and approach, see also notes 32, 48, and 107.

106. I have dealt with these issues in "Introduction: Time and the Fallacy of Misplaced Concreteness" in *Physics and the Ultimate Significance of Time*; there is a brief discussion of apparent precognition on 30–31. See also Jule Eisenbud, *Parapsychology and the Unconscious*, 45. Although Stephen Braude has not changed his earlier opinion that arguments against the very intelligibility of backward causation are unconvincing, perhaps because he has not developed a general theory of causation (*The Limits of Influence*, 261), he has concluded that the idea is very problematic, and that ostensible precognition can be explained without resort to this idea (261–77).

107. Frederick Suppe has pointed out that most discussions of the idea of knowledge as "justified true belief" have assumed that "knowing that X is true" entails "knowing that one knows that X is true," i.e., having adequate evidence to defend the claim to know that it is true (*The Structure of Scientific Theories*, 717–28). This unjustified requirement, which leads to a vicious infinite regress, lies behind Hume's skeptical attacks on the possibility of knowledge and most recent rejections, by Kuhn, Feyerabend, and others, of the relevance of the correspondence notion of truth to scientific beliefs (718, 719, 723). Suppe argues rightly for "a separation of the role of evidence in the rational evaluation and defense of knowledge claims from the role evidence plays in obtaining knowledge" (725). With that separation, we can maintain the traditional definitions of knowledge as justified true belief and of truth as correspondence of belief to reality. None of this entails, I would insist perhaps more strongly than Suppe, that the modern scientific worldview is true, or that any of the current scientific theories gives us anything approaching the whole truth about their referents. Indeed, it is only if we hold to these traditional definitions of truth and knowledge that we have a rational standard in terms of which to criticize the dominant contemporary knowledge-claims.

108. The issue of correspondence was broached above, in the discussion related to notes 27 through 34. The way in which panexperiential philosophy can make sense of a notion of correspondence is to be dealt with in essays in Volume 4 of this series.

109. These principles, especially the latter four, have all, in fact, been denied by modern science-related thought. However, their explicit denial has been accompanied by implicit affirmation, producing massive incoherence. The reason for their explicit denial is *not* that they conflict with the implications of any other equally universal principles but that they conflict with the implications of contingent beliefs of modernity, which have been discussed above.

110. Stephen Toulmin, *The Return to Cosmology: Postmodern Science and the Theology of Nature*, 224, 226.

111. *Ibid.*, 233, 237, 247, 8.

112. As indicated on pages 13–14 and exemplified in Parts I and II of the book.

113. *Ibid.*, 13, 16, 268, 274.

114. *Ibid.*, 16.

115. *Ibid.*, 1, 260, 265, 272.

116. *Ibid.*, 248, 254, 255–56, 257, 262. Toulmin says in one place that issues of methodology, attitude, and social organization in modern science have been more important for the rejection of genuine cosmology than novelties in content (227). However, he points out that changes in content are closely interrelated with changes in methodology (228), and that it was the dualism between "rational, thinking humanity" and "causal, unthinking nature" that led to the notion of science as a value-neutral, objective, purely theoretical activity (238–47). Also, although Toulmin usually speaks only of reintegrating humanity into nature (253, 254, 257, 262), he notes that once nature was thought of as composed of "insensate" physical objects the problems related to vitality became almost as intractable as those related to mentality (241, 248). He is, furthermore, critical of the anthropocentric treatment of other creatures as mere means to our ends (272). Hence, the larger issue is reintegrating *life* into nature.

117. I wish to stress both that this book represents only one of the first steps, and that it is a first step in which only some of the necessary elements are contained. One of the major omissions is the lack of any feminine perspectives of the kind cited in notes 31 and 45. (I had hoped to have an essay by Carolyn Merchant, who was a participant at the conference from which many of the essays were drawn, but her schedule required that hers be postponed until a later volume. Liberation from sexism plays a more central role in Volume II, and Catherine Keller's essay therein draws importantly upon Merchant's work.) Also, while the relevance of a reenchanted science to ecological liberation is dealt with explicitly, this volume hardly broaches the question of the ways in which postmodern science might be emancipatory in relation to the racist, classist, and imperialist oppression supported by modern science (see Brian Easlea, *Liberation and the Aims of Science: An Essay on Obstacles to the Building of a Beautiful World* [Totowa, N. J.: Rowman and Littlefield, 1973], as well as the writings of Easlea, Gould, Greene, and Harding mentioned in notes 2 and 26).

2

THE COSMIC CREATION STORY

Brian Swimme

Our planetary difficulties: our technologies have resulted in 50,000 nuclear warheads; our industrial economies have given us ecocide on every continent; our social distribution of goods and services has given us a billion underdeveloped and starving humans. One thing we can conclude without argument: as a species and as a planet we are in terrible shape. So as we consider proposals for leading us out of this dying world, we need to bear in mind that only proposals promising an immense efficacy need be considered. Anything less than a fundamental transformation of our situation is hardly worth talking about.

And yet, given this demand, my own suggestion is that we tell stories— in particular, that we tell the many stories that comprise the great cosmic story. I am suggesting that this activity of cosmic storytelling is the central political and economic act of our time. My basic claim is that by telling our cosmic creation story, we inaugurate a new era of human and planetary health, for we initiate a transformation out of a world that is—to use David Griffin's thorough formulation—mechanistic, scientistic, dualistic, patriarchal, Eurocentric, anthropocentric, militaristic, and reductionistic!

A *cosmic creation story* is that which satisfies the questions asked by humans fresh out of the womb. As soon as they get here and learn the language, children ask the cosmic questions. Where did everything come from? What is going on? Why are you doing such and such anyway? The young of our species desire to learn where they are and what they are about in this life. That is, they express an inherent desire to hear their cosmic story.

By *cosmic creation story* I also mean to indicate those accounts of the universe we told each other around the evening fires for most of the last 50,000 years. These cosmic stories were the way the first humans chose to initiate and install their young into the universe. The rituals, the traditions, the taboos, the ethics, the techniques, the customs, and the values all had as their core a cosmic story. The story provided the central cohesion for each society. *Story* in this sense is "world-interpretation"—a likely account of the development and nature and value of things in this world.

Why story? Why should "story" be fundamental? Because without storytelling, we lose contact with our basic realities in this world. We lose contact because *only* through story can we fully recognize our existence in time.[2]

To be human is to be in a story. To forget one's story is to go insane. All the tribal peoples show an awareness of the connection between health and storytelling. The original humans will have their cosmic stories just as surely as they will have their food and drink. Our ancestors recognized that the universe, at its most basic level, is story. Each creature is story. Humans enter this world and awaken to a simple truth: "We must find our story within this great epic of being."

What about our situation today? Do we tell stories? We most certainly do, even if we do not call them stories. In our century's textbooks—for use in grade schools and high schools—we learn that it all began with impoverished primitives, marched through the technical inventions of the scientific period, and culminated—this is usually only implied, but there is never much doubt—in the United States of America, in its political freedom and, most of all, in its superior modes of production. For proof, graphs of industrial output compare the United States with other countries. Throughout our educational experiences, we were drawn into an emotional bonding with our society, so that it was only natural we would want to support, defend, and extend our society's values and accomplishments. Of course, this was not considered story; we were learning the facts.

Obviously, Soviets reflecting on their educational process recall a different story, one that began with the same denigration of the primal peoples, continued through a critique of bourgeois societies, and culminated in the USSR. And the French or British, reflecting on *their* educations, remember learning that, in fact, *they* were the important societies, for they were extending the European cultural tradition, while avoiding both the superficiality of the Americans and the lugubriousness of the Soviets.

Although we told ourselves such human stories, none of us in the industrial countries taught our children cosmic stories. We focused entirely on the human world when telling our stories of value and meaning. The universe and Earth taken together were merely backdrop. The oceans were large, the species many, yes—but these immensities were just the stage for the humans. This mistake is the fundamental mistake of our era. In a sentence, I summarize my position this way: *all our disasters today are directly related to our having been raised in cultures that ignored the cosmos for an exclusive focus on the human.* Our uses of land, our uses of technology, our uses of each other are flawed in many ways but due fundamentally to the same folly. We fail in so grotesque a manner because we were never initiated into the realities and values of the universe. Without the benefit of a cosmic story that provided meaning to our existence as Earthlings, we were stranded in an abstract world and left to invent nuclear weapons and chemical biocides and ruinous exploitations and waste.

How could this have happened? How could modern Western culture escape a 50,000-year-old tradition of telling cosmic stories? We discovered science. So impressed were we with this blinding light, we simply threw out the cosmic stories for the knowledge that the sciences provided. Why tell the story of the Sun as a God when we knew the sun was a locus of thermonuclear reactions? We pursued "scientific law," relegating "story" and "myth" to the nurseries and tribes. Science gave us the real, and the best science was mathematical science. We traded myth for mathematics and, without realizing it, we entered upon an intellectual quest that had for its goal a complete escape from the shifting sands of the temporal world. As Ilya Prigogine summarizes: "For most of the founders of classical science—even for Einstein—science was an attempt to go beyond the world of appearances, to reach a timeless world of supreme rationality—the world of Spinoza."[3]

What a shock it has been to have *story reappear*, and this time right in the very center of the mathematical sciences! Someday someone will tell the full story of how "story" forced its way into the most antistory domain of modern science—I mean mathematical physics. Here I would like to indicate in broad strokes what has happened.

For physicists during the modern period, "reality" meant the fundamental interactions of the universe. In a sense, the world's physical essence was considered captured by the right group of mathematical equations. Gravity and the Strong Nuclear Interaction were the real actors in the universe. The actual course of events was seen as of secondary importance, as the "details" structured by the fundamental dynamics of physical reality. The Story of Time was regarded as secondary, even illusory—time was simply a parameter that appeared in the equations. That is, nothing was special about the time today, as opposed to some time one billion years from now. Each time was the same, for the mathematical equations showed no difference between any two times.

The best story I know concerning this dismissal of time concerns Albert Einstein. Out of his own amazing genius, he arrived at his famous field equations, the mathematical laws governing the universe in its physical macrodimensions. What most alarmed Einstein—and we must remember that here was a man who had the courage to stick to his mathematical insights no matter how shocking they might seem to the world—what most disturbed Einstein about his own equations was their implication that the universe was expanding. Such a notion made no sense in the Newtonian cosmology of a static universe, which held that the universe today is essentially the same as the universe at any other time. In Newton's universe motion could exist *in* the universe, but the idea that the universe as a whole was changing was hardly thinkable. For these reasons, Einstein's equations stunned him when they whispered their secret—that the universe is not static; that the universe is expanding each moment into a previously nonexistent space; that the universe is a dynamic developing reality.

To avoid these alarming implications, Einstein altered his equations to eliminate their predictions. If only the truth of the universe could be so easily contained! Soon after Einstein published his equations, the Russian mathematician Alexander Friedmann found solutions to Einstein's equations—these solutions were theoretical universes, some of which expanded, some of which contracted, and some of which oscillated in and out. Einstein's response to Friedmann's communication was a polite dismissal of what seemed to be an utterly preposterous mathematical fiction.

But when Edwin Hubble later showed the empirical evidence for an expanding universe, Einstein realized his failure of nerve. He later came to regard his doctoring of the field equations as the "biggest blunder of my life."[4] My point is the complete surprise this discovery was for the scientists involved. If Einstein had left the equations as he had come to them, he would have made the greatest prediction in the entire history of science. But such a leap out of a static universe into a cosmic story was simply beyond the pale for our century's greatest scientist.

Even so, we now realize—following the work of Einstein, Hubble, and others—that ours is a universe that had a beginning in time and has been developing from 15 to 20 billion years. And every moment of this universe is new. That is, we now realize that we live not in a static Newtonian space; we live within an ongoing cosmic story.

Story forced its way still further into physics when in recent decades scientists discovered that even the fundamental interactions of the universe *evolved* into their present forms. *The laws that govern the physical universe today and that were thought to be immutable are themselves the results of developments over time.* We had always assumed that the laws were fixed, absolute, eternal. Now we discover that even the laws tell their own story of the universe. That is, the Cosmic Story, rather than being simply governed by fixed underlying laws, draws these laws into its drama.

Story inserts itself still further into the consciousness of contemporary physicists when the very status of physical law is put into a new perspective. Where once we listed a set of laws that, we were certain, held everywhere and at all times, we now ponder the violations of each of these laws. A preeminent physicist of our time, John Archibald Wheeler, concludes that in nature "there is no law except the law that there is no law." Wheeler's inclination is to question our fixation with law; he demands that the details of nature be given the same attention we give to the unifying ideas. As Wheeler sings, "Individual events. Events beyond law. Events so numerous and so uncoordinated that, flaunting their freedom from formula, they yet fabricate firm form."[5]

What happens when physicists begin to value not just the repeatable experiment but history's unrepeatable events, no longer regarding each event as simply another datum useful for arriving at mathematical law but as a revelation all by itself? A reenchantment with the universe happens. A new love affair between humans and the universe happens.

Only when we are surprised in the presence of a person or a thing are we truly in love. And regardless how intimate we become, our surprise continues. Without question we come to know the beloved better and are able to speak central truths about her or him or it, but never do we arrive at a statement that is the final word. Further surprises always occur, for to be in love is to be in awe of the infinite depths of things.[6] What I am suggesting by remembering Einstein's astonishment at the time-developmental nature of the universe and by underlining Wheeler's fascination with the individual event is that scientists have entered a new enchantment. Having been raised and trained in the disenchanted world of classical Newtonian physics, they are suddenly astonished and fascinated in an altogether new way by the infinite elegance which gathers us into its life and existence.

A central desire of scientists in the future will be to explore and celebrate the enveloping Great Mystery—the story of the universe, the journey of the galaxies, the adventure of the planet Earth and all of its life forms. Scientific theories will no longer be seen simply as objective laws. Scientific understanding will be valued as that power capable of evoking in humans a deep intimacy with reality. That is, the value of the electromagnetic interaction as objectively true will be deepened by our awareness that study and contemplation of the electromagnetic interaction allows humans to enter a rich communion experience with the contours of reality in the stellar cores, as well as in the unfolding dynamics of our sun and forests.

I am convinced, finally, that the story of the universe that has come out of three centuries of modern scientific work will be recognized as a supreme human achievement, the scientific enterprise's central gift to humanity, a revelation having a status equal to that of the great religious revelations of the past.

Of course, these are my speculations. I may be wrong. Instead of scientists devoting themselves to a further exploration and celebration of the cosmic story, they may be entirely captured by the militaries of the planet. But I do not think so, and for a number of reasons. The one reason I mention here concerns the planetary implications of the cosmic creation story.

I discussed Einstein's resistance to highlight an obvious and significant fact of the cosmic creation story—*its power to draw humans into itself.* Einstein did not want to discover an expanding, time-developmental universe. Another famous physicist, Arthur Eddington, found the whole notion "abhorrent." But the story convinces regardless. Its appeal to humans is virtually irresistible. The cosmic creation story has the potency to offset and even to displace entirely every previous worldview. Often, this displacing of traditional stories has resulted in cultural tragedy, and this reality must be discussed. What I want to bring to the readers' attention here is that the human being, as constituted today, finds the cosmic story undeniably tied to the truth, and this is great news indeed.

For suddenly, the human species as a whole has a common cosmic story. Islamic people, Hopi people, Christian people, Marxist people, and Hindu people can all agree in a basic sense on the birth of the Sun, on the development of the Earth, the species of life, and human cultures. For the first time in human existence, we have a cosmic story that is not tied to one cultural tradition, or to a political ideology, but instead gathers every human group into its meanings. Certainly we must not be naive about this claim of universality. Every statement of the cosmic story will be placed in its own cultural context, and each context is, to varying degrees, expressive of political, religious, and cultural perspectives. But given that fact, we have even so broken through to a story that is panhuman; a story that is already taught and developed on every continent and within every major cultural setting.[7]

What does this mean? Every tribe knows the central value of its cosmic story in uniting its people. The same will be true for us. We are now creating the common story which will enable *Homo sapiens* to become a cohesive community. Instead of structuring American society on its own human story, or Soviet society on its own human story, and so on, we have the opportunity to tell instead the cosmic story, and the oceanic story, and the mammalian story, so that instead of building our lives and our society's meanings around the various human stories alone, we can build our lives and societies around the Earth story.

This is a good place to make my final comment on the meaning of *cosmic creation story.* Although with this phrase I refer in general to the account of our emergence out of the fireball and into galaxies and stars and Earth's life, I also think of the cosmic story as something that has not yet emerged. I think we will only have a common story for the human community when poets tell us the story. For until artists, poets, mystics, nature lovers tell the story—or until the poetic and mystical dimensions of humans are drawn forth in every person who sets out to tell us our story—we have only facts and theories.[8]

Most tribal communities understand the necessity of developing storytellers—people who spend their lives learning the cosmic story and celebrating it in poetry, chant, dance, painting, music. The life of the tribe is woven around such celebrations. The telling of the story is understood both as that which installs the young and that which regenerates creation. The ritual of telling the story is understood as a cosmic event. Unless the story is sung and danced, the universe suffers from decay and fatigue. Everything depends on telling the story—the health of the people, the health of the soil, the health of the sun, the health of the soul, the health of the sky.

We need to keep the tribal perspective in mind when we examine our situation in the modern period. Instead of poets, we had one-eyed scientists and theologians. Neither of these high priests nor any of the rest of us was capable of celebrating the cosmic story. It is no wonder then that so many of us are sick and disabled, that the soils have gone bad, that the sky is covered with soot, and that the waters are filled with evils. Because we had no celebrations inaugurating us into the universe, the whole world has become diseased.

But what will happen when the storytellers emerge? What will happen when "the primal mind," to use Jamake Highwater's term,[9] sings of our common origin, our stupendous journey, our immense good fortune? We will become Earthlings. We will have evoked out of the depths of the human psyche those qualities enabling our transformation from disease to health. They will sing our epic of being, and stirring up from our roots will be a vast awe, an enduring gratitude, the astonishment of communion experiences, and the realization of cosmic adventure.

We must encourage cosmic storytellers because our dominant culture is blind to their value. Is it not remarkable that we can obtain several hundred books on how to get a divorce, how to invest money, how to lose fat, and yet there is nothing available to assist those destined to sing to us the great epic of reality?

I suggest that when the artists of the cosmic story arrive, our monoindustrial assault and suicide will end and the new beginnings of the Earth will be at hand. Our situation is similar to that of the early Christians. They had nothing—nothing but a profound revelatory experience. They did nothing—nothing but wander about telling a new story. And yet the Western world entered a transformation from which it has never recovered.

So too with our moment. We have nothing compared to the massive accumulation of hate, fear, and arrogance that the intercontinental ballistic missiles, the third world debt, and the chemical toxins represents. But we are in the midst of a revelatory experience of the universe that must be compared in its magnitude with those of the great religious revelations. And we need only wander about telling this new story to ignite a transformation of humanity. For this story has the power to undo the mighty and arrogant and to ignite the creativity of the oppressed and forgotten. As the Great Journey of the Universe breaks into human self-awareness, nothing can dam up our desire to shake off the suffocation of nationalism, anthropocentrism, and exploitation and to plunge instead into the adventure of the cosmos.

Let me end with an imaginary event—a moment in the future when children are taught by a cosmic storyteller. We can imagine a small group gathered around a fire in a hillside meadow. The woman in the middle is the oldest, a grandmother to some of the children present. If we can today already imagine such an event, we can be assured that tomorrow someone will begin the journey of bringing such dreams into practice.

The old woman might begin by picking up a chunk of granite. "At one time, at the beginning of the Earth, the whole planet was a boiling sea of molten rock. We revere rocks because everything has come from them— not just the continents and the mountains, but the trees, the oceans and your bodies. The rocks are your grandmother and your grandfather. When you remember all those who have helped you in this life, you begin with the rocks, for if not for them, you would not be."

She holds the rock before them in silence, showing each person in turn. "Do you hear the rock singing? In the last era, people thought there was no music in rocks. But we know that is not true. After all, some rocks became Mozart and showed their music as Mozart. Or did you think that the Earth had to go to Mars to learn how to play its music? No, Mozart is rocks, Mozart is the music of the Earth's rocks."

Now she slowly sinks her hands into the ground and holds the rich loamy soil before her. "Every rock is a symphony, but the music of soil soars beyond capture in human language. We had to go into outer space to realize how rare and unique soil is. Only the Earth created soil. There is no soil on the moon. There are minerals on the moon, but no soil. There is no soil on Mars. There is no soil on Venus, or on Sun, or on Jupiter, or anywhere else in the surrounding trillion miles. Even the Earth, the most extraordinarily creative being of the solar system, required four billion years to create topsoil. We worship and nurture and protect the soils of the Earth because all music and all life and all happiness come from the soil. The soils are the matrix of human joy."

She points now to a low-hanging star in the great bowl of the nightsky. "Right now, that star is at work creating the elements that will one day live as sentient beings. All the matter of the Earth was created by the Grandmother Star that preceded our Sun. She fashioned the carbon and nitrogen and all the elements that would later become all the bodies and things of Earth. And when she was done with her immense creativity, she exploded in celebration of her achievement, sharing her riches with the universe and enabling our birth.

"Her destiny is your destiny. In the center of your being you too will create, and you too will shower the world with your creativity. Your lives will be filled with both suffering and joy; you will often be faced with death and hardship. But all of this finds its meaning in your participation in the great life of Earth. It is because of your creativity that the cosmic journey deepens."

She stares into the distance. In the long silence, she hears the thundering breakers on the ocean shore, just visible in the evening's light. They listen as the vast tonnage of saltwater is lifted up in silence, then again pounds up the sand.

"Think of how tired we were when we arrived here, and all we had to do was carry our little bodies up the hills! Now think of the work that is being done ceaselessly as all the oceans of the world curl into breakers against the shores. And think of all the work that is done ceaselessly as the Earth is pulled around the Sun. Think of all the work that is done ceaselessly as all 100 billion stars of the Milky Way are pulled around the center of the galaxy.

"And yet the stars don't think of this as work. Nor do the oceans think of their ceaseless tides as work. They are drawn irresistibly into their activities, moment after moment. The Earth finds itself drawn irresistibly to the Sun, and would find any other path in life utterly intolerable. What amazing work the stars and the planets accomplish, and never do we hear them complain!

"We humans and we animals are no different at all. For we find ourselves just as irresistibly drawn to follow certain paths in life. And if we pursue these paths, our lives—even should they become filled with suffering and hardship—are filled as well with the quality of effortlessness. Once we respond to our deepest allurements in the universe, we find ourselves carried away, we find ourselves on the edge of a wave passing through the cosmos that had its beginning 15 to 20 billion years ago in the fiery explosion of the beginning of time. The great joy of human being is to enter this allurement which pervades everything and to empower others—including the soil and the grasses and all the forgotten—so that they might enter their own path into their deepest allurement."

The light of dusk has gone. She sits with them in the deepening silence of the dark. The fire has died down to become a series of glowing points, mirroring the ocean of starlight all above them.

"You will be tempted at times to abandon your dreams, to settle for cynicism or greed, so great will your anxieties and fears appear to you.

"But no matter what happens, remember that our universe is a universe of surprise. We put our confidence not in our human egos but in the power that gathered the stars and knit the first living cells together. Remember that you are here through the creativity of others. You have awakened in a great epic of being, a drama that is 15 to 20 billion years in the making. The intelligence that ignited the first minds, the care that spaced the notes of the nightingale, the power that heaved all 100 billion galaxies across the sky now awakens as you, too, and permeates your life no less thoroughly.

"We do not know what mystery awaits us in the very next moment. But we can be sure we will be astonished and enchanted. This entire universe sprang into existence from a single numinous speck. Our origin is mystery; our destiny is intimate community with all that is; and our common species' aim is to celebrate the Great Joy which has drawn us into itself.'

Rocks, soils, waves, stars—as they tell their story in 10,000 languages throughout the planet, they bind us to them in our emotions, our spirits, our minds, and our bodies. The Earth and the universe speak in all this. The cosmic creation story is the way in which the universe is inaugurating the next era of its ongoing journey.

NOTES

1. This summary is found in the "Statement of Beliefs and Purposes" of the Center for a Postmodern World, which is available from the Center at 2060 Alameda Padre Serra #101, Santa Barbara, Calif. 93103.

2. Paul Ricoeur, "On Interpretation," Kenneth Baynes, James Bohman, and Thomas McCarthy, eds., *After Philosophy* (Cambridge, Mass.: MIT Press, 1987), 358.

3. Ilya Prigogine, *From Being to Becoming* (San Francisco: Freeman, 1980), 215. On this point in general, see David Ray Griffin, ed., *Physics and the Ultimate Significance of Time: Bohm, Prigogine, and Process Philosophy* (Albany: State University of New York Press, 1986).

4. Charles W. Misner, Kip S. Thorne, and John Archibald Wheeler, *Gravitation* (San Francisco: Freeman, 1970), 410–11.

5. Quoted by Freeman Dyson in Dean W. Curtin, ed., *The Aesthetic Dimension of Science* (New York: Philosophical Library, 1982), 54.

6. See, for example, Erich Jantsch, *The Self-Organizing Universe* (New York: Pergamon Press, 1980), 176.

7. The first to celebrate the emergence of a new creation story were Loren Eiseley in *The Immense Journey* (New York: Random House, 1957) and Teilhard de Chardin in *The Phenomenon of Man* (New York: Harper & Row, 1959). The person who first realized the cultural and planetary significance of a common creation story was Thomas Berry; see his *The New Story* (Chambersburg, Penn.: Anima Books, 1978). For a superb contemporary telling of the entire cosmic story, see Nigel Calder, *Timescale* (New York: Viking Press, 1983).

8. My version of the cosmic story is *The Universe is a Green Dragon* (Sante Fe, N. M.: Bear and Co., 1985).

9. Jamake Highwater, *The Primal Mind* (New York: New American Library, 1981).

3

POSTMODERN SCIENCE
AND A
POSTMODERN WORLD

David Bohm

I. MODERN PHYSICS AND THE MODERN WORLD

With the coming of the modern era, human beings' view of their world and themselves underwent a fundamental change. The earlier, basically religious approach to life was replaced by a secular approach. This approach has assumed that nature could be thoroughly understood and eventually brought under control by means of the systematic development of scientific knowledge through observation, experiment, and rational thought. This idea became powerful in the seventeenth and eighteenth centuries. In fact, the great seal of the United States has as part of its motto "the new secular order," showing the way the founders of the country were thinking. The main focus of attention was on discerning the order of the universe as it manifests itself in the laws of nature. The principle path to human happiness was to be in the discovery of these laws, in complying with them, in utilizing them wherever possible for the benefit of humankind.

So great is the change in the whole context of thought thereby brought about that Huston Smith and some others have described it as the onset of the modern mind. [1] This mind is in contrast with the mind of the medieval period, in which it was generally supposed that the order of nature was beyond human comprehension and in which human happiness consisted in being aware of the revealed knowledge of God and carrying out the divine commandments. A total revolution occurred in the way people were aiming to live.

The modern mind went from one triumph to another for several centuries through science, technology, industry, and it seemed to be solidly based for all time. But in the early twentieth century, it began to have its foundations questioned. The challenge coming from physics was especially serious, because it was in this science that the modern mind was thought to have its firmest foundation. In particular, relativity theory, to a certain extent, and quantum theory, to a much greater extent, led to questioning the assumption of an intuitively imaginable and knowable order in the universe. The nature of the world began to fade out into something almost indescribable. For the most part, physicists began to give up the attempt to grasp the world as an intuitively comprehensible whole; they instead restricted their work mostly to developing a mathematical formalism with rules to apply in the laboratory and eventually in technology. Of course, a great deal of unity has emerged in this work, but it is almost entirely in the mathematical formalism. It has little or no imaginative or intuitive expression (whereas Newton's ideas were quite easily understandable by any reasonably educated person).

A similar current of thought has been developing at the same time in other fields. In philosophy, the trend has been to relinquish any notion that the general nature of reality could be known through some kind of metaphysics or worldview. Existentialists like Kierkegaard and Nietzsche and others following this line have emphasized instead what is personal and peculiar to each human being. Other philosophers have emphasized language as the main point, and positivists have said that the role of science is nothing more than a systematic and rationally ordered way of organizing our observational data. In art, as in literature and other fields, universal values have also generally been dropped, replaced for the most part by a focus on personal reactions or on some kind of formal structure.

Clearly, during the twentieth century the basis of the modern mind has been dissolving, even in the midst of its greatest technological triumphs. The whole foundation is dissolving while the thing is flowering, as it were. The dissolution is characterized by a general sense of loss of a common meaning of life as a whole. This loss of meaning is very serious, as meaning in the sense intended here is the basis of *value*. Without that, what is left to move people to work together toward great common aims sensed as having high value? Merely to operate at the level of solving problems in science and technology, or even of extending them into new domains, is a very narrow and limited goal which cannot really captivate the majority of the people . It cannot liberate humanity's highest and most comprehensive creative energies. Without such liberation, humanity is sinking into a vast mass of petty and transitory concerns. This leads, in the short run, to meaningless activity that is often counterproductive; in the long run, it is bringing humankind ever closer to the brink of self-destruction.

Needless to say, the development described above will have serious consequences for the individual human being, for society as a whole, and for the overall quality of relationships among human beings and between human beings and the rest of nature. Our entire world order has, in fact, been dissolving away for well over a century. This dissolution has tended further to erode all our basic values on which the stability of the world order must depend. Hence, we are now confronted with a worldwide breakdown which is self-evident not only at the political level but also in smaller groups and in the consciousness of the individual. The resort to mindless violence is growing and behind it all is the even more mindless threat of mutual annihilation, which is implicit in our current international situation and which could make everything we are doing quite pointless. I suggest that if we are to survive in a meaningful way in the face of this disintegration of the overall world order, a truly creative movement to a new kind of wholeness is needed, a movement that must ultimately give rise to a new order, in the consciousness of both the individual and society. This order will have to be as different from the modern order as was the modern from the medieval order. We cannot go back to a premodern order. A postmodern world must come into being before the modern world destroys itself so thoroughly that little can be done for a long time to come.

Even though physics is by now a rather specialized profession and even though the question of metaphysics or worldview is discussed seriously by only a few people within this profession, the worldview that physics provides is clearly still playing a crucial role as a foundation for the general mode of thinking which prevails throughout society. That is the worldview that physics provided from the sixteenth through the nineteenth centuries. It is therefore important to ask whether twentieth-century physics actually implies a universe that is beyond intuitive and imaginative comprehension, as well as whether this universe is without any deep meaning, being only something to be computed mathematically and manipulated technically. For example, one of the leading physicists at this time, Steven Weinberg, has said that the more he looks at the universe the less it seems to have any meaning, that we have to invent our own meaning if any is to exist. But, if we find that that is the wrong conclusion to be drawn from recent physics, this discovery may help open the way to the truly original and creative step that is now required of humankind. We *cannot* go on as we are; we must have something really new and creative. This step cannot be merely a reaction to the breakdown of the modern world order, but it must arise out of a fresh insight that would make it possible to move out of this morass into which we have been sinking.

The possibility of a postmodern physics, extended also to postmodern science in general, may be of crucial significance for this sort of insight. A postmodern science should not separate matter and consciousness and should therefore not separate facts, meaning, and value. Science would then be inseparable from a kind of intrinsic morality, and truth and virtue would not be kept apart as they currently are in science. This separation is part of the reason we are in our present desperate situation.

Of course, this proposal runs entirely contrary to the prevailing view of what science should be, which is a morally neutral way of manipulating nature, either for good or for evil, according to the choices of the people who apply it. I hope in this essay to indicate how a very different approach to science is possible, one that it is consistent and plausible and that fits better the actual development of modern physics than does the current approach.

II. MECHANISTIC PHYSICS

I begin by outlining briefly the mechanistic view in physics, which was characteristic of the modern view and which reached its highest point toward the end of the nineteenth century. This view remains the basis of the approach of most physicists and other scientists today. Although the more recent physics has dissolved the mechanistic view, not very many scientists and even fewer members of the general public are aware of this fact; therefore, the mechanistic view is still the dominant view as far as effectiveness is concerned. In discussing this mechanistic view, I start by listing the principal characteristics of mechanism in physics. To clarify this view, I contrast it with that of ancient times, which was organic rather than mechanistic.

The first point about mechanism is that the world is reduced as far as possible to a set of basic elements. Typically, these elements take the form of particles. They can be called atoms or sometimes these are broken into electrons, protons, and neutrons; now the most elementary particles are called quarks, maybe there will be a subquarks. Whatever they may be called, the assumption is that a basic element exists which we either have or hope to have. To these elementary particles, various continuous fields, such as electromagnetic and gravitational fields, must be added.

Second, these elements are basically external to each other; not only are they separate in space, but even more important, the fundamental nature of each is independent of that of the other. Each particle just has its own nature; it may be somewhat affected by being pushed around by the others, but that is all. The elements do not grow organically as parts of a whole, but are rather more like parts of a machine whose forms are determined externally to the structure of the machine in which they are working. By contrast, organic parts, the parts of an organism, all grow together with the organism.

Third, because the elements only interact mechanically by sort of pushing each other around, the forces of interaction do not affect their inner natures. In an organism or a society, by contrast, the very nature of each part is profoundly affected by changes in the other parts, so that the parts are internally related. If a man comes into a group, the consciousness of the whole group may change, depending on what he does. He does not push people's consciousnesses around as if they were parts of a machine. In the mechanistic view, this sort of organismic behavior is admitted, but it is explained eventually by analyzing everything into still smaller particles out of which the organs of the body are made, such as DNA molecules, ordinary molecules, atoms, and so on. This view says that eventually everything is reducible to something mechanical.

The mechanistic program has been very successful and is still successful in certain areas, for example, in genetic engineering to control heredity by treating the molecules on which heredity depends. Advocates do admit that the program still has much to achieve, but this mechanistic reductionistic program assumes that there is nothing that cannot eventually be treated in this way—that if we just keep on going this way we will deal with anything that may arise.

The adherence to this program has been so successful as to threaten our very existence as well as to produce all sorts of other dangers, but, of course, such success does not prove its truth. To a certain extent the reductionistic picture is still an article of faith, and faith in the mechanistic reductionistic program still provides the motivation of most of the scientific enterprise, the faith that this approach can deal with everything. This is a counterpart of the religious faith that people had earlier which allowed them to do great things.

How far can this faith in mechanism be justified? People try endlessly to justify faith in their religions through theology, and much similar work has gone into justifying faith in mechanism through the philosophy of science. Of course, that the mechanism works in a very important domain is given, thereby bringing about a revolution in our life.

During the nineteenth century, the Newtonian worldview seemed so certain and complete that no serious scientist was able to doubt it. In fact, we may refer to Lord Kelvin, one of the leading theoretical physicists at the time. He expressed the opinion that physics was more or less finished, advising young people not to go into the field because further work was only a matter of minor refinements. He did point, however, to two small clouds on the horizon. One was the negative results of the Michelson-Morley experiment and the other was the difficulty in understanding black-body radiation. Now he certainly chose his clouds well: the first one led to the theory of relativity and the second to quantum theory. Those little clouds became tremendous storms; but the sky is not even as clear today as it was then—plenty of clouds are still around. The fact that relativity and quantum together overturned the Newtonian physics shows the danger of complacency about worldview. It shows that we constantly must look at our worldviews as provisional, as exploratory, and to inquire. We must have a worldview, but we must not make it an absolute thing that leaves no room for inquiry and change. We must avoid dogmatism.

III. The Beginning of Nonmechanistic Physics: Relativity Theory

Relativity theory was the first important step away from the mechanistic vision. It introduced new concepts of space, time, and matter. Instead of having separate little particles as the constituents of matter, Einstein thought of a field spread through all space, which would have strong and weak regions. Some strong regions, which are stable, represent particles. If you watch a whirlpool or a vortex, you see the water going around and you see that the movement gets weaker the farther away it is from the center, but it never ends. Now the vortex does not actually exist; there is only the moving water. The vortex is a pattern and a form your mind abstracts from the sensations you have of moving water. If two vortices are put together, they will affect each other; a changing pattern will exist where they modify each other, but it will still be only one pattern. You can say that two exist, but this is only a convenient way of thinking. As they become even closer together, they may merge. When you have flowing water with patterns in them, none of those patterns actually has a separate existence. They are appearances or forms in the flowing movement, which the mind abstracts momentarily for the sake of convenience. The flowing pattern is the ultimate reality, at least at that level. Of course, all the nineteenth-century physicists knew this perfectly well, but they said that *really* water is made of little atoms, that neither the vortices nor the water are the reality: the reality is the little atoms out of which it is all made. So the problem did not bother them.

But with the theory of relativity, Einstein gave arguments showing that thinking of these separate atoms as existent would not be consistent. His solution was to think of a field not so different from the flowing water, a field that spreads through all space and time and in which every particle is a stable form of movement, just as the vortex or whirlpool is a temporarily stable form that can be thought of as an entity which can be given a name. We speak of a whirlpool, but one does not exist. In the same way, we can speak of a particle, but one does not exist: *particle* is a name for a certain form in the field of movement. If you bring two particles together, they will gradually modify each other and eventually become one. Consequently, this approach contradicted the assumption of separate, elementary, mechanical constituents of the universe. In doing so, it brought in a view which I call *unbroken wholeness* or *flowing wholeness:* it has also been called *seamless wholeness.* The universe is one seamless, unbroken whole, and all the forms we see in it are abstracted by our way of looking and thinking, which is convenient at times, helping us with our technology, for example.

Nonetheless, relativity theory retains certain essential features of mechanism, in that the fields at different points in space were thought to exist separately and not to be internally related. The separate existence of these basic elements was emphasized by the idea that they were only locally connected, that the field at one point could affect a field only infinitesimally nearby. There was no direct effect of a field here on something far away. This notion is now being called *locality* by physicists; it is the notion of no long-distance connection. This notion is essential to the kind of mechanistic materialism developing throughout the science of the modern era, the notion of separate elements not internally related and not connected to things far away. The animistic view of earlier times was that spirits were behind everything and that these spirits were not located anywhere. Therefore, things far away would tend to be related. This view was taken to be most natural by astrologers and alchemists. But that view had been turned completely around in the modern period, and the modern view seemed so fruitful and so powerful that there arose the utter conviction of its truth.

IV. MORE FULLY NONMECHANISTIC PHYSICS: QUANTUM THEORY

With quantum theory, a much bigger change occurred. The main point is that all action or all motion is found in a discrete indivisible unit called a *quantum.* In the early form of the theory, electrons had to jump from one orbit to the other without passing in between. The whole idea of the continuous motion of particles, an idea at the heart of mechanism, was thereby being questioned. The ordinary visible movement, like my hand moving, was thought to comprise a vast number of quantum movements, just as, if enough fine grains of sand are in the hourglass, the flow seems continuous. All movements were said to comprise very tiny, discrete movements that do not, as it were, go from one place to another by passing through the space in between. This was a very mysterious idea.

Second, matter and energy had a dual nature; they manifest either like a wave or like a particle according to how they were treated in an experiment. An electron is ordinarily a particle, but it can also behave like waves, and light which ordinarily behaves like waves can also behave like particles; their behavior depends on the context in which they are treated. That is, the quality of the thing depends on the context. This idea is utterly opposed to mechanism, because in mechanism the particle is just what it is no matter what the context. Of course, with complex things, this is a familiar fact; it is clear, for example, that organs depend very much on context, that the brain depends on the context, that the mind functions differently in a different context. The new suggestion of quantum theory is that this context-dependence is true of the ultimate units of nature. They hence begin to look more like something organic than like something mechanical.

A third point of quantum theory was the property of nonlocal connection. In certain areas, things could apparently be connected with other things any distance away without any apparent force to carry the connection. This "nonlocality" was very opposed to what Einstein wanted and very opposed to mechanism.

A fourth new feature of quantum physics, which was against mechanism, was that the whole organizes the parts, even in ordinary matter. One can see it doing so in living matter, in organisms, where the state of the whole organizes the various parts in the organism. But something a bit similar happens in electrons, too, in various phenomena such as superconductivity. The whole of chemistry, in fact, depends on this idea.

In summary, according to quantum physics, ultimately no continuous motion exists; an internal relationship between the parts and the whole, among the various parts, and a context-dependence, which is very much a part of the same thing, all do exist. An indivisible connection between elements also exists which cannot be further analyzed. All of that adds up to the notion that the world is one unbroken whole. Quantum physics thereby says what relativity theory said, but in a very different way.

These phenomena are evident only with highly refined modes of observation. At the ordinary order of refinement, which was available during the nineteenth century, there was no evidence that any of this was occurring. People formed the mechanistic philosophy on the basis of fairly crude observations, which demonstrates the danger of deciding a final philosophy on the basis of any particular observations; even our present observations may be too crude for something still deeper.

Now one may ask: if there has been such a disproof of mechanism, why is it that most scientists are still mechanistic? The first reason is that this disproof takes place only in a very esoteric part of modern physics, called *quantum mechanical field theories*, which only a few people understand, and most of those only deal with it mathematically, being committed to the idea they could never understand it beyond that level. Second, most other physicists have only the vaguest idea of what quantum mechanical field theorists are doing, and scientists in other fields have still less knowledge about it. Science has become so specialized that people in one branch can apply another branch without really understanding what it means. In a way this is humorous, but it has some very serious consequences.

V. Unbroken Wholeness and
Postmechanistic Physics

I propose a view that I have called *unbroken wholeness*. Relativity and quantum physics agree in suggesting unbroken wholeness, although they disagree on everything else. That is, relativity requires strict continuity, strict determinism, and strict locality, while quantum mechanics requires just the opposite—discontinuity, indeterminism, and nonlocality. The two basic theories of physics have entirely contradictory concepts which have not been brought together; this is one of the problems that remains. They both agree, however, on the unbroken wholeness of the universe, although in different ways. So it has seemed to me that we could use this unbroken wholeness as our starting point for understanding the new situation.

The question is then how to understand this wholeness. The entire language of physics is now analytic. If we use this language, we are committed to analyzing into parts, even though our intention may be quite the opposite. Therefore, the task is quite difficult.

What I want to suggest is that one of the most important problems is that of *order*. Worldviews have always had views of order. The ancient Greeks had the view of the earth as the center of the universe and of various spheres in order of increasing perfection. In Newtonian physics, the order is that of the particles and the way they move. That is a mechanical order, and coordinates are used mathematically to express that order. What kind of order will enable us to consider unbroken wholeness?

What *is* order? That is a very deep question, because everything we say presupposes order. A few examples: There is the order of the numbers, the order of the words here, the order of the walls, the order in which the body works, the order in which thought works, the order in which language works. We cannot really define order, but we nevertheless understand order somewhat, because we cannot think, talk, or do anything without beginning from some kind of order.

The order physics has been using is the order of separation. Here the lens is the basic idea. If one takes a photograph, one point on the object corresponds to one point on the image. This fact has affected us very greatly, suggesting that everything is made of points. The camera was thereby a very important instrument for helping to strengthen the mechanistic philosophy. It gives an experience that allows everybody to see what is meant by the idea that the universe is nothing but separate parts.

Another instrument, the *holograph*, can also illustrate this point. The Greek word *holo* means *whole*, and *graph* means *to write*; consequently, a holograph writes the whole. With the aid of a laser, which produces highly ordered light, the waves of light from everywhere can be brought to one spot, and just the waves, rather than the image of the object, can be photographed. What is remarkable is that in the resulting picture, each part of it can produce an image of the whole object. Unlike the picture produced by a camera, no point-to-point correspondence with the object obtains. Information about each object is enfolded in each part; an image is produced when this enfolded information is unfolded. The holograph hence suggests a new kind of knowledge and a new understanding of the universe in which information about the whole is enfolded in each part and in which the various objects of the world result from the unfolding of this information.

In my proposal of unbroken wholeness, I turn the mechanistic picture upside down. Whereas the mechanistic picture regarded discrete objects as the primary reality, and the enfolding and unfolding of organisms, including minds, as secondary phenomena, I suggest that the unbroken movements of enfolding and unfolding, which I call the *holomovement,* is primary while the apparently discrete objects are secondary phenomena. They are related to the holomovement somewhat as the vortex, in the above example, is related to the unbroken flow of water. An essential part of this proposal is that the whole universe is *actively* enfolded to some degree in each of the parts. Because the whole is enfolded in each part, so are all the other parts, in some way and to some degree. Hence, the mechanistic picture, according to which the parts are only externally related to each other, is denied. That is, it is denied to be the primary truth; external relatedness is a secondary, derivative truth, applicable only to the secondary order of things, which I call the explicate or unfolded order. This is, of course, the order on which modern science has focused. The more fundamental truth is the truth of internal relatedness, because it is true of the more fundamental order, which I call the implicate order, because in this order the whole and hence all the other parts are enfolded in each part.

In my technical writings,[2] I have sought to show that the mathematical laws of quantum theory can be understood as describing the holomovement, in which the whole is enfolded in each region, and the region is unfolded into the whole. Whereas modern physics has tried to understand the whole reductively by beginning with the most elementary parts, I am proposing a postmodern physics which begins with the whole.

VI. POSTMODERN SCIENCE AND QUESTIONS OF MEANING AND VALUE

We have seen that fragmentary thinking is giving rise to a reality that is constantly breaking up into disorderly, disharmonious, and destructive partial activities. Therefore, seriously exploring a mode of thinking that starts from the most encompassing possible whole and goes down to the parts (subwholes) in a way appropriate to the actual nature of things seems reasonable. This approach tends to bring about a different reality, one that is orderly, harmonious, and creative. For this actually to happen, however, a thoroughgoing end to fragmentation is necessary.

One source of fragmentation—perhaps the *major* one—is the belief that our thinking processes and what we are thinking about are fundamentally distinct. In this essay, I have stressed that everything is internally related to everything through mutual enfoldment. And evidently the whole world, both society and nature, is internally related to our thinking processes through enfoldment in our consciousness. For the content of our thought is just the world as we perceive it and know it (which includes ourselves). This content is not just a superficial part of us. Rather, in its totality, it provides us with the ground of all meaning in our lives, out of which arise our intentions, wishes, motivations, and actions. Indeed, even imagining what life could mean to us without the world of nature and society enfolded within us is impossible.

The general way we think of this world will thus be a crucially important factor of our consciousness, and thus of our whole being. If we think of the world as separate from us, and constituted of disjoint parts to be manipulated with the aid of calculations, we will tend to try to become separate people, whose main motivation with regard to each other and to nature is also manipulation and calculation. But if we can obtain an intuitive and imaginative feeling of the whole world as constituting an implicate order that is also enfolded in us, we will sense ourselves to be one with this world. We will no longer be satisfied merely to manipulate it technically to our supposed advantage, but we will feel genuine love for it. We will want to care for it, as we would for anyone who is close to us and therefore enfolded in us as an inseparable part.

Vice versa, however, the idea of implicate order means that we are enfolded in the world—not only in other people, but in nature as a whole. We have already seen an indication of this fact in that, when we approach the world in a fragmentary way, its response is correspondingly fragmentary. Indeed, it can be said that, as we are not complete without the world which is enfolded in us, so the world is not complete without us who are enfolded in it. It is a mistake to think that the world has a totally defined existence separate from our own and that there is merely an external "interaction" between us and the world. It follows that if we approach the world through enfolding its wholeness in our consciousness and thus act with love, the world, which enfolds our own being within itself, will respond in a corresponding way. This can obviously happen in the world of society. But even the world of nature will cease to respond with degeneration, due to pollution, destruction of forests, and so on, and will begin to act in a more orderly and favorable way.

I want to emphasize this point. Because we are enfolded inseparably in the world, with no ultimate division between matter and consciousness, *meaning and value are as much integral aspects of the world as they are of us.* If science is carried out with an amoral attitude, the world will ultimately respond to science in a destructive way. Postmodern science must therefore overcome the separation between truth and virtue, value and fact, ethics and practical necessity. To call for this nonseparation, is, of course, to ask for a tremendous revolution in our whole attitude to knowledge. But such a change is now necessary and indeed long overdue. Can humanity meet in time the challenge of what is required? The coming years will be crucial in revealing the answer to this question.

NOTES

1. See Huston Smith, *Beyond the Post-Modern Mind* (New York: Crossroad, 1982), esp. chap. 8, "Beyond the Modern Western Mind-set."

2. See David Bohm, *Wholeness and the Implicate Order* (London: Routledge & Kegan Paul, 1980) and other references given therein.

4

THE POSTMODERN CHALLENGE TO BIOLOGY

Charles Birch

The dominant model of life in biology today is strictly mechanistic (substantialist) and reductionist. But it is not the model of life of the founders of modern biology in the sixteenth and seventeenth centuries. Vesalius, Harvey, and others had a more organic view of life. What they discovered was later set in a mechanistic framework by their successors, particularly René Descartes. The methodology of mechanistic biology is to investigate the living organism as if it were a machine. Many biologists, probably most of them since Descartes, take the next step, a metaphysical one, and conclude that the living organism *is* a machine.

To be critical of the mechanistic model in biology is not to deny that it has been highly successful. The triumphs of molecular biology in describing and manipulating genes are triumphs of the mechanistic and reductionist approach. There are mechanical aspects of living entities. Limbs operate as levers. The heart operates as a pump. As Levins and Lewontin say:

> The great success of Cartesian method and the Cartesian view of nature is in part a result of a historical path of least resistance. Those problems that yield to the attack are pursued most vigorously, precisely

69

because the method works there. Other problems and other phenomena are left behind, walled off from understanding by the commitment to Cartesianism. [1]

To be critical of the mechanistic model is not to deny a role to this way of thinking. It is to recognize that there are some problems in biology that have been singularly unresponsive to the mechanistic approach. These are developmental biology, the function of the central nervous system, aspects of animal behavior, and the evolution of mind and consciousness.

I. Contrast between the Mechanistic and the Ecological Models

The mechanistic model of life recognizes only one set of causes as operative in a living organism. These are external relations—those components of the organism's environment that push it or pull it. Descartes wanted to reduce the laws of biology to the laws of matter in motion. "Give me matter and motion," he said in effect, "and I shall construct a universe." Mind was recognized to exist only in human beings. The rest of the created things on our planet, including the human body, were understood in strictly mechanistic terms.

The postmodern challenge to biology is to recognize a second set of causes in addition to external relations. This second set is internal relations. We recognize internal relations in ourselves when our lives are profoundly influenced by a compelling purpose. Human lives are changed by such influences. I am what I am partly as a consequence of all the external relations that have impinged on me since conception. But I am also what I am by virtue of internal relations—the ways I have chosen to respond to those external conditions. An internal relation determines the nature of the entity, indeed even its very existence.

The notion of internal relation as causal strikes at the heart of the strictly mechanistic and reductionistic model. The ideal of this model is to divide the world into next to nothing as possible—call those entities "atoms" or what you will—and then try to build the world up again from those building blocks. When you do that, of course, you get a machine. In the mechanistic model the building blocks are substances. They have no internal relations. The definition of a substance is something that exists independently of anything else. In substance thinking, an atom of hydrogen is the same atom of hydrogen whether it be in the heart of the sun or in the molecules of my brain. It is what it is independently of its environment. That is the substance notion of a hydrogen atom. The idea of internal relations is that a human being, let us say, is not the same person independent of his or her environment. The human being is a subject and not simply an object pushed around by external relations. To be a subject is to be responsive, to constitute oneself purposefully in response to one's environment. The postmodern view that makes most sense to me is the one that takes human experience as a high-level exemplification of entities in general, be they cells or atoms or electrons. All are subjects. All have internal relations. Consequently, in biology a distinction is made between a biology that is *compositional* (substantialist) and one that is *relational* (ecological).

As one moves up levels of organization—electrons, atoms, molecules, cells, etc.—the properties of each larger whole are given not merely by the units of which it is composed but also by the new relations between these units. It is not simply that the whole is more than the sum of its parts. The parts are themselves redefined and recreated in the process of evolution from one level to another. This means that the properties of matter relevant at, say, the atomic level do not begin to predict the properties of matter at the cellular level, let alone at the level of complex organisms. That is why, already 50 years ago, the Danish physicist Niels Bohr advised his students that the new laws of physics were most likely to be discovered in biology. This introduces a principle unrecognized by the mechanistic model, that as well as interpreting the higher levels in terms of the lower, we also interpret the lower levels in terms of the higher.

I have drawn a contrast between an organism or natural entity and a machine. The parts of a machine are subject only to the laws of mechanics, with its external forces acting on these parts. In some modern machines, such as computers, nuts and bolts are replaced by transistors and microchips. There is no evolution of computers in any real sense, but only change in design brought about by the designer outside the machine. There is of course also natural selection—in the market place! Likewise, in the mechanical model of life, no real evolution occurs, merely rearrangements of parts and natural selection among the different arrangements.

Nuts and bolts cannot evolve! They can only be rearranged. This means that a completely mechanistic account of evolution is a gross abstraction from nature. Whitehead perceived this critical distinction when he wrote:

> A thoroughgoing evolutionary philosophy is inconsistent with materialism. The aboriginal stuff, or material, from which a materialistic philosophy starts, is incapable of evolution. This material is in itself the ultimate substance. Evolution, on the materialistic theory, is reduced to the role of being another word for the description of the changes of the external relations between portions of matter. There is nothing to evolve, because one set of external relations is as good as any other set of external relations. There can be merely change, purposeless and unprogressive . . . . The doctrine thus cries aloud for a conception of organism as fundamental to nature.[2]

Evolution, according to the ecological or organic model, is the evolution not of substances but of subjects. The critical thing that happens in evolution is change in internal relations of subjects.

II. PUTTING THE ECOLOGICAL MODEL
INTO PRACTICE

It is one thing, says Lewontin,[3] to call for a biology that is relational rather than compositional. It is quite another to put it into practice. Lewontin makes some attempt to do this in relation to his model of dialectical materialism. I want to do this in relation to the ecological model which I find more illuminating than dialectical materialism. What follows are some examples.

A mechanistic brain physiologist analyses my sitting at a word processor in terms of light waves impinging on my retina from the keyboard and the screen which set in train chemical processes in my nerves and brain. Messages from the brain to my muscles cause them to contract in ways that result in very complex movements of my fingers as I sit at the machine. This interpretation is fine as far as it goes—but it does not go very far. It does not account for the fact that I have some thoughts in mind that I purpose to put into writing. My thoughts initiate the complex sequence of events the physiologist studies. What the physiologist describes are external relations. The influence of my thoughts are internal relations. The distinction between these two sorts of causes in human behavior was clearly made by Socrates as reported in Plato's dialogue the *Phaedo*. There are some, he tells us, who argue that the cause of his actions as he sits in prison awaiting death are the mechanical forces on his bones and muscles and sinews. But the real cause of his sitting in prison was that he made a *choice* to bow to the Athenians' sentence. In the mechanistic analysis, an immense gap exists between what the scientist describes and what I experience. This is recognized by some brain physiologists, notably Sperry,[4] who considers that a thought itself can initiate chemical and electrical impulses in cells in the brain. His attempt to bring the mental and the physical together provides a richer understanding than the view that regards the physical account as exclusive and sufficient.

Some activities, such as the movement of fingers, appear to be represented in the brain in particular groups of cells. But in the case of visual memory, the brain does not seem to store information locally but widely. Karl Pribram and his colleagues[5] produced a holographic model of the brain in which the image is not represented in the brain as a point-to-point image from an object to a photographic plate. Rather, it is represented such that if some cells of the brain are removed, this removal does not destroy just one part of the image but reduces the clarity of the image as a whole. Dissecting the visual image down to particular cells is not possible. The image is a consequence of the interrelation of many cells as a whole. This is a far more ecological model of the brain than the strictly mechanistic model provided by most brain physiologists.

A mechanistic student of animal behavior seeks to interpret all behavior in terms of stimulus and response, analogously to the way in which a photoelectric cell receives a message from our approach to a door and responds with a message to a motor to open the door. These sorts of relationships can be made quite complex by incorporating negative feedback (cybernetic) mechanisms. We can then construct complex robots that perform quite complex activities. Such models add something to our understanding of animal behavior. But the environment of these robots is extremely simple compared to the environment of any animal in the wild. The nonmechanistic student of animal behavior tries to study animals in their complex relations with a complex world, as Jane Goodall has done with chimpanzees in Gombe Reserve.[6] Her success was dependent upon her establishing a rapport with the chimpanzee and, presumably, vice versa. She tried to think like a chimpanzee and to imagine what it was like to be one. She was, in fact, taking into account what she perceived to be critically important internal relations in their lives.

Hartshorne provided evidence that supports his view that birds have some musical feeling and that their song is not simply a matter of attracting the attention of mates.[7] In more general terms, Donald R. Griffin argues that the needed step in research in animal behavior is to attempt to understand the mind of the animal and he suggests ways to approach this.[8] I cannot really know what it is to be a chimpanzee, let alone a bee, unless I am one. Nor can I know what it is to be you instead of me. But in this latter case, we struggle imaginatively to enter one another's lives. Why should we not seek to do the same with other living organisms? Is not our neighbor all that participates in life? If so, the implication for ethics is revolutionary. If the needs of neighbors stretch beyond human need, so does the reach of love.

A mechanistic sociobiologist argues that individual human limitations imposed by genes place constraints on society. The nonmechanistic student of societies argues that social organizations are able to negate individual limitations. Lewontin makes the analogy of human beings and flight.[9] Human beings cannot fly by flapping their arms and legs. Yet we do fly because of the existence of aircraft, pilots, fuel production, radios—all products of social organization. Moreover, it is not society that flies, but the individuals who have acquired this property as a consequence of socialization. The individual can be understood only in terms of the total environment. In different environments we have different properties. We are indeed different.

The naively mechanistic geneticist says that genes are particles located on chromosomes, that genes make proteins, proteins make us, and that genes replicate themselves. The nonmechanistic geneticist says genes are not like particles at all. What a gene is depends upon neighboring genes on the same and on different chromosomes and upon other aspects of its environment in the cell. The gene (DNA) makes nothing by itself. It does not even make more DNA. It depends on enzymes in the cell to do all these things. Geneticists no longer teach "particulate genetics." And molecular biology is properly called *molecular ecology*. We know that a particular DNA molecule can express itself in a great variety of ways—*which* way depends upon the environent of the cell and therefore of the molecule at the time.

The molecule and its chemical environment are in a state of perpetual dynamic equilibrium depending upon the magnitude of the physical forces and the concentrations of chemicals inside the cell. Which chemical pathway is *chosen* is a matter of probability rather than absolute determinism. The difference between 100 percent determinism and even 99.99 percent determinism is all the difference in the world. It is the difference between being completely determined by the environment and having a degree of self-determination. A thoroughgoing mechanist might argue that the difference between 100 percent and 99.99 percent may be due to defective functioning of a deterministic system, which is precisely the point. If accidents can happen in the system, determinism by the environment is not complete. Self-determinism or choice is therefore possible. The substance or billiard–ball concept of the gene is no longer credible. The classical notion that genes were pellets of matter that remained in all respects self-identical, whatever the environment, has to be abandoned in the light of modern knowledge.

The challenge of postmodern thought to molecular biology is to pursue further this avenue of thought. I would claim that to exhibit self-determination is to exhibit mind. It is to have some degree of freedom, no doubt minute at the molecular level. I am not saying that, having investigated the life of the cell, biologists have found mind. I am saying that what they have found is *more consistent with* the proposition that the cells and their DNA molecules are mind-like in the sense of having internal relations than with the proposition that they are machine-like. They take account of their environment in the deep sense of taking account: They are constituted by their relations. Molecular genetics was the last into mechanistic biology. Maybe it will be the first out.

Mechanistic developmental biologists thought that an organism developed in complexity from a single fertilized egg into a complex living organism in the way a motor car is built up from individual bits and pieces. But we now know that if you cut out the limb bud of a developing frog embryo at a very early stage, shake the cells loose and put them back at random in a lump, a normal leg develops. It is not as though each cell in its particular place was initially destined to become a particular part. Each cell could become any part of the leg (but not of the eye) depending upon its total environment. Unlike a machine, which can be pulled to pieces and reassembled, the bits and pieces of the embryo seem to come into existence as a consequence of their spatial relationships at critical moments in the development of the embryo. Says Lewontin:

If development is really, in an important sense, a consequence of the relations between things, how are we to reduce the incredible complexity of relationships to a manageable set of regularities? And how are we to do this using an experimental method that is itself so wedded to Cartesian analysis?[10]

An example of how developmental biology was misled along the Cartesian path was the hunt for the so-called organizer in development. For 60 years biochemists hunted for a single molecule or group of molecules that might be responsible for "organizing" the development of the parts of the embryo, such as a leg or an eye. But they found no "organizer." This reductionist program was a colossal distraction.[11] Development evidently cannot be reduced to the action of single chemicals.

The mechanistic evolutionist seeks to interpret all in terms of chance and necessity. "Chance alone," said Monod, "is at the source of every innovation, of all creation in the biosphere."[12] He contrasts his position with those who sought to find in every detail of nature evidence of deterministic design. The choice he gives us is complete chance or complete determinism.

Darwinism was a shattering blow to those who conceived of nature as completely determined, be it by an outside designer or some inbuilt principle in nature. To take chance seriously is the first step in moving away from the concept of deterministic design. This was a problem for Darwin. It seems he could not admit the reality of chance, despite the role he attributed to it. In this respect, he was like Einstein who could not believe that God plays dice. "I cannot think," said Darwin, "that the world . . . is the result of chance; yet I cannot look at each separate thing as the result of Design . . . I am, and shall ever remain, in a hopeless muddle." So wrote Darwin in a letter to the Harvard botanist Asa Gray. Again and again Darwin's letters reiterate this refrain—is it all determined or is it all a result of chance? But are these the only possibilities?

Hartshorne hits the nail on the head when he says: "Neither pure chance nor the pure absence of chance can explain the world."[13] He goes on to say: "There must be something positive limiting chance and something more than mere matter in mattter, or Darwinism fails to explain life."

The *something positive* that limits chance and the *something more* than mere matter in matter is the degree of self-determination exercised by natural entities in response to possibilities of their future. In other words, a causal role in evolution is played by internal relations as well as the external relation of natural selection about which Darwin wrote. Chance (plus natural selection) alone cannot explain the evolution of life. Chance and purpose together provide a more substantial base for thinking about evolution.

This thought is not as revolutionary as it might at first appear. Evolutionary biologists have accepted an important role for purpose in human evolution in what is called *cultural evolution*. Cultural choices have determined the direction of genetical evolution. Cultural evolution and genetical evolution go hand in hand. But we can also recognize a role that choice and purpose play in the lives of other animals. For them, too, cultural evolution is a reality. How far down the line are we prepared to go with this argument? Logically there is no need to draw a line anywhere in the total evolutionary sequence from atoms to humans. This is a challenge of postmodern thought to evolutionary biology today—to propose a role for purpose together with chance in evolution all down the line. This is to propose that, in addition to external relations as causal, internal relations are causal also in determining the direction of evolution.

Evolution raises a profound question: Why did atoms evolve into cells and into plants and animals? Why didn't creativity stop with the first DNA molecule? Mechanism provides no answer. The ecological model opens up ways to explore it in terms of lure and response, or purposive influence and self-determination. Self-determination is minimal at the atomic level. It is greatest in the higher organisms. Because natural entities are always, with their own particular degree of freedom, in process of relating to the lure to fulfillment, a constant tension between chaos and order occurs in nature.

Implicit in what I have said is that the scientists' methodology and the way in which they interpret the data depend upon their metaphysical stance. Scientists always take sides. I have given one alternative to Cartesian mechanistic biology. There are others and we need to see the parallels and differences between them.

In addition to the biologists I have already mentioned, others provide a challenge to mechanistic reductionistic biology, including Sewall Wright[14] in evolutionary biology, C. H. Waddington[15] in developmental biology, Ilya Prigogine and Isabelle Stengers[16] in molecular biology, and, in the broad field of all biology, J. Z. Young,[17] Rupert Sheldrake,[18] and John Cobb and me.[19]

The contrast between a bits-and-pieces view of nature and an holistic one is captured by Henry Reed in his poem, "Naming of Parts," which begins:

> Today we have naming of parts, Yesterday
> we had daily cleaning. And tomorrow morning
> we shall have what to do after firing. But today,
> Today we have naming of parts. Japonica
> Glistens like coral in all of the neighboring gardens,
> And today we have naming of parts.

NOTES

1. Richard Levins and Richard Lewontin, *The Dialectical Biologist* (Cambridge, Mass.: Harvard University Press, 1985), 2-3.

2. A. N. Whitehead, *Science and the Modern World* (Cambridge: Cambridge University Press, 1933), 134–35.

3. Richard Lewontin, "The Corpse in the Elevator," *New York Review of Books* 30 (1983), 14–37, esp. 36.

4. Roger Sperry, *Science and Moral Priority: Merging Mind, Brain and Human Values* (Oxford: Blackwell, 1983); "Interview with Roger Sperry," *Omni* 5/ii (1983), 69–100.

5. Karl H. Pribram, "Holonomy and Structure in the Organization of Perception," John M. Nicholas, ed., *Images, Perception and Knowledge* (Dordrecht: Reidel, 1977), 155–85; K. H. Pribram, M. Nuwer, and R. Baron, "The Holographic Hypothesis of Memory Structure in Brain Function and Structure," R. Atkinson, O. Krantz, R. Luce, and P. Suppes, eds., *Contemporary Developments in Mathematical Psychology,* Vol. 2 (San Francisco: Freeman, 1974), 416–57.

6. Jane van Lawick Goodall, *In the Shadow of Man* (Boston: Houghton Miflin Co., 1971); *The Chimpanzees of Gombe: Patterns of Behavior* (Cambridge, Mass.: Harvard University Press, 1986).

7. Charles Hartshorne, *Born to Sing: An Interpretation and World Survey of Bird Song* (Bloomington: Indiana University Press, 1973); *Omnipotence and Other Theological Mistakes* (Albany: State University of New York Press, 1984).

8. Donald R. Griffin, *The Question of Animal Awareness: Evolutionary Continuity of Mental Experience* (New York: Rockefeller University Pess, 1976); *Animal Thinking* (Cambridge, Mass.: Harvard University Press, 1984).

9. Lewontin, "The Corpse in the Elevator," 37.

10. *Ibid.*, 36.

11. Mae-Wah Ho and P. T. Saunders, *Beyond Neo-Darwinism: An Introduction to the New Evolutionary Paradigm* (New York: Harcourt Brace Janovich, 1984), 10, 267–90; Jam Witowski, "The Hunting of the Organizer: An Episode in Biochemical Embryology," *Trends in Biochemical Science* 10 (1985), 379–81.

12. Jacques Monod, *Chance and Necessity: An Essay on the Natural Philosophy of Modern Biology* (London: Fontana/Collins, 1974), 110.

13. Charles Hartshorne, *Omnipotence and Other Theological Mistakes*, 69.

14. Sewall Wright, "Biology and the Philosophy of Science," W. L. Reese and E. Freeman, eds., *Process and Divinity* (La Salle, Ill.: Open Court, 1964), 101–25.

15. C. H. Waddington, ed., *Toward A Theoretical Biology*, Vol. 2, *Sketches* (Edinburgh: Edinburgh University Press, 1969), 72–81.

16. Ilya Prigogine and Isabelle Stengers, *Order out of Chaos: Man's New Dialogue with Nature* (New York: Bantam Books, 1984).

17. J. Z. Young, *Programmes of the Brain* (Oxford: Oxford University Press, 1978).

18. Rupert Sheldrake, *A New Science of Life: The Hypothesis of Formative Causation* (London: Blond and Briggs, 1981).

19. Charles Birch and John B. Cobb, Jr., *The Liberation of Life: From the Cell to the Community* (Cambridge: Cambridge University Press, 1981).

5

THE LAWS OF NATURE AS HABITS: A POSTMODERN BASIS FOR SCIENCE

Rupert Sheldrake

The universe of classical physics, formulated near the outset of the modern age, was a vast and eternal machine, composed of indestructible particles of matter, propelled by indestructible energy, and governed by changeless mathematical laws.

By contrast, the universe of the new cosmology is an evolving organism. It recalls the mythological accounts of the Cosmic Egg, from which the universal organism grew, forming within itself all that is. It is said to have arisen in a primal explosion about 15 billion years ago, and has been growing and cooling ever since. In the early stages of its growth, subatomic particles and simple atoms appeared within it; and then through the condensation of the primal gas the galaxies and stars; and then through the nuclear reactions in the great heat of the stars the atoms of the various chemical elements; and then through the aggregation of the cooling residues of exploded stars the solid bodies of planets, moon, asteroids, comets, meteorites, and dust clouds. And within and around these solid bodies ever more complex types of molecules evolved, and as liquids and solutions crystallized, a great variety of crystal forms arose. On at least one planet, living forms appeared in the primal oceans. Then within the seas and, later, on the land as well, evolved the vast diversity of microorganisms, plants, and animals that we find on the earth today. Human beings arose from primate ancestors; and human culture and technology evolved at first slowly, then more rapidly with the development of agriculture, and more rapidly still with the rise of industries, and so on at an ever-accelerating pace.

We ourselves have grown up in a world preoccupied with development and innovation. Our culture is permeated with a consciousness of change, and all our major social, historical, economic, and political theories are cast in an evolutionary framework. Science itself has evolved, and within science, the evolutionary perspective has dominated geology and biology for well over a century. But, seemingly insulated from this pervasive evolutionism, physics has, until very recently, remained the stronghold of a very different vision: the vision of an eternal universe governed by immutable laws, with a changeless amount of matter and energy.

Since the late 1960s, physics has found itself within the framework of an evolutionary cosmology. The old paradigm of changelessness is now in radical conflict with the paradigm of evolutionary change. Questions arise that we have hardly begun to answer. Let us consider just one of these. If the universe has evolved and is still evolving, then has it done so against the background of changeless laws of nature which already existed in a virtual form before the Big Bang? Or do the laws of nature themselves come into being in time and evolve along with the universe? Is it impossible for them to evolve because they represent an eternal system of mathematical order that governs all things in the universe? Or do they depend on what has actually happened; could they be more like habits, as C. S. Peirce suggested a century ago? [1]

Such a change in our understanding of the "laws of nature" would be consistent with a change of paradigm from the machine to the organism, which would be a change from a modern to a postmodern basis for science. The ordering of machines comes from designs imposed on them by their creators; the ordering of organisms depends on habits and dispositions they have inherited or acquired. All organisms, and the universal organism itself, may be creatures of habit, rather than mechanisms following eternally given, changeless laws.

But the idea of changeless laws has a powerful hold on our thinking, and itself has the force of a deeply established habit with a long tradition behind it, harkening to the dawn of European thought. The mathematical discoveries of the Pythagoreans both arose from and reinforced their vision of a timeless mathematical order behind and beyond all things; and in the closely related philosophy of the Platonists, the phenomenal world we experience with our senses is not the ultimate or real world, but a reflection of changeless Forms or Ideas where existence transcends both time and space. In Christian Neoplatonism, these Ideas subsist within the external Mind of God; they are aspects of the divine Logos.

The great founders of modern science—Copernicus, Kepler, Galileo, Descartes, and Newton—were all in various ways illuminated by this Pythagorean or Platonic vision, and it has continued to inspire the leading thinkers of physics, not least Einstein and the pioneers of the quantum theory.[2]

The other great legacy of Greek thought to modern science was the philosophy of atomism. The notion of changeless particles of matter impelled by a changeless amount of motion was brought together with the vision of changeless mathematical laws in the mechanical philosophy of the seventeenth century; this hybrid of Platonism and materialism has dominated modern science ever since. It is dualistic, with an eternal quantity of matter and energy on the one hand and the mathematical laws on the other: the material reality of the universe is governed by the universal and immutable invisible principles.

Sceptical philosophy, from Hume onwards, has failed to find any justification in experience or in logic for the assumption that these universal laws exist independently of our own minds; nevertheless, an implicit Platonism continues to permeate the thinking of scientists and the practice of science. We usually take it for granted; indeed, the very methodology of science depends on it: experiments can be repeatable only in principle if the laws of nature are the same everywhere and do not change. This assumption cannot be explained by a science that presupposes it. As Karl Popper says:

> The assertion of the universality or constancy of our causal laws through space (and time) amounts to asserting a structural regularity—a regularity of co-existence which seems to be in principle causally inexplicable since it cannot be explained by any causal law or law of succession . . . . The structural homogeneity of the world seems to resist any 'deeper' explanation: it remains a mystery.[3]

But if at least some of the laws of nature *evolve*, perhaps a deeper insight into the structural regularity of the world might be possible. Now that the new cosmology has placed all of nature under the aspect of evolution, this possibility invites exploration.

One avenue of exploration is provided by the hypothesis of formative causation.[4] This hypothesis postulates that the characteristic forms taken up by molecules, crystals, cells, tissues, organs, and organisms are shaped and maintained by specific fields called *morphogenetic fields* (from the Greek *morphe* meaning *form* and *genesis* meaning *coming-into-being*). The structures of these fields are derived from the morphogenetic fields associated with previous similar systems; the morphogenetic fields of past systems become present to subsequent similar systems by a process called *morphic resonance*.

The concept of morphogenetic fields is by no means new, although it has not previously been interpreted in this way. For more than 50 years, embryologists and developmental biologists have used this term to refer to the unknown structuring and organising factors that enable animals and plants to develop from eggs, through various embryonic stages into their characteristic adult forms. These fields have been regarded as responsible not only for the coming-into-being of biological forms, but also for the "holistic" properties of organisms, shown, for example, by their ability to regenerate after damage. The trouble is that no one has ever been able to say what these fields are or the way they work. Some biologists, such as the late C. H. Waddington, have considered them to be a mere "descriptive convenience," a sort of shorthand for complicated sets of conventional physical and chemical interactions, the details of which remain unknown. In this case, morphogenetic fields provide little more than a suggestive terminology and cannot, as such, lead to testable predictions. By contrast, the hypothesis of formative causation enables them to be interpreted as a new type of physical field with effects that can be detected experimentally.

All processes of development start from systems that already possess characteristic patterns of organization. For example, an embryo develops from a fertilized egg containing nucleic acids and proteins, which are organized in particular ways and are specific to each species. The hypothesis of formative causation proposes that these morphogenetic starting points, or *morphogenetic germs*, enter into morphic resonance with previous systems of which structures similar to these morophogenetic germs were a part. A morphogenetic germ thus becomes surrounded by, or embedded within, the morphogenetic field of the higher-level system, which then shapes or molds the process of development toward this characteristic form. Although morphogenetic fields play a causal role in the organization of the developing system, they are not themselves energetic; they act by patterning probabilistic events, by restricting the possible outcomes of energetically indeterminate processes.

The hypothesis proposes that the influence of past systems on present systems by morphic resonance is not significantly attenuated by spatial or temporal separation. Consequently, all past systems of a given type influence subsequent similar systems; their influence is, in fact, cumulative. As these past systems are similar rather than identical, when a subsequent system comes under their collective influence by morphic resonance, its morphogenetic field will not be sharply defined, but it will consist of a kind of composite of previous similar forms. Thus, morphogenetic fields not only act upon probabilistic events, but also are themselves probabilistic in nature.

The hypothesis of formative causation leads to an interpretation of the inheritance of form in animals and plants that is very different from the conventional theory. According to the latter, the way in which organisms develop is somehow "programmed" in their DNA. But while DNA undoubtedly codes for the sequence of amino acids in proteins, according to the hypothesis of formative causation the form and organization of the cells, tissues, organs and organisms as a whole are governed by a hierarchy of morphogenetic fields which are not inherited chemically but given directly by morphic resonance from past organisms of the same species.

By extending the concept of morphogenetic fields to the organization and patterning of probabilistic events within the nervous system, we can interpret the inheritance of instinctive patterns of behavior in a comparable manner.

These ideas are extremely unfamiliar and are, perhaps, easier to grasp with the help of an analogy. Imagine an intelligent and curious person who knows nothing about electricity or electromagnetic radiation. He is shown a television set for the first time. He might at first suppose that the set actually contained little people, whose images he saw on the screen. But when he looked inside and found only wires, condensers, transistors, and so on, he might adopt the more sophisticated hypothesis that the images somehow arose from complicated interactions among the components of the set. This idea would seem particularly plausible when he found that the images became distorted or disappeared when components were removed and that the images were restored to normal when these components were put back. If the suggestion was put to him that the images in fact depended on invisible influences entering the set from far away, he might reject it on the grounds that it was unnecessary and obscurantist. His opinion that nothing came into the set from outside would be reinforced by the discovery that the set weighed the same switched on or off. While admitting that he could not explain in detail how the images were produced from complicated interactions within the set, and nothing more, he might well claim that such an explanation was possible in principle, and that it would, in fact, eventually be achieved after a great deal of further research. This point of view resembles the conventional approach to biology. By contrast, the hypothesis of formative causation does not involve a denial of the importance of DNA, protein molecules, and so on (corresponding in the analogy to wires, transistors, and the like); but it recognizes in addition the role of influences transmitted from outside the system, the "transmitters" being past organisms of the same species. Genetic changes can affect the inheritance of form or instinct by altering the "tuning" or by introducing distortions into the "reception." Genetic factors alone, however, cannot fully account for the inheritance of form and instinct, any more than the particular pictures on the screen of a television set can be explained in terms of its wiring alone.

The hypothesis of formative causation can be tested in a variety of ways. One involves studying the crystallization of chemicals that have never been synthesized before. According to the hypothesis, prior to the first crystallization, no specific morphogenetic field for the crystals should exist. After the first crystals have formed, however, subsequent crystallizations should be influenced by the morphogenetic fields of earlier crystals. The more often a substance is crystallized, the more readily should it do so.

New compounds are, in fact, generally difficult to crystallize and do indeed form crystals more readily as time progresses. The conventional explanation for this phenomenon is that fragments of previous crystals that serve as "seeds" are carried from laboratory to laboratory on the beards or clothing of migrant scientists. When the effect still happens in the absence of any such identifiable carrier, seeds are usually assumed to have travelled around the world as microscopic dust particles in the air.

The hypothesis of formative causation predicts that such crystallizations should still occur more readily even when dust particles are filtered out of the air and peripatetic scientists, especially those with beards, are kept at bay. It should not be too difficult to design experiments to test for this effect.

In the biological realm, the hypothesis gives rise to a wide range of testable predictions. Perhaps the most striking involves the learning by animals of new patterns of behavior. If a number of rats, for example, learn to carry out a task that rats have never done before, then other rats everywhere else in the world should be able to learn the same task more easily in the absence of any known type of physical connection or communication.

Remarkably enough, evidence suggests that this effect actually occurs. In a long series of experiments started at Harvard University in 1920, William McDougall found that the rate at which successive generations of rats learned to escape from a specially designed water maze increased noticeably. In each generation, the rats were bred from parents that had already learned to perform the task. McDougall considered that these results provided evidence in favor of inheritance of acquired characteristics, or "Lamarckian" inheritance.

In order to answer the criticism that this effect might have been due to the selection of quicker-learning rats as parents, despite the fact that they were chosen by a seemingly random procedure, McDougall carried out a further series of experiments in which he bred only from the slowest-learning rats in each generation. In this case, genetic selection might have been expected to result in a *decrease* of the rate of learning in successive generations. But, in fact, the rate of learning once again *increased*.[4]

In view of the controversial implications of these findings, other workers—F. A. E. Crew in Edinburgh and W. E. Agar and his colleagues in Melbourne—repeated McDougall's experiments using the same type of water maze. However, at both locations, the first generation of rats learned at much faster rates than McDougall's early generations had. Indeed, Crew found that some of the first rats he tested "learned" the task immediately without making a single error.

Agar and his colleagues compared the performance of successive generations of rats descended from trained parents with that of rats from a control line in which the parents of each generation had never been near the water maze. The performance of successive generations of trained rats improved, just as McDougall had found. *But so did the performance in the control line.* The rats in this line were descended from untrained parents, so this result showed that their improvement could not be explained in terms of the passing on of modified genes from parents to offspring, as Lamarckian theory requires. Thus, McDougall's *conclusions* were refuted. Nevertheless, his *results* were confirmed, and to this day they have not been satisfactorily accounted for in conventional terms. But they are in good agreement with the hypothesis of formative causation.

In experiments specially designed to test for the effects of morphic resonance, comparing the rate at which rats learned a particular task in one location, say New York, before and after a large number of rats had been trained to carry out the same task at another, say London, would probably be advisable. Obviously, appropriate precautions would have to be taken to avoid any conscious or unconscious bias on the part of the experimenters. One precaution would be for those in New York to go on testing the rate of learning of fresh classes of rats at, say, monthly intervals over a one-year period. Then, in London, the time at which the training began would be selected at random within this period; for example, it might be five months after the regular tests started in New York. If the experimenters in New York, who would not have been told what was going on in London, detected a marked increase in the rate of learning only after the rats in London had been trained, then the result would provide evidence in favor of the hypothesis of formative causation.

Currently, this hypothesis is being tested in the realms of chemistry, biology, and psychology. Perhaps the findings of these empirical investigations will support the hypothesis. The fields that order molecules, crystals, and living organisms may indeed depend on what has happened before; they may undergo evolution and be more akin to habitual patterns than to changeless laws.

How far might this principle be extended? Theoretical physicists are already speculating about the evolution of the known fields of physics from a primal Unified Field;[5] and what new perspective might open if we begin to explore the relationships of these fields to the morphogenetic fields of chemistry and biology?

The notion of repeatable experiments depends on the presupposition that the laws of nature are the same everywhere and at all time. But if fields evolve, then certain kinds of experiments may be intrinsically unrepeatable. Consider, for example, experiments on the learning of rats of the type discussed above: if the ability of rats to learn a new task is tested in one laboratory after it has been tested in another, the results will not be the same because the subsequent rats will be influenced by morphic resonance from the previous rats. But this raises the embarrassing possibility that such effects may already be influencing the results of conventional scientific experiments. Do new kinds of nuclear particles, for example, become easier to detect if they have already been detected in other laboratories?

The more often patterns of coming-into-being of form have been repeated, the more fields will be stabilized by morphic resonance; the deeper will the grooves of habit become; and the more the phenomena will appear to be governed by immutable laws.

We know from our experience of ourselves and other people that the more habitual our behavior becomes, the more it appears to follow a quasi-mechanical predictability; we behave in certain ways "like clockwork."

If the universe is like an eternal machine, and all organisms within it are more or less complex mechanistic systems, then all their spontaneity of evolution and behavior must ultimately stem from blind chance. This has been the dominant modern view and is still the predominant orthodoxy of biology. But if the universe is more like a living organism, whose regularities depend on habits, mechanistic phenomena become a limiting case, the idealization of which classical physics took as its model. At present, we can only begin to imagine the consequences that will flow from moving beyond the modern model into a radically evolutionary, postmodern understanding.

NOTES

1. M. G. Murphy, *The Development of Peirce's Philosophy* (Cambridge, Mass.: Harvard University Press, 1961).

2. Ken Wilber, ed., *Quantum Questions* (Boulder, Col.: Shambhala, 1984).

3. Karl Popper, *Realism and the Aim of Science* (London: Hutchinson, 1983).

4. Rupert Sheldrake, *A New Science of Life: The Hypothesis of Formative Causation* (London: Blond & Briggs, 1981).

5. P. C. W. Davies, *Superforce* (London: Heinemann, 1984).

6

RELIGIOUS WORLD MODELING AND POSTMODERN SCIENCE

Frederick Ferré

Modern science has dealt notorious blows to religions concerned for the spiritual health of human beings. In a series of retreats, theologians have been forced to concede specific issues like the peripheral location of the earth in the universe, the kinship of *Homo sapiens* with the ancestral ooze, the depths of human unreason, and even the molecular basis for valued traits. But by far the most anguishing effect of modern science on the religious confidence of the industrial civilization built by its technologies and shaped by its values lies deeper. It is the sense of alienation from responsible agency, from community with nature, and from personal inwardness. The images of the universe that are naturally drawn from the ideals of modern science—ideals contributory to three centuries of intellectual and technological achievements—provide no home for such qualities.

I. WORLD MODELS FROM MODERN SCIENCE

I stress the images and the ideals of modern science because these are the evocative and value-laden aspects of the scientific phenomenon that flow most directly into the religious consciousness of an age. Science cannot function without ideals. Every measurement, however carefully taken, is laced with error and only approximates the ideal of perfect precision. Every significant theoretical concept reflects an idealization—point masses, frictionless surfaces, instantaneous velocities, and the like—not directly met in the unkempt world of experience. And every explanation finally depends on what Stephen Toulmin calls an "ideal of the natural order," [1] which gives the scientific reach for understanding a stopping point for the incessant "why?" by offering a sense of rightness or appropriateness or inevitability of the answer given.

These ideals generate images of how things are. For example, the important scientific ideal that things be perfectly regular, despite the apparent randomness of much in crude experience, suggests the image of the Perfect Machine. By it the universe is thought—and felt—in terms of an ideal clockwork mechanism in which nothing ever goes awry and in which every part is determined by the springs and gears which require its every motion. The ideal is fundamental to scientific activity; it is hard even to imagine a science in which apparent disorder might be accepted with a shrug at face value. And the world modeled after the Perfect Machine supports that ideal and encourages the devotion of years to the search for the hidden regularities and what Margenau calls *subsurface connections*, which comprise the triumph of scientific genius. The world model of the Perfect Machine has further consequences: it gives a sense of the ideal unity of all things, organized in principle within one great system; and it gives a sense, also, of the kind of security that comes from feeling that all things are working together and are continuing as they must without accident, flaw, or mischance.

These last consequences, of course, are religious attitudes. The images that evoke or embody them are what I call *religious world models* when they are used not only to focus attitudes toward the world but also to think about it and to grapple with it through policies of life rooted in a vision of what the world is like.

The image of the Perfect Machine is only one of several religious world models generated from the ideals of modern science as they have contributed to shaping human consciousness since the seventeenth century. Another important example is the image of the Ultimate Particle. The method of analysis sponsored by Galileo and codified by Descartes is basic to modern science. This method requires dividing problems into their smallest components, reducing issues from the complex to the simple, and solving them separately. In like manner, looking for explanation tended to become a quest for the smallest unit, something simple underlying all other things. If only the fundamental particle (or particles) could be identified and understood, then those complexes built up from the ultimate particles in combination also would be thoroughly understood. Explanation would proceed by reduction. To know what a thing really is, in terms of this ideal, would be to know as much as possible about the parts that comprise it. The lure of the atomic theory, and deeper yet the lure of subatomic particles and finally of the quark (if the quark is indeed that from which all other particles derive) is the ideal image of the Ultimate Particle. It represents Being in and of itself. Its properties define those of reality; all other properties are mere appearance. To discover its nature is to stand before the deepest secrets of what all things are like in essence, which turns out to be most austere. It excludes color, sound, texture, or quality of the sort we are accustomed to experiencing in the everyday world. Those are joint products of "reality" interacting with subjective mentality. Mentality itself has no secure place in the image of the Ultimate Particle; it is something different from the rest of what counts as reality. Perhaps it, too, is merely derivative Appearance?

A third image, that of the Pure Object, reinforces the other two. One of the principal ideals of modern science has been to rid the world of the merely subjective, whether it be at the level of scientific belief (where objectivity must rule the tendency to whim and delusion) or at the level of subject matter (where remnants of Aristotelian "final causation" must be rigorously excised in every area). The objective is highly valued; the subjective is shunned. Even laboratory ritual, such as the highly impersonal manner of writing up results, obeys and strengthens the ideal of commitment to the objective and the object.

Unfortunately, the religious world models that spring naturally from these ideals of modern science are not easily reconciled with profound human cravings. If we venerate the qualities implicit in the image of the Perfect Machine—those of regularity, predictability, control—we lose the values of spontaneity, creativitiy, responsibility. And those are the values of the personal. If all reality should be seen and felt as perfectly regular clockwork, with each happening being determined by its preceding circumstances, then we are not free to do otherwise than whatever it is we find ourselves actually doing. We are then not responsible agents, capable of initiating chains of events, but we are only necessary links in the causal sequence which looms indefinitely into the future and ties us remorselessly to the conditions of the past. We can never truly say with Harry Truman that "the buck stops here." The "buck" never stops; all events are conditioned in a Perfect Machine by the state of the machine in its previous moment, and so on, *ad infinitum*. Personal responsibility falls victim to the deterministic ideals of regularity and predictability. And with this loss come serious social and psychological consequences for modern civilization. Human beings, perceived as without essential responsibilities or need for personal creativity, will more easily be placed into economic bondage to assembly-line production techniques; overwhelming bureaucracies will show less communication in mechanically administering our lives not only without spontaneity but (worse) without personal assumption of moral accountability, from birth to burial.

The consequences of the religious world model drawn from the ideal of the Ultimate Particle are no less depressing. The reductionist vision sees the whole as an aggregate of the parts; and what the parts are, so the whole is. Nature, thus modeled, is in reality "a dull affair, soundless, senseless, colourless; merely the hurrying of material, endlessly, meaninglessly."[2] If we value reality and disdain mere appearance, we will be free to build the Ugly Society on this religious world model, because aesthetic values are merely in the subjective eye of the beholder, and commitment to reality is best acted out through single-minded devotion to the amassing and manipulation of material. Further, because physical nature has no mentality or values of its own, we are free to treat all of our environment, without compunction, as resource pit and garbage dump. Even animals, as Descartes assured us, deserve no more consideration than would the chemicals composing them.[3]

Thus, the reductionist ideal, although vital to science since Descartes, leads quickly to a "nothing but" attitude towards our surroundings and, together with the discounting of the qualitative aspect of experience and the loss of place in the universe for mentality, drives us to a state of deep alienation from the universe in which we live.

Likewise, we find the influence of the ideal of the Pure Object leading to dismaying consequences of spirit and action. By worshiping the Object at the cost of the Subject, this religious world model alienates us from our own inwardness, from our own intuitions of meaning and our own structures of purpose. Not only are we cut off from the world of nature, but the world of other persons becomes the domain of I-it perception, and the stage is set for both the great and the little atrocities of modern life.

The French reductionist biologist Jacques Monod, who embraces the key religious world models of modern science and advocates them despite acknowledging their incompatibility with profoundly rooted human needs and values, summarizes the painful religious legacy of modern science by urging that if the human race truly accepts the import of modern science,

> then man must at last wake out of his millenary dream; and in doing so, wake to his total solitude, his fundamental isolation. Now does he at last realize that, like a gypsy, he lives on the boundary of an alien world. A world that is deaf to his music, just as indifferent to his hopes as it is to his suffering or his crimes.[4]

II. RELIGION AND SCIENCE

What I have been calling *modern science* is of course only one of many possible approaches to the problems of *natural philosophy* (as science used to be called), and alternatives to it and its ideals have not been lacking. Modern science was itself an alternative to premodern forms of natural philosophy, mainly rooted in the thinking of Aristotle. It is a verbal matter whether we choose to call such approaches, including the highly developed astrological and alchemical traditions of the Middle Ages and the Renaissance, *premodern science* or *prescientific*. I prefer the former because I believe that modern science, with its bleak value-consequences, does not deserve a monopoly on the whole meaning of the honorific word *science*.

Something importantly new, however, came into the world with modern natural philosophy, and (despite the yearnings of some, like Theodore Roszak)[5] returning to premodern forms of science is not possible. The requirements of empirical testability, for one thing, and the powerful linkage of explanatory theory to mathematics, for another, have brought us too far and given us too much unprecedented control over (and responsibility for) nature to be simply "gotten round"[6] as merely another mythology. However humane (and this point itself is debatable), premodern sciences like astrology and alchemy cannot on value-grounds alone compete with the demonstrable results of three centuries of modern scientific achievement.

Indeed, the proper role of intellectual regulation in the governance of belief is a question of basic values; and, as such, this question falls within the domain of the religious if religion, as I believe, is primarily a value-phenomenon.[7]

The procedure of some religious traditions, we know, is indifferent or hostile to the values of critical intelligence. Some strands of Christianity, which has on the main tended to value the virtues of the mind, view the intellect as a temptation, something to be mortified rather than fulfilled. The *sacrificium intellectus*, however, is always subject to ethical assessment. A religious stance that requires the mutilation of any great aspect of life is to that extent faulted. The richer the wholeness that religious imagery supports in individuals and in communities, the better.

If this is so, then for religious adequacy itself there must be found a place for the values of critical intelligence. It is possible to scoff at the demands for logical consistency and coherence or for evidential relevance and adequacy, but only at the expense of the human capacity for thought itself, including even that of the scoffer. Although religion's root is in the life-oriented domain of practical reason, it is pushed by its own drive toward comprehensiveness to include the values of theoretical reason as well. In principle, therefore, an enterprise devoted to the support of intellectual needs will be valued positively within an adequate religious framework; science, on its deepest intention, is such an enterprise; therefore science, for any valuationally comprehensive religion, will be acknowledged as having just claim on the loyalties of religious persons. An antiscientific religious posture shows its valuational inadequacy on its face.

III. Ecology and Postmodern Science

If neither cognitive nor valuational justification exists for abandoning modern science for premodern modes of thinking, but if at the same time the images and values of modern science are threatening to the spiritual health—and indirectly even the survival—of contemporary civilization, then our best hope will be the emergence of a postmodern form of science that will preserve the virtues of rigorous thinking without absolutizing the alienating religious world models of Machine, Particle, and Object. Is this a futile hope?

Some, like Jacques Monod, argue that science shows no signs of weakening in its headlong antihumanistic tendency, and that it cannot escape being perceived as a danger to contemporary society.

> Here, I am not referring to the population explosion, to the destruction of the natural environment, nor even to the stock pile of megatons of nuclear power; but to a more insidious and much more deep-seated evil: one that besets the spirit. One that was begot of the sharpest turning point ever taken in the evolution of ideas. An evolution, moreover, which continues and accelerates constantly in the same direction, ever increasing that bitter distress of the soul.[8]

Monod's proposed solution is to try to root out the craving for meaning and purpose despite the depth of its hold within the psyche. But this solutions calls for capitulation to alienated consciousness and depersonalized society. Is there no alternative? Are there no grounds for hope for genuine science and human meaning at once? I believe it is possible, first, to challenge Monod's assertion that the evolution of science is in fact linear, accelerating "constantly in the same direction" and, second, to see what implications any important changes in direction from modern to postmodern ideals and images might have for generating religious world models appropriate for our lives now and for our future.

It is easy to see how a scientist like Monod, steeped both in modern scientific ideals and in the Cartesian cultural tradition, might see the historical development of science as a clean, straight line leading from the heroic days of seventeenth-century quantifiers, analyzers, abstracters, and reducers through the Newtonian mechanists, to his own highly reductionist and analytical science of molecular biology. Not only Monod but a great many persons today see the wave of the scientific future in the study of the Ultimate Particles drawn from living things considered as collections of physical and chemical parts conforming to the ideal of the Perfect Machine and treated as approximating the image of the Pure Object. From huge new plans for fighting cancer to genetic engineering, and from test-tube babies to rumors of cloning, the news columns are filled with discussions that suggest the potency, for good or ill, of this scientific development and its associated technologies. All this seems new and startling as it vaults into public consciousness.

And yet from another perspective there is nothing quite so familiar. Molecular biology and its offspring sociobiology are the fulfillment and at the same time apotheosis of tendencies central to the old ideals of modern science, leading to what might paradoxically be called an "old future," in the sense that it will bring basically more of the same alienating results. And yet, as we have noted, these old ideals are powerful, well designed to bite deeply into hitherto unknown territory. Because this is the case, we should not be surprised at the effectiveness of these well-honed ideals and abstractions when they are directed at the pertinent aspects of living things.

We need not suppose, however, that all aspects of living organisms are in fact pertinent to ideals and images, no matter how powerful, that have their historical origin in astronomy and physical dynamics. These specific ideals are both limited and accidental. They are *limited* in ways I have discussed at the outset and shall return to, by way of contrast, in what follows. They are *accidental* for science, but not in the sense that it is difficult to understand just why astronomical subject matter, with negligible frictional disturbance giving rise to its great simplicities and highly visible regularities, became a paradigm for clocklike explanatory representations; or why physics, with its relatively uncomplicated, inert and docile subject materials, became the fountainhead of reductionist and objectivist presuppositions. These make sense in the historical context of a nascent science, but precisely this historical context reminds us that there is nothing logically essential in such ideals for all science in every period or mode of development. They may, indeed, be essential to understanding the specific cultural phenomenon of modern science in the tradition of Galileo and Newton; without these ideals and images, we would have a very different science. But they are historically accidental so far as science itself, taken simply as a logically controlled and empirically responsible way of understanding, is concerned. Different interests might have led to other, less abstract, images and ideals.

To demonstrate that this is no empty possibility in the current scientific world, we find among us *bona fide* sciences that have broken sharply with the ideals and assumptions long identified with modern science. These postmodern sciences are the really exciting developments in the evolution of science, culture, and value today.

Harold Schilling writes of a "new consciousness" breaking out in all of the traditional disciplines, including his own field of physics.[9] His evidence is welcome that postmodern concepts and values are becoming pervasive, if not by any means yet dominant, in the various sciences. For the purposes of illustration, an examination of the science of ecology as a young but immensely significant specimen of a postmodern science will serve.

Ecological science, first, involves a whole way of thinking that is radically different from the epistemological model of modern analytical science. Ecologists need and use analysis, of course, in their methodological toolbox. They need chemical analyses, such as of complex compounds, and geophysical analyses of estuarial systems. But for the ecologist, these analyses always become means to a wider end, the end of a conceptual synthesis that preserves awareness of living systems in dynamic interaction. As the leading ecologist Eugene P. Odum states:

> . . . it is important to emphasize that findings at any one level aid in the study of another level, but never completely explain the phenomena occurring at that level. When someone is taking too narrow a view, we may remark that "he cannot see the forest for the trees." Perhaps a better way to illustrate the point is to say that to understand a tree, it is necessary to study both the forest of which it is a part as well as the cells and tissues that are part of the tree.[10]

The science of ecology does not, then, reject analysis. It incorporates and employs all the rigor of modern analytical technique, but it neither stops with analysis nor worships antiseptic analytical values. It includes and transcends analysis in a holistic way essential to its conceptual task. Thus, ecological science becomes a model for a postmodern consciousness that is neither reductionistic nor antirational.

Second, ecological science involves a vision of reality that is wholly at odds with the typically sterile, alien images generated from the modern sciences. The postmodern images of reality that come from ecology portray the world as an endlessly complex network of organic and inorganic systems locked in constant interaction.[11] In each system the lesser parts—far from being the basis for all explanation—are intelligible only with reference to the larger unities in which they play a role. These unities, in addition, are themselves not merely an assemblage of parts. Some of them are entities with interests and projects of their own. They need to be "let be" to allow for full appreciation of their importance in their own right and not merely in terms of human needs or concerns. Nonhuman centers of value exist in the ecologist's world. At the same time, alienation from the matter being studied is overcome; the ecologist is personally and inevitably part of the total subject matter.[12] The esprit, from the sense of being involved, from participating in what is of scientific interest rather than being merely the disinterested observer, places the science of ecology quite apart from other sciences in obvious ways. It is no coincidence that an ecology *movement* intent on reforms for present society and zealous with the inspiration of a new consciousness has grown up around it. It is ludicrous, but instructive, to ponder what a "chemistry movement" or an "astronomy movement" might be like, and why there is no reason to expect such movements to appear. Ecological science is essentially different, in content and in style, from the modern framework's methods and beliefs, from which it has departed.

Third, the postmodern science of ecology involves a set of values that differ sharply from the manipulative and Promethean values characteristic of outlooks inspired by modern science. By contrast, the values appropriate to ecological consciousness are modest, self-limiting, and integrative. Human exploitation is not accepted uncritically as a justification for bending nature to our will. Human intervention is, of course, acknowledged as a fact—and as a necessity as long as a human race exists. Ecological values are not misanthropic; but neither are postmodern ecological values anthropocentric, as the controlling consciousness bred by the alienating dichotomies of modern science has tended to be. The essential values of ecological consciousness acknowledge a variety of legitimate interests, human and nonhuman, interacting in dynamic equilibrium. The world is portrayed neither as a mere resource pit to be mined nor as a sheer wilderness to be shunned, but as a complex garden to be tended, respected, harvested, and loved.

The image of the Garden, then, bids to replace the religious world model of the Machine in postmodern consciousness, if holistic ecology becomes the paradigmatic science of our future. Modern attitudes and values, however, are still overwhelmingly dominant in our universities, and it may be that the most vital religious struggles of our time are occurring within the discipline of ecology itself in the fight for the soul of this science. As Donald Worster observed in his study of the history of ecology, the internal reductionist counterattack, in the name of "responsible" (modern) science, may be winning the day.

> By the 1960s, orthodox scientific thought was virtually monopolized by thermodynamics and bioeconomics. The organicists' vision of relatedness was confined to the ecosystem model of the New Ecologists, who were quite as reductive in their way as Whitehead's *bêtes noires*, the eighteenth-century *philosophes*. From most professional circles, at least, the metabiological, idealizing tendencies of organicism had been firmly exorcised: Ecology at last had got its head out of the clouds, its feet on solid ground, and its hands on something to measure. [13]

But the battle remains in flux. "It was thought that, to qualify as a field of objective knowledge, ecology could have no further dealings with the private, muddled realms of value, philosophy, and ethics. How long the discipline will remain so carefully sterilized is another matter: Organicism has a way of gaining a foothold on even the most unpromising surface." [14]

It is not for us to prejudge the outcome. If the image of the Garden, in which humanity and the rest of nature interact with balance and mutual benefit, becomes a fundamental image for our world, it will, of course, be easier to see how the Machine can fit—as an inorganic simplification and servant of the organic—than it is now to understand how a Garden could come to grow in the cosmic Machine. The intellectual and spiritual fruits of this reintegration of understanding with valuational intuition will be immense; the consequences for social sanity will be beyond calculation.

But if these specific hopes are dashed within the field of ecology itself, as seems possible, there is still no need to capitulate to the values of the Machine, the Particle, or the Object. Religious insight into value should not dictate what the scientist claims as fact, but the profound attractions of the Garden are not likely to die. "There is no reason for believing that this science cannot find an appropriate theoretical framework for the ethic of interdependence. If the bioeconomics of the New Ecologists cannot serve, then there are other, more useful, models of nature's economy that await discovery." [15]

Once we see the religious world modeling functions of scientific ideals for what they are and succeed in distinguishing them logically from the more limited techniques and tentative findings of science as a human enterprise, then we are freed from the painful choice between respect for science as such and regard for essential values. Modern science, in portraying the world as a Machine, alienated modern consciousness from the purposive, the responsible, and the whole; the task for postmodern science is to let us keep the modern tools of analysis sharp in their proper role as tools and to send us back into the Garden to work with respect and caution.

NOTES

1. Stephen Toulmin, *Foresight and Understanding: An Enquiry into the Aims of Science* (Bloomington: Indiana University Press, 1961), chaps. 3 and 4.

2. Alfred North Whitehead, *Science and the Modern World* (New York: The Free Press, 1967), 54.

3. René Descartes, *Discourse on Method* (1637; Indianapolis, Ind.: Bobbs-Merrill, 1960), Part V.

4. Jacques Monod, *Chance and Necessity: An Essay on the Natural Philosophy of Modern Biology,* Austryn Wainhouse, trans. (New York: Vintage Books, 1972), 172–73.

5. Theodore Roszak, *Where the Wasteland Ends* (Garden City, N. Y.: Doubleday & Co. 1973), 203.

6. Theodore Roszak, *The Making of a Counter-Culture* (Garden City, N. Y.: Doubleday & Co., 1969), 215.

7. Frederick Ferré, *Basic Modern Philosophy of Religion* (New York: Charles Scribner's Sons, 1967), chaps. 2 and 3.

8. Monod, *Chance and Necessity,* 164.

9. Harold K. Schilling, *The New Consciousness in Science and Religion* (Philadelphia: United Church Press, 1973).

10. Eugene P. Odum, *Ecology* (New York: Holt, Rinehart & Winston, 1963), 4.

11. See, for example, Theodore C. Foin, Jr., *Ecological Systems and the Environment* (Boston: Houghton Mifflin Co., 1976).

12. See, for example, Jack B. Bresler, ed., *The Environments of Man* (Reading, Mass.: Addison-Wesley Publishing Co., 1968).

13. Donald Worster, *Nature's Economy: The Roots of Ecology* (Garden City, N. Y.: Anchor Books, 1979), 332.

14. *Idem.*

15. *Ibid.*, 339

7

ECOLOGY, SCIENCE, AND RELIGION: TOWARD A POSTMODERN WORLDVIEW

John B. Cobb, Jr.

The ecological movement is religious, and Biblical thought (like most religious thought), from which Christianity arose, is ecological. But on the whole, the ecological movement is not Christian and contemporary Christianity is not ecological. The explanation lies in the participation of Christianity in the modern worldview. If, as I believe, the ecological movement is a prime bearer of an emerging postmodern worldview, this movement is important for Christians.

In this essay I (1) discuss "worldview" in its intimate connection with both science and religion; (2) describe the roles of science and religion in the rise of the modern worldview; (3) propose that the ecological movement is supporting the emergence of a new worldview; (4) indicate two candidates for this new ecological worldview; and (5) point out implications for understanding the divine. I do this as a Christian theologian, but one who has rejected the modern as well as the premodern forms of Christian faith.

I. Science, Religion, and Worldview

Both an assumption and a conclusion of this essay is the view that compartmentalization of thought is always artificial. This view runs against the grain of twentieth-century teaching, which has gone through great pains to clarify the differences among disciplines, levels of thought, or "language games." Special emphasis has been placed on the difference between religion and science. For some, the concern has been to protect a realm of religious discourse from the criteria appropriate to science. For others, it has been to show the vacuity of religious thought.

To accomplish either of these goals, science must be defined more and more narrowly. Increasingly, "science" appears to occur only where a discipline, its conceptuality, and its methods are well established and can be applied to new data. On this view, the formation of a science, the working out of its conceptuality, and the determination of appropriate methods cannot themselves be "science." The great paradigm shifts cannot be "science." Indeed, because the majority of what is most interesting in the history of science cannot be separated from speculative philosophy and questions of worldview, it cannot be "science," according to this view. Furthermore, speculative philosophy and worldview cannot be separated from religious belief. In a recent essay on which I am here quite dependent, David Griffin has summarized the impressive evidence that, in the formation of what we know as modern science, explicit commitments to particular forms of Christian theology played a large role.[1] Denying that an antireligious conviction played a comparable role in developing positivistic views of science is difficult.

In the context of the history of global human thought, this recent Western passion for compartmentalization appears eccentric. In Greece, in China, in India, in the Middle Ages of Europe, in Muslim Spain and the Near East, no such compartmentalization was conceivable. It was certainly not envisioned or desired by such founders of modern science as Bacon, Descartes, and Newton. It arose in the nineteenth century for particular historical reasons, and its role as orthodoxy in the twentieth century is profoundly unstable.

The normal human condition is to live out of a relatively unified understanding of the nature of things, which is partly conscious while being partly and unconsciously taken for granted. The new consciousness resulting from historical study of worldviews along with the encounter of alternative living worldviews has brought more of this unconscious material into consciousness, thereby relativizing every worldview, making all problematic. Because religion traditionally has involved the celebration, articulation, and practical implications of a worldview, the relativizing of worldviews also involves the relativization of all the religious traditions of humankind. Individual freedom to transcend worldviews entails individual freedom to decide about aspects of religious belief that were once simply given.

The matter is not, however, quite so simple. Those who distance themselves from commitment to worldviews are not without a point of view. Sometimes this point of view can be readily recognized by an observer as itself a worldview of a quite conventional sort. For example, some of those who deny commitment to any worldview and its accompanying religious meaning for life are, in fact, committed to a mechanist worldview, which is as problematic as any other. Others, however, may be committed to the impossibility of any unifying vision, holding that any worldview transcends the capacity of the human mind or belies the actual nature of things. This commitment, too, leads to a total way of thinking and responding to the issues of the day, thereby resembling a worldview. But it will be better to speak of it as an antiworldview and an antireligion. Of course, it may allow room for religion in another sense, for example, an apophatic mysticism or a Christianity that has redefined itself as dissociated from any worldview.

Worldviews are always and necessarily universal generalizations made from some aspect or aspects of the world as experienced. An organic worldview generalizes from observed organisms. A mechanist worldview generalizes from observed machines. A spiritualist worldview generalizes from particular qualities of human experience. A dualistic worldview may generalize from both human self-experience as mind and human experience of the world as matter. When a worldview is articulated philosophically, the claim is made that the really real things are of the sort, or sorts, posited.

Stephen Pepper has called worldviews *world hypotheses*.[2] When we become conscious of alternative worldviews, thereby recognizing them in their relativity, we can adopt one or another in this form. But we should beware of the notion that hypotheses are held, even by the most detached scientists, in a fully open way. Most of the hypotheses, at least the important ones, elicit considerable commitment, such that they are not quickly set aside because of apparent disconfirmation. At the level of world hypotheses, these commitments are very strong indeed. Even extensive disconfirmation does not cause ready abandonment of such hypotheses, whether they are religious, antireligious, or nonreligious.

I find this true in my own case. In general, I fancy that I am quite open to evidence and prepared to make adjustments in my beliefs in its light. However, my worldview entails that the future does not actually exist and can have no causal efficacy in the present; I am also convinced that the present has some capacity to determine itself. Although many aspects of the future are now determined, I conclude that the future in its entirety and in its exact shape is not now determined and therefore cannot now be known, even by God. If I were eager to check all this out as an interesting hypothesis that I entertained in a detached way, I would no doubt study the evidence for precognition carefully. I have not done so. I am prejudiced against it. I will go to considerable lengths to explain it in terms satisfactory to my present world hypothesis. Where evidence resists such explanation, I will resist acknowledging its validity. In short, it would take overwhelming evidence to dislodge me from my "hypothesis." I think, therefore, it is better to speak of it as a conviction.[3]

I can provide some justification for my resistance to evidence in this area. My conviction seems to work very well with regard to much other evidence. It proves fruitful in new areas as I try to apply it. The world hypotheses that are supported by the idea of perfect precognition seem less fruitful or satisfactory with respect to other evidence. In addition, I have invested myself, and my personal identity, so fully in this "hypothesis" or conviction that my self-image and my pride are very much involved. My religious faith and practice are also bound up with this conviction. Nevertheless, my worldview and my religious faith both require that I not cling to them forever in the face of evidence that they are false. They would cease to be what they are if I were forced to acknowledge that they blinded me to the truth. Change is possible, but such change would be a radical conversion, and conversions do not come easily.

I have stated this quite personally so as to express my understanding of what goes on in the establishment and change of worldviews and antiworldviews. They are enormously resistant to change. A great deal is at stake. We must collectively move (and are to some extent moving) from mechanistic and dualistic worldviews and positivist and other antiworldviews to an ecological worldview. Such a change entails profound alterations in both science and religion.

II. Science and Religion in the Rise of the Modern Worldview

The above-mentioned paper by David Griffin (some of the ideas of which are incorporated in the Introduction to this volume) shows the unity of the scientific, religious, philosophical struggle that resulted in the victory of the Newtonian worldview. He shows that this victory, with its strong support for a Calvinistic theism, was short-lived, and that the term *Newtonian worldview* was transferred to a quite different, thoroughly mechanist worldview, against which Newton had himself fought vigorously. This section is derived from Griffin's work.

Three movements struggled for supremacy during the seventeenth century: the fading power of Aristotelian philosophy, the continuing power of the "magical" vision, and the emerging power of mechanistic thinking. The latter eventually won, and accordingly history has been written as if this were *the* scientific theory. The actual evidence, long-resisted and even concealed by the advocates of the mechanistic worldview, is that the magical movement provided the initial context for the rise of modern science.

This movement drew on the traditions of Pythagoras, Plato, Neoplatonism, Hermetic mysticism, and the Cabala. It was fascinated by number, and it turned to mathematics and science as the earlier Italian Renaissance had not. Ficino, Paracelsus, and Bruno were among its early leaders. It inspired also Copernicus, Kepler, and Francis Bacon.

Whereas the Aristotelian tradition had emphasized the teleological element in all things, the magical tradition went much further: it sought to ally itself with spiritual forces immanent in all things so as to bend them to human use and control. For it, nature was alive with spirit, and the explanations of natural events were to be found in these immanent spiritual forces. These forces could act at a distance as well as in proximity.

The primary objection to this tradition was not that it inhibited scientific investigation or blinded its adherents to empirical data. It did not. The primary objection was that it threatened belief in a God who transcended nature as its omnipotent creator. By seeing a miraculous aspect in many natural events, it undercut the arguments of the Christian church for validating supernatural miracles. It was for this reason that Fr. Marin Mersenne, the senior correspondent of Descartes, favored Artistotelianism over the magical tradition but saw even more promise in mechanism. Robert Boyle opposed the magical tradition because it united God with matter in a way theologically unacceptable to him. Accordingly, he denied to natural creatures any power to move themselves, attributing all power of motion to the external, omnipotent God. The physical world is purely objective matter, completely passive in relation to God. I stress that the "physical world" did not include the human mind or soul. The human mind or soul was regarded as a spiritual substance, wholly different from the bits of matter composing bodies.

Newton was influenced by both traditions, but for theological reasons he moved to the mechanistic camp. By denuding physical nature of all power of self-motion, he magnified the power of God. In gravity, he found apparent action at a distance that seemed to support the proponents of magic. In explaining this, he refused to allow any mechanistic account such as that of the Cartesians, but also any magical or animistic account. He ridiculed the idea that material bodies at a distance could exercise any influence on each other by any inherent power. The explanation had to be in terms of "spiritual forces," which meant, ultimately, God. Like Boyle, he magnified the power of God by denying power to the creatures.

The emergence of a mechanistic view of nature, which denied to nature any purpose, capacity for self-movement, or interiority, was not a necessity of science. At least, in part, it was designed to support theological voluntarism, the idea that the transcendent God imposes "His" will by fiat upon the world. Ironically, the mechanistic account of the way matter operated became so satisfactory to many people that they freed the mechanistic view from its original association with the imposed will of God and a dualistic view of human beings as composed of a spiritual soul in a mechanistic body. A world composed of purely material, and therefore purely passive, entities became completely self-sufficient. This materialistic, atheistic view came to be known as the Newtonian worldview!

This mechanistic-materialistic worldview was never adequate to the evidence, but its success in guiding theory-formation and experimentation in some areas was so great that it became entrenched as common sense. When Hume undercut it empirically, Kant reestablished it as grounded in the universal structure of mind. When this view could no longer be applied in subatomic physics, much of the scientific and philosophical community concluded that we are condemned to paradox and unintelligibility, because "reason" remained identified with mechanistic materialism. Surely this "hypothesis" had become a very powerful conviction! Even those who acknowledge that it may not be objectively true as a worldview still usually insist that there is no other alternative *methodologically* than to assume it. When we remember that modern science arose out of a quite different way of thinking, we cannot but be impressed by the success with which the victorious tradition suppressed even the memory of its opponent.

III. ECOLOGY AND THE RISE OF A POSTMODERN WORLDVIEW

The dominance of the materialistic-mechanistic worldview has never been complete. Most of its supporters have made some place for human beings outside the otherwise all-inclusive machine—for example, by at least tacitly presupposing the distinct existence of the human mind. This place was greatly enlarged and developed in German Idealism. The Romantic movement challenged the view of nature as machine, appealing to some of the intuitions that had been expressed in the magical tradition. Some biologists (vitalists) insisted that life could not be understood mechanically. Existentialists and counterculturalists deplored the effects of this worldview on human beings. Occultism flourished in reaction to it. More and more developments in physics pointed away from it. Positivists, while affirming its methodological implications, rejected it as worldview. Nevertheless, it is not a mistake to single out the ecological movement as of particular importance in helping to break the hold of the modern worldview on scientific thinking and common sense. Whereas the earlier reactions functioned chiefly restrictively and negatively, accepting the modern worldview for the most part, ecology has suggested essential ingredients for a postmodern worldview.

Ecologists are those biologists who study living things in relation to their natural environment. There they find an infinitely complex interconnectedness of living things with each other and with the inorganic world. They are impressed by the complex outworking of the effects of change in one part of the system and by the adaptability and resilience of the whole when it is not subjected to too great a stress by human intervention. But they have also been impressed by the increasing massiveness of human intervention and its often extreme degradation of once-flourishing ecosystems.

They see that these changes are often irreversible, because species die out, topsoil disappears, and weather is changed. They see that not only is the nonhuman world impoverished by these changes, but that an environment is being created that will not be able to support the increasing human population. They see that other species sometimes increase in population to the point that their environment cannot support them and then die out drastically. They see the danger that human beings will bring upon themselves a similar catastrophe. Toward the end of the 1960s, their cries of alarm finally caught the ear of the public. Although the initial response included faddish elements, a widespread change of consciousness has since occurred that is not likely to be reversed.

Once we are forced to attend to the destructive consequences of our exploitation of our environment, the facts are indisputable. Because the destruction has been vastly accelerated by the industrial revolution, we ask ourselves why in recent times we have been so oblivious. The answer is that we see what our worldview encourages us to see. We see especially through the eyes of our scientific disciplines, both natural and human, and these disciplines have all been established in the context of the materialistic or dualistic worldview. In the context of dualism, the human sciences along with ethics and theology take nature as the given stage for the human drama. They do not encourage attention to changes in the stage. In the context of mechanism nature appears as unhistorical. Hence, only those who actually went and looked noticed the changes; and, because they did not develop mechanistic theories of what they saw, they had the lowest status among the scientists.

Those who are committed to the rejection of all worldviews were at least equally responsible for the long obliviousness to this crucial feature of reality. For them there is no knowable reality apart from that which is treated in one department of knowledge or another. Nature does not have an independent existence which could allow it to have a history outside of human knowledge. The history of reality is accordingly identified with the history of human thought, which is fragmented among the disciplines. The modern university is a tribute to the success of this antiworldview, but is hardly a support for an appropriate response to the threat of catastrophe.

The majority of people, of course, have not been converted to an ecological worldview. Many people have incorporated *some elements* of the new awareness into the old ones. Systems theory has enabled those wedded to mechanism to envision far more complex machines replete with all manner of feedback loops. Dualists can talk about the crisis as fundamentally a human crisis to be dealt with by enhanced concern for justice among human beings. The opponents of worldviews can pay more attention to the discipline of ecology, while still berating the tendency for too great generalization from limited data. In the public realm, the issues raised by ecologists must compete for attention with those that come from other sources, especially immediate economic concerns and military policy.

Nevertheless, there are others for whom the vision of the interconnectedness of all things has become the inclusive context within which the other sciences, as well as issues raised by economic needs and military policy, are viewed. This change of vision has been for some a fundamental conversion, for others, a development of already strong intuitions. At this point, ecology becomes a worldview. The remainder of this chapter explores two forms of this worldview: the first, very briefly; the second, to which I subscribe, at greater length.

IV. Two Ecological Worldviews

The first ecological worldview is sometimes called *deep ecology.*[4] It stresses the interdependent and unified character of the ecosystem as a whole. It is in this total system rather than in individual creatures that value lies. The individuals exist as participants in this whole and have value as they contribute to the complex network of relations which is the whole. To this whole, a strong sense of sacredness attaches itself; to its violation, a strong sense of evil.

Deep ecology entails a drastically different understanding of the place of the human from that of the heretofore dominant views. Especially in the West, the emphasis has been on human separateness from nature. This separateness is especially accentuated in dualism. But evolutionary theory can also encourage a view of humanity as the supreme product of nature for whose sake the remainder exists. This view can corroborate the basic ideas of Biblical believers. In all of these views, human beings stand in some measure above nature (or, at least, above the rest of nature) and rightfully shape it to human purposes. Their basic understanding of themselves is of how they transcend nature rather than of how they belong to it.

The deep ecologists reject all of this as human pretension that is not only false but also the cause of our destructive behavior. In truth, they say, the human species is one of many, neither better nor worse than the others. It has its place in the ecosystem as a whole and can have its value as contributory to it. But humanity has no special value, and its pretense to have special value has led to its massive violations of that ecological order on which its good, and all good, depend.

Deep ecology, like most worldviews, is a profoundly religious vision. Among traditional religious doctrines it comes closest to pantheism but, if it is pantheism, it is pantheism in a new form. Its rituals and practices are only beginning to be worked out, but that it has radical implications for all of life cannot be questioned. Indeed, the implications are so shattering with respect to all that we have inherited from our civilized ancestors that one wonders how widely the worldview can be assimilated.

The second form of ecological worldview does not depart as radically from the Western tradition. It calls for a modification of science and religion but retains recognizable continuity with existing trends and in some ways returns to classical religious sources. Instead of focusing initially on the whole, it attends primarily to the individuals comprising it. I call this the *postmodern ecological worldview.*

A very simple idea impressed upon us by ecology is that things cannot be abstracted from relations to other things. They may be moved from a natural set of relations to an artificial one, such as in a laboratory, but when these relations are changed, the things themselves are changed. The effort to study things in abstraction from their relations is based on a misunderstanding. This misunderstanding is that things exist as independent entities and only incidentally are related to one another. This is the misunderstanding that lies at the base of the materialistic view of nature (which is shared by both the dualistic and the materialistic worldviews). This materialism is articulated philosophically in terms of "substance." A *substance* is that which depends on nothing else for its existence. It is a thing that remains fundamentally the same regardless of its relations. An atom was defined by the Greeks to be a unit of substance. Modern mechanism is built on this notion. Everything that is not an atom is nothing but a structure of atoms. The atoms are not affected by the structures in which they are arranged. The structures behave like machines and are not inherently affected by their relations to other things. They can be externally affected by other things by having some of their parts separated from others, but the character of the separated parts is not affected by this separation. The laboratory is the ideal place to do science, in this view, because it is designed for abstracting things from their relations, taking them apart, and putting them back together again, often in new ways.

The expectation of substantialist thinking would be that the properties of the compound structures, apart from shape, would be the sum of the properties of the substantial parts as they exist independently of the compound. It is now a commonplace idea that this is not so. Salt has properties other than shape not found in any of its components (when these are not structured as salt). This point is an embarrassment for mechanistic materialism, but it is glossed over as an instance of the "emergence" of properties, a quite nonmechanistic notion. The importance of arrangement of atoms in the determination of properties is so great that "structure" is now a fundamental category of analysis. This fact should not be so if the world were really composed of material substances.

An explanation for this fact is not difficult to find, but it requires that the notions of *material* and *substance* be rejected. According to this explanation—an ecological one—the properties of an atom are always the properties of that atom as its existence is determined by its relations to its environment. Atoms acquire different properties when they are arranged in different molecular structures because these different structures constitute different environments. Instead of viewing molecules as machines, we should view them as ecosystems. Science may continue to ask what properties a certain type of atom continues to have in great varieties of contexts, but it should add the question as to the diverse properties the atom acquires in different relationships. This ecological approach to the study of atoms can subsume the materialistic one, whereas the materialistic approach cannot subsume the ecological.

The situation does not change to the advantage of the idea of material substance when we shift to a still more primitive level. Indeed, it has long been recognized that ideas of material substance cannot be consistently applied at the subatomic level. Atoms cannot be understood as machines; they are much better envisioned as ecosystems.

That things are related is no news to mechanistic-materialists, but for them the relations of a material substance must be wholly external. That is, the substance is not different *in itself* because it is related. This doctrine makes understanding how atoms can acquire new properties when they are in new relationships impossible. If this is the case, the atoms must be affected by the relationships. That is, the relationships must be *internal* to the atoms; they must participate in the *constitution* of the atoms. The ecological worldview holds that all the units of reality are internally related to others. All units or individuals are constituted by their relations.

This notion of internal relations requires further reflection. Although much evidence is found for internal relatedness, a felt contradiction exists between what we first think of when we image a molecule and the notion of internal relations. I can explain this contradiction better at the familiar level of interpersonal relations. It is an oft-noted fact that I can think of another person in two ways. One way is as I experience him or her through my senses, especially vision. What I think of then is a body bounded by its skin. That body has spatial relations with other bodies and can be affected by the contact of other bodies. But it is hard to understand what it would mean to say that it is internally related to those other bodies. The relation *appears* to be external (although the behavior I observe testifies to something else). However, I can also think of other persons as ones who feel and think much as I do. In that case, I imagine them to experience objects in their environment through their senses. Those objects are then partly constitutive of, or internally related to, their experiences. Their experiences would be different if the objects in their field of vision were different. Thus, when I think of them not as objects of my experience but as subjects of their own, it is natural to think of them as constituted by their relations to others.

An ecological worldview of the sort I am here proposing requires that we adopt this double view of every real individual. Each such individual exists for my objectifying thought and experience. But each exists also as its own center of experience. In most cases this experience is not *conscious* experience. But it *is* an activity of taking account of its world and thereby constituting itself out of its relations.

If we ask why it goes against the grain of so many contemporary thinkers to attribute activity or agency to atoms and subatomic entities, the answer is not that this idea is inherently absurd. It was a very natural idea for some of those in the magical tradition whose work was foundational for modern science. It became strange only through the victory of those physicist-theologians who wanted to denude nature of all life and feeling for the sake of attributing all action to the will of God, and of keeping God wholly external to the world. The ecological worldview restores *inherent reality*, hence activity and experience, to nature.

A further point entailed by the above discussion needs to be drawn out. An activity is not an agent that acts. To think of an agent that acts is to move back to the idea of substance. The agent would have to exist first apart from the activity and to be essentially unaffected by the activity. There is no evidence of such agents in nature. The activity itself constitutes nature. The relatively enduring aspects of nature are the results of the repetitiveness of many activities. Also, the way in which one activity takes account of others may be highly unique. But for the ecological vision, behind the sensory display of apparently passive substances is a world of interrelated activities. What happens in the superficial world of passive substances is a function of what happens in the dynamic world of interrelated activities.

Perhaps the most radical implication for human self-understanding is that, just as there are no agents of activity separable from the activity in the rest of the world, so there is no self who is the subject of experience apart from the activity that is the experience in the human being. The ecological worldview here agrees with Hume and with the Buddhist analysis. There is a flow of experience that has just that richness and just that degree of identity through time that it factually possesses. There is nothing more (and nothing less).

The cellular activities throughout the human body and the acts of human experience which grow out of the complex patterns of structure in the brain are among these interrelated activities that constitute nature. This postmodern ecological vision agrees with deep ecology at that point. Human beings are, without remainder, part of the ecosystem. Everything is both subject and object, and human beings are no exception. Dualism is excluded.

This form of ecological vision also agrees with deep ecology in seeing value in the way each individual, each activity, contributes itself to all the others. But, unlike deep ecology, it also affirms the unique value of each activity in itself. This affirmation leads to a doubly differentiated valuation of individual things. They have diverse values for others, and they have diverse values in themselves. Some of the entities that have the least value for others have the greatest value in themselves and some that have the most value for others (at least in large numbers) have the least value in themselves. However, because of the fundamental character of internal relations, the realization of value in one entity tends to enhance the value of others.

The human species in overall perspective has very little value for other species in nature. The whole biosphere today would in fact be much healthier if evolution had not led to the appearance of human beings. If our species were to disappear under circumstances that did not poison the atmosphere or destroy numerous other species, we could expect a gradual recovery of the biosphere from our depredation.

But human experience has introduced into this planet dimensions of experience that are, as far as we know, impossible for other species. The qualities of enjoyment characteristic of human relationships and creativity have unique intrinsic worth. That we are fully part of nature does not undercut the distinctiveness of the values we have realized. Furthermore, in principle, according to this ecological vision, the realization of special value at one point does not take away from value somewhere else. On the contrary, it provides a new possibility of realizing values to those who come after because the value that can be realized in any act of experience is largely a function of the values of the activities that have come before it, and to which this new act is internally related.

This concluding emphasis is important in overcoming the substantialist idea that what is of value is in limited supply and that human beings therefore relate to one another and to other creatures in a primarily competitive way. There is truth to this doctrine with respect to many of the goods on which the economist focuses. But the greater goods of human relations and of aesthetic enjoyment are mutual rather than competitive. Furthermore, the person informed by the ecological vision can show that full employment and more efficient and democratic use of resources, far from being "trade-offs," can be attained together. There are many instances of interspecies adjustment for mutual benefit throughout the ecosystem. Competition is not the ultimate principle.

However, neglecting the fact of competition would be sentimental. Individual plants compete for space and light; animals compete for habitat and food; animals kill plants and carnivores kill other animals. Life is robbery. Far more animals are born than can reach maturity. The ecosystem works well for the species, but the sacrifice of individuals is enormous.

Furthermore, the dominant human role continues to be that of mindless butchery and habitat destruction, often for minor short-term goals. Even if everyone shared the ecological vision, there would be no easy solution to the pressures of human population on remaining habitat for "wild" animals. A participant in the ecological worldview is in permanent mourning for the accelerating destruction which impoverishes us all. Nevertheless, the ecological vision does suggest new policies based on a *synergistic* rather than competitive model.

The modern worldview initially intended the unity of natural science. But this unity was always only a hope and, in fact, the natural sciences multiplied. In the substantialist perspective, one can isolate any set of elements from their context in the real world and study them analytically in their own terms. There is no necessary reference to other elements of the world. The social sciences, which grew up on the other side of the great divide between material and mental substances, multiplied in a similar fashion.

With time, the methods and conceptualities of each science became well entrenched within that science and quite differentiated with respect to others. Although there may be influences from one science on another, these are random. Basically each one models itself on the supposedly substantial character of the subject matter.

It is notorious that many of our most important questions cannot be dealt with within the confines of any existing science. For that reason they are likely to be ignored, or else misleadingly treated as if they did belong to some one of the disciplines. Occasionally interdisciplinary teams are organized to deal with such problems. But the results are only modestly encouraging. The questions need to be treated in their integrity, not as the sum of questions formulated according to the traditions of several discrete disciplines. For example, nothing is more important than charting the right course for development in third world countries. This task is generally treated as a problem in economics. But, in fact, cultural anthropology, political science, ecology, agriculture, and forestry are almost always centrally involved. Decisions reached by teams with representatives of many disciplines are usually better than those made by economists alone. But their multiple specialties do not add up to a unified picture. The practical results, humanly and environmentally, have been disastrous.

The ecological worldview tells us that our initial mistake was the supposition that we could isolate some elements from the whole and learn the truth about them in this abstraction. A conceptuality developed to deal with them in abstraction from their real embedment in the whole will not accurately describe them in that embedment. A sum of distortions based on the different abstractions of the several disciplines will not give us the truth about the concrete reality. Of course much can be learned, but the addition, for example, to economics of political theory and sociology still does not bring us very close to what is really going on in our society unless the economics is richly informed from the outset by political theory and sociology. Only a knowledge that is ecologically related to all knowledge is appropriate to a reality that is ecologically interconnected. The implications run markedly counter to most current trends.

V. THE POSTMODERN ECOLOGICAL WORLDVIEW AND THE DIVINE

This postmodern ecological worldview, like deep ecology, is profoundly religious while rejecting the modern, Newtonian God. It resembles more the magical vision against which the theological voluntarists reacted. But, unlike deep ecology, it cannot be pantheistic, because every individual has its own indissoluble reality, activity, and value in and for itself and not only for others. The Whole for which it is also a value must itself be an activity numerically distinct from all the others, although internally related to all.

The contrast of the thought of the divine in the substantialist and ecological worldviews deserves emphasis. Boyle and Newton thought of both God and creatures as substances. There could be no internal relations among them. Power is fundamentally power to cause locomotion. On this view, if creatures had the power to move themselves, they would compete with or displace the divine power. Hence, God is glorified by the denial of all capacity for self-motion to the creatures. They are held to be purely passive, that is, purely material. God is the one source of all motion.

For the postmodern ecological worldview the "Adventure in the Universe as One" is internally related to the world. That is, she is constituted by Her relations to the activity and value of the world. The more value is attained in the world, the richer is the divine life. Similarly, the creature is constituted in part by its internal relation to the Divine Eros. From Her, it receives the power of freedom as self-determination. Apart from Her, it would be at most the outcome of its relations to past events, determined by their relative strength. From Her, it receives the ability to transcend that determination by the past in light of relevant unrealized possibilities.

In this paragraph, I have used the language of Alfred North Whitehead in *Adventures of Ideas*,[5] except that I have employed the feminine pronoun. It would be more convenient simply to speak of *God*, as Whitehead did in *Process and Reality*. But that word is so heavily freighted with the meanings that apply to the Newtonian God that, at least provisionally, it is well to think in another language. In many respects, the ecological vision of the divine suggests feminine aspects as opposed to the stereotypically masculine ones of the Newtonian deity. Another alternative to Whitehead's language of Adventure and Eros is simply to speak of the *Goddess*, but that would falsely exaggerate discontinuity with the God of the Bible.

It would be possible to leave off these last paragraphs and present the ecological vision of the world with its obvious religious meaning without reference to divinity. There are those who share much of the ecological worldview I have outlined without feeling the need to speak of the divine. But I believe that approach to be truncated. At least two things are lost.

First, although the locus of value in this postmodern vision is dispersed throughout the myriad individual activities, there is a need to speak of better and worse states of the world as a whole. We are concerned to maintain a healthy biosphere replete with human life because such a world will be more valuable than one of molten rock. But that conviction is hardly intelligible unless we can say *from what perspective* it is more valuable. The appropriate perspective is the Whole. But if the Whole is a perspective, that perspective is divine, and all the parts must be constitutive for it. As many ethicists have also discovered, if we do not affirm the reality of an inclusive and impartial perspective, we must yet think as if there were one in order to make sense of our valuations.

Second, without the Divine Eros, the ecological vision tends to become static. The emphasis in ecology tends to be on repetitive patterns. But the real world is radically historical. There would be less reason to heed the ecologists' warning if there were not the likelihood of drastic destruction and the need for drastic new action historically. These things are hard to conceive if there be no real relevance of novel possibility initiating real freedom for alternative activity.

Clearly, this talk of the Divine adds additional religious dimensions to an already religious vision. For me, it adds to the continuity I feel with my Biblical and Christian heritage. To rescue that heritage from its bondage to the materialist and dualist substantialist forms of thought which have captured much of it in the modern world seems to me an important calling.

NOTES

1. David Ray Griffin, "Theology and the Rise of Modern Science," unpubl. ms. Many of the relevant ideas have been incorporated into the Introduction to this volume.

2. Stephen Pepper, *World Hypotheses: A Study in Evidence* (Berkeley: University of California Press, 1942); *Concept and Quality* (La Salle, Ill.: Open Court, 1969).

3. See James W. McClendon, Jr. and James M. Smith, *Understanding Religious Convictions* (Notre Dame, Ind.: University of Notre Dame Press, 1975).

4. For a good statement, see Bill Devall and George Sessions, *Deep Ecology: Living as if Nature Mattered* (New York: Peregrine Smith, 1985).

5. Alfred North Whitehead, *Adventures of Ideas* (1933; New York: The Free Press, 1967). On the Divine Eros, see 11, 198, 277; the phrase "Adventure in the Universe as One" occurs on 295.

8

THE POSTMODERN HERESY: CONSCIOUSNESS AS CAUSAL

Willis W. Harman

This paper explores some of the indications that a profound shift is taking place in the metaphysical assumptions underlying the modern world. If, in fact, this turns out to be the case, one can be sure that the new world that emerges will be so discrepant with the present as to fully justify the appellation *postmodern world*.

In discussing this topic, I want to put myself clearly in the role of *reporter*, as distinct from that of philosopher or pundit. We have seen many signs over the past quarter century that the Western world (in particular—but because of our contemporary global interconnectedness, the entire world) appears to be undergoing a transition of sea-change proportions. If so, it is because *vast numbers of people are apparently changing their minds about some of the tacit assumptions that underlie the modern world.* Any new idea that has the power of thus changing the world must be *simple*—simple in form, however profound in its implications. Thus, I want to deal with some simple concepts. Eventually, these ideas will come to be dealt with in full philosophical and scholarly sophistication. But, at the moment, I am concerned with a different task—that of interpreting this change that appears to be taking place in the way ordinary people are experiencing the world. I propose to put it in terms they would understand.

An apt example of what I mean is what is ordinarily thought of as the "Copernican heresy"—the assertion that the sun, rather than the earth, is at the center of the universe. This is by no means an adequate statement of the "scientific heresy" (or "scientific revolution") to which Copernicus' theories led, but it does delineate the issue in terms the public could understand.

I. Indications of a "New Heresy"

We are seeing, I believe, indications of a "new heresy" that is challenging modern secular authority at a level as profound as the "scientific heresy" challenged ecclesiastical authority in the seventeenth century. If so, this means that *the postmodern world will be as different from the modern world as that is from the world of the Middle Ages.*

Perhaps the most central aspect of this heresy occurs in the peculiarity of science. Although modern science has an ever-increasing amount to say about the human brain and central nervous system, it has had surprisingly little to say about *mind* or *consciousness*. Science has even in the past described mind as a mere "epiphenomenon" of the process in the brain, implying its relative nonimportance. Nobel laureate Roger Sperry marked a watershed point with his 1982 paper "Changing Priorities" in which he asserted:

> Current concepts of the mind-brain relation involve a direct break with the long-established materialist and behaviorist doctrine that has dominated neuroscience for many decades. Instead of renouncing or ignoring consciousness, the new interpretation gives full recognition to *the primacy of inner conscious awareness as a causal reality.* [1]

It is not immediately apparent how thoroughgoing a change this implies. Every known society rests on some set of largely tacit, basic assumptions about *who we are, what kind of universe we are in, and what is ultimately important to us.* Some such set of assumptions can be found to underlie the institutions and mores, patterns of thought, and systems of value that characterize the society. They are typically not formulated or taught, because they need not be. They are absorbed by each person born into the society as though by osmosis. (The process by which each culture teaches its members how to perceive reality is probably closely akin to hypnotic suggestion.) These assumptions are accepted as given, as obviously true, and are throughout most of history, by most people, never questioned.

When they have been questioned, when a widening group of people found that the assumptions no longer fit their experience, then what followed comprised a major societal transformation. There have been relatively few such instances in history; one of these was the transformation from medieval to modern times.

The shift Sperry postulates, essentially a shift in the assumptions about how we should interpret our own inner conscious awareness, is at such a fundamental level that it is bound to affect everything else. Thus, somewhat as "the earth goes around the sun" became the inadequate summary of the post-Copernican view, so "consciousness as causal reality" may come to identify (also inadequately) the "new heresy."

II. THE "SCIENTIFIC HERESY" MARKING THE END OF THE MEDIEVAL WORLD

It will be useful to examine in slightly more detail the impact of the "scientific heresy." We need no persuasion that this change of worldview that took place in Western Europe around the seventeenth century comprised a major shaping influence on the modern world. The heresy was directed against the traditional way of thinking and of educating known as Scholasticism. The latter assumed a world created and guided by God for human benefit. Its understandings were largely arrived at by citing authorities, either philosophical or scriptural. The primary function of this knowledge was to rationalize sense-experience in harmony with revealed religion. In contrast, the new way was to be empirical: What is true is what is found by scientific inquiry to be true. Ultimate authority lies in experiment and disciplined observation, rather than tradition.

This was not simply a change in beliefs; it was, literally, a change in the world perceived. An educated man in the year 1600 (most educated persons were men) perceived the Earth—the seat of change, decay, and Christian redemption—at the center of the cosmos, while above it circle the planets and stars, themselves pure and unchanging, but moved by intelligent or divine spirits, and signalling and influencing human events by their locations and aspects. One hundred years later his equally Christian descendant perceived (unless he lived in a Church-controlled Catholic country) the Earth as but one of many planets orbiting around one of many stars, moving through and separated by unimaginable distances.

In both cases the person would see the world to be under the overall guidance of God; however, in the intervening century an important change had taken place. The outlook of the individual in 1600 was theological: The universe is enchanted and imbued with purpose. Rocks, trees, rivers, and clouds are wondrous and alive. All creatures are part of a Great Chain of Being, with humans between the angels and the lower animals; events are explained by divine purpose or by their function in a meaningful world.

The cosmos is a place of *belonging*, of feeling at home, of being related in a way that gives meaning to life. To the person in 1700, by contrast, this is essentially a dead universe, constructed and set in motion by the Creator, with subsequent events accounted for by mechanical forces and lawful behaviors; divine purpose is considered an anthropocentric notion. The earlier person would confidently accept the overwhelming evidence for the working of enchantments, the occurrence of miracles, the existence of witches and other beings with supernatural powers; the later one, with equal certainty, would dismiss all those stories as the results of charlatanry and delusion. (A rich description of the difference between these two worlds is found in Morris Berman's *The Reenchantment of the World*.)[2]

The term *scientific revolution* focuses on certain important aspects of the change that occupied Western Europe in the seventeenth century. An "economic revolution," which involved not only new capitalist institutions but also a new emphasis in values and logic, also exerted an important influence on the modern world. So did the political shifts attending the Treaty of Westphalia, wherein the autonomy of the nation-state became a new factor in the world. And all of these were closely interconnected; all were part of one fundamental mind-change that in the end determined the modern world.

It would not have been easy for someone in the early part of the seventeenth century to recognize that such a fundamental belief-system shift was taking place, let alone to forecast what the consequences of the paradigm shift would be. We are in a similar position. Unequivocal signs of a shift to a postmodern world are hard to come by, and we can only sense some broad characteristics of a postmodern world. Nonetheless, the endeavor to understand this transition is vitally important because all our decisions will be influenced by that understanding, or the lack of it.

III. THE EVOLUTION OF THE
SCIENTIFIC WORLDVIEW

Bearing in mind that the shift from modern to postmodern has many other dimensions than the scientific, let us remind ourselves how this preeminently influential knowledge-system came to have its present form. Throughout most of the history of most kinds of science, scientific research and theory have been based on a foundational set of metaphysical assumptions that included *positivism*—the assumption that what is (scientifically) real is what is physically measurable; and *reductionism*—the assumption that (scientific) understanding is to be found in the reducing of phenomena to more elemental events (such as explaining the temperature of a gas in terms of the motion of its molecules, or human behavior in terms of stimulus and response).

This metaphysical bias was a useful one for many purposes. It was especially so for distinguishing scientific explanations from such pre-scientific interpretations as the whims of the gods, or the intervention of Divine grace, or "natural tendencies" such as bodies seeking to come to rest near the center of the universe or nature abhorring a vacuum.

When the modern worldview began to take shape, it involved, said Joseph Wood Krutch, "a revolt of common sense against everything that was repugnant to it." The revolt involved "a declaration of faith in the senses . . . and in the visible world as opposed to the unseen."[3] Although Krutch's statement must be qualified, it points in the right direction. For good reason the founders of modernity emphasized the empirical, as a reaction against the authoritarianism of the Scholastics, and the reductionist, as a more fruitful kind of explanation than the medieval concepts of ruling spiritual forces.

There were also ample grounds for science's separating the objective, which can be viewed by all, from the subjective, which the individual experiences in the privacy of his or her own mind—and good reasons to concentrate on the former. One such reason was that concentrating on the objective accelerated scientific progress; but an equally cogent one was to avoid a territorial clash with the institutions of religion, which viewed the soul and spirit as their special domain.

As Western Europe and North America put increasing emphasis on industrializing economic production, they naturally supported research into knowledge that would improve the abilities to predict and control, and to generate new technologies. This bias in the support pattern strengthened still further the deterministic and behavioristic tendencies in science.

Despite the impressive accomplishments of positivistic, reductionistic science, a puzzling question remained: How to deal with consciousness? It could not be ignored or explained away. After all, the only *direct* experience of reality that we have is our own conscious awareness. There was, many felt, something unnatural about a science that denied consciousness as a causal reality when everyday experience seemed to confirm again and again that my *decision* to act causes action.

There were other poses, which felt artificial, that one had to assume in order to be in accord with the sophisticated scientific view of the day. One tried to accept that it is the brain that is real, while conscious awareness in only an "epiphenomenon." The question, "Does mind exist?" seemed an important one. The complex products of creative imagination were supposed to have come about through some sort of random cycling of a brain-computer, together with some kind of selection of "best fit." One was supposed to believe that the complex instinctual behaviors of animals, and complex and seemingly purposeful physiological systems, such as the two eyes that give us binocular vision, had developed through our evolutionary past exclusively as a result of random mutations plus natural selection.

One was also supposed to ignore or explain away any spiritual feelings or inner conviction of transcendental reality. Positivistic science encouraged us to ignore the accumulated experience of the world's spiritual traditions, including thousands of years of sophisticated exploration of the further reaches of inner experience carried out in those research laboratories called monasteries. Spirituality was repressed but it never disappeared.

Besides these discrepancies, the anomalies reminded us that all was not well with the orthodox scientific worldview. Through the centuries, a variety of anomalous phenomena, including clairvoyant remote viewing, telepathic communication, levitation, teleportation, "instantaneous" spiritual healing, and other so-called psychic phenomena, have been reported. Various explanations have been offered as to why these reports were probably mistaken. Famous and competent scientists have arrayed themselves on both sides of the debate. One half century ago it seemed fairly clear that, in spite of the claims of a few persons doing research in parapsychology or "psychic research," the better educated and more sophisticated public felt confident that scientific advance was making the genuineness of the phenomena decreasingly plausible.

Common to all of these anomalous phenomena was that *mind* seemed to have some effects in the physical world—directly, as in the reported instances of dramatic healing, or indirectly, as in the presumed telepathic communication. But that is true in everyday and commonplace phenomena as well. I decide to raise my right arm, and up it goes! Attitudes toward one's work bring about tension and stress, and a peptic ulcer results. Patients told that a plain sugar pill has curative powers experience remission of the symptoms of their illness (the placebo effect). In our everyday experience, denying that what goes on in our minds has effects on our actions seems strained and artificial. Yet *as scientists*, more than one generation of students were trained to engage in that denial. It is in the light of these decades of *denial* of consciousness as causal reality that Roger Sperry's pronouncement comes with such impact.

IV. CHALLENGING THE BASIC ASSUMPTIONS OF WESTERN SCIENCE

Discovering that the prevailing knowledge-system of our culture, Western science, contains inherent and fundamental bias specific to this culture perhaps should not surprise us. This discovery would not surprise a cultural anthropologist.

It is well known to anthropologists that people who grow up in different cultures literally perceive different realities. The phenomenon is basically the same as hypnosis. A hypnotized subject, having accepted into the (partially unconscious) belief-system a suggestion, perceives reality in accordance with that suggestion. Similarly, people who are "hypnotized" by the suggestions implicit in one culture will perceive differently, experience different limits, etc., from those with a different "cultural hyponosis."

One pertinent example is the recent popularity in the United States of firewalking workshops. There had been ample evidence, for many generations, that people in certain cultures traditionally find it possible to walk barefoot over burning coals without hurting their feet. Until very recently, that possibility was not a part of reality in modern industrial culture. However, within the past several years, thousands of well-educated professional and business persons have demonstrated to themselves the power of their minds, by walking unharmed over a bed of burning coals after only a few hours' psychological preparation. This preparation centers around accepting and internalizing the suggestion that the fire will not burn them.

Another example is the phenomenon of clairvoyant "remote viewing"—"sending one's mind out" as far as hundreds or thousands of miles to "see" what is going on at some remote location. Primitive tribes had long used this ability to check up on distant relatives or strayed cattle, but its possibility was not a part of modern cultural reality. Only in the last two decades have military intelligence groups in both the United States and the Soviet Union put the phenomenon to their own uses. (As have archaeologists searching for ruins buried under many feet of sand, and energy companies seeking where to drill for oil.) Training to bring out the latent remote-viewing ability consists primarily in overcoming the negative belief that one cannot do it—that it is "physically" impossible.

It has been humbling for scientists to come to recognize (as they have been doing in increasing numbers over the past one-quarter century) that science is in a sense a cultural artifact. A different society, with a different "cultural hypnosis" (or different unconscious assumptions about reality), would have created a different science.

This observation poses a perplexing puzzle. Research in hypnosis and other areas of experimental psychology has amply demonstrated that once a person (or a society) has an internalized picture of reality, the world thenceforth tends to be experienced in accordance with that picture. Thus, for example, people of a certain ethnic origin tend to be experienced as having characteristics expected of that ethnic group. The hypnotized subject not only sees reality in accordance with the internalized suggestions from the hypnotist, but has very logical-sounding explanations as to why reality "really" is that way. Persons "hypnotized" by a particular culture to perceive in the way taught by that culture's prevailing belief-system tend to find their experience conforming to the approved "reality."

Thus, we have the very important dual relationship between the experienced world and the science that is developed. Advancing scientific knowledge influences the way we perceive the world. *But, the way the world is experienced in our culture influences what kind of science gets developed.* As Western society after the Middle Ages became increasingly secular, it created a science based on the positivistic assumption that only what can be measured physically is scientifically real. That science then finds that everywhere it looks in the universe it sees nothing save that which is measurable! A basic tenet of the new science was that scientific explanations are deterministic and reductionistic; that science then peers out into the universe and discerns nothing resembling purpose!

This thought—that a society's basic experiencing of reality shapes its science as well as the reverse—may be quite disturbing as one pursues its implications. When the shift took place from medieval to modern society, it was not a matter of the medieval paradigm's being proved wrong. Rather, the gradual secularization of values that had been taking place over several centuries had brought the culture to the point where an empirical science served its needs better than the outmoded Scholasticism. Similarly, if the adequacy of the scientific authority-system is being challenged today, it is first of all not a matter of its having been proved wrong so much as a question of whether the needs of persons, societies, and the planet are being well served.

That brings us to the question: If the underlying assumptions of Western society are changing, *why* are they? Mainly for two reasons. One is the accumulation of evidences that remind us that the contemporary scientific worldview does not jibe with the totality of human experience; some of these we have already indicated. The psychologically prior reason is the many ways in which the consequences of the modern paradigm are not good for people, and not good for the planet. The serious global problems of our day—from the threat of nuclear weapons and toxic chemical concentrations, to hunger, poverty and environmental deterioration, to insults to the Earth's life-support systems—are the direct consequence of the Western industrial mind-set which began to dominate the world several centuries ago.

We cannot take space here to explore in detail how changing metaphysical assumptions are already being reflected in a new sense of what societies and their institutions are about, and, hence, leading to basic changes in those institutions and their behaviors. Nor can we detail how, as people have increasingly looked to their own inner experience as the realm in which matters of value and meaning are resolved, and as they increasingly look to their own deep intuition as the ultimate authority, the "secret" has been more and more openly shared: *Experienced reality does not conform to the "reality" they taught us in science class; the "scientific worldview" is not an adequate guide for living life or for managing a society.*

V. THE POSSIBILITY OF A COMPLEMENTARY SCIENCE

If the positivistic and reductionistic assumptions no longer serve well, what are the replacement assumptions? How is "consciousness as causal reality" to be accommodated?

One possible way is through a "complementary science." This additional body of knowledge, like the present science, would be experimental and cumulative (in a broad sense at least). However, it would take as its particular focus subjective experience, consciousness, unconscious processes, etc. It would have special concern for purpose, value choices, search for meaning, total human development, etc. Among its emphases would be attention and volition; teleological explanations; explorations of alternate states of consciousness, particularly "deep intuition." Compared to present science, it would adopt a weaker stance with regard to positivism, determinism, reductionism, and objectivism. Models and metaphors would tend to be more holistic; teleological explanations would complement reductionistic kinds of explanations. (The present discipline of cognitive science could conceivably develop in this direction.)

A number of philosopher-scientists, recognizing that the extreme positivist position simply does not square with experience, have proposed an approach similar to this. (Nobel laureates Roger Sperry and Sir John Eccles are two examples.) Whereas the implicit assumption in positivistic science is that the basic stuff of the universe is matter-energy, this alternate approach makes a different assumption: *The basic stuff of the universe exhibits two fundamentally different kinds of properties: matter-energy properties and mind-spirit properties.* The former are studied with the present tools of science; mind-spirit properties must be explored in other ways more appropriate to the subject (e.g., inner, subjective exploration). Thus there develop, in essence, two complementary kinds of scientific knowledge. In areas where these overlap (e.g., the role of the mind in healing, the field of psychic phenomena), complementary understandings ensue from the two kinds of investigation.

We need to note here that previous attempts in science to bring in self-reports of subjective experience as primary data (e.g., introspectionism, phenomenological approaches, and Gestalt psychology) have tended to be considered failures. But those attempts did not involve a shift in basic assumptions; the bases on which they were judged nonfruitful do not apply if there is a fundamental paradigm shift.

We must also note that it has been widely assumed that science does not and cannot have anything to say about values. That assumption is false; the health sciences, for instance, deal very explicitly with value issues. Consider, for example, the mounting evidence that certain attitudes—e.g., resentment, frustration, rage, anxiety—are unwholesome in that they tend to interfere with the functioning of the body's immune system and foster ulcers, cancer, and other illness. Other attitudes—e.g., humor, joy, love—promote wellness and healing. But attitudes are intimately related to beliefs. Thus some beliefs (about oneself, one's relationship to others and to the planet) are wholesome while others are unwholesome. Some beliefs strongly encouraged by modern society are distinctly unwholesome—think, for instance, of the beliefs that underlie stress or feelings of alienation. While much of science may not have seemed to deal with values, the sciences relating to health and human development have the most profound value implications.

One of the hopes for a "complementary science" is that it might deal more satisfactorily with value issues. As noted earlier, conventional science developed around the desire to predict and control, and to manipulate the physical environment through technologies. This characteristic has contributed to the current confusion about values: With ever-increasing technological "know-how," modern industrial society is more capable of *doing* than any society in history; at the same time, it seems most unsure of what is *worth* doing. The belief in value-free science, once widely taught, has tended to lead toward moral relativism if not nihilism. Development of a complementary science could potentially contribute to clarification of these perplexing questions of value.

Yet is is doubtful that such a quasidualistic approach will in the end be satisfactory, for a reason stated below. Besides the positivistic/reductionistic assumptions of modern science and the quasidualistic assumption, a third possible position exists, which I now examine.

VI. A THIRD KIND OF METAPHYSICAL ASSUMPTION

This third kind of metaphysical assumption finds *the ultimate stuff of the universe to be consciousness.* Mind or consciousness is primary, and matter-energy arises in some sense out of mind. Individual minds are not separate (although individual brains may appear to be); they connect at some unconscious level. The physical world is to the greater mind as a dream image is to the individual mind. Ultimately reality is contacted not through the physical senses, but through the deep intuition. Consciousness is not the end-product of material evolution, having had to await development of complex neuronal networks in the human cortex. Rather, consciousness was here first!

At first thought, this way of looking at reality seems so alien to the Western-educated mind that it is difficult to take it seriously. Upon closer examination, however, it appears to build upon and expand, not violate, the accumulated experience of empirical science. Furthermore, it allows inclusion of, rather than forced ignoring or denial of, all those aspects of consciousness so puzzling in the conventional scientific view. These points require elaboration.

Let us first try to get the "feel" of the reality-picture wherein consciousness is the fundamental stuff of the universe. The analogy with a dream has already been mentioned. When we dream, there is typically a "story line"—events happen, and a causal relationship seems to exist among them. While we are dreaming, everything in the dream seems real enough. Then we awaken, and we recognize that it was actually a dream. The law of causality is other than it seemed to be when we were asleep. In the dream it may have seemed that one event was the cause of something else and so on. To the awakened self, it is apparent that "I, the dreamer" am cause of the dream—events, interrelationships, and all.

Now try to imagine the analogue. In our ordinary state, the physical world seems real; various kinds of events take place, and apparent causal relationships exist between them. Some of these relationships are so dependable that we discover "scientific laws" to describe them. (Only rarely does mind seem to intrude in the physical world in such a way that anomalous phenomena occur.) But suppose one "awakens" from the "dream" of the physical world. It then becomes apparent that the causality law is different than we thought (and were taught): "I, the dreamer" (or "We, the collective dreamer") am the cause of the events and the relationships. The out-of-consciousness collective/universal mind is creator of the world the individual mind experiences.

We should not think of this picture of reality as some abstract theological or philosophical theory to be debated. Rather, it seems to be a universal insight of which at some level of our selves we are already aware. It has appeared again and again in the "perennial wisdom" esoteric understandings of the world's spiritual traditions. In these traditions, we are urged not to analyze it or argue about it, but through meditative and other disciplines to "get in there and experience it." (It is not insignificant that a widening group of people are exhibiting interest in the "perennial wisdom" traditions, as well as being involved in meditation, yoga, and other "spiritual fitness" disciplines.)

Because each of us is going to spend most of his/her life in the "reality dream," and because present science works very well there in many respects, much of science remains unchanged even if the underlying metaphysical assumptions change. Somewhat as Newtonian physics still holds in many aspects of our lives even after the relativistic-quantum revolution, so physics and chemistry and much of the life sciences will still apply after the metaphysical shift. New kinds of holistic concepts (e.g., the "Gaia hypothesis") will gain increased credibility. Psychology will of course be totally different.

An interesting example is evolution. According to the generally accepted theory, as recently refined, the present universe began some 15-20 billion years ago, with the "Big Bang." Approximately four billion years ago, the first life appeared; two-tenths of a billion years ago, the first mammals. Through mutations and natural selection, evolution has proceeded to create organisms of increasing complexity. Extremely recently (cosmologically speaking) the first humans appeared, experiencing consciousness—a nonmaterial attribute arising out of the material universe.

In sharp contrast to this accepted theory, the third metaphysic starts from a totally different assumption. *Consciousness is.* Out of universal mind is created the evolution of the physical universe. The development of life forms is "pushed" by natural selection, "survival of the fittest," but it is also "pulled" in certain preferred directions (e.g., increasing awareness, freedom, complexity). Humans are—in one sense now; in another sense potentially—cocreators of the universe.

VII. SUMMARY

Oversimplifying somewhat for clarity,[4] three alternative kinds of metaphysical assumption that might underlie science and society have been explained:

M–1 Materialistic Monism (Matter Giving Rise to Mind): The basic stuff of the universe is matter-energy. We learn about reality from studying the measurable world. (The positivist assumption is that that is the only way we *can* learn.) Whatever consciousness is, it emerged out of matter (i.e., the brain) when the evolutionary process had progressed sufficiently far. Whatever we can learn about consciousness must ultimately be reconciled with the kind of knowledge we get from studying the physical brain.

M–2 Quasidualism: The fundamental stuff of the universe has matter-energy aspects and also mind-spirit aspects. The former are studied by something such as conventional science; the latter by a complementary science especially adapted to the exploration of "inner space."

M–3 Transcendental Monism (Mind Giving Rise to Matter): The basic stuff of the universe is mind or consciousness; the world of matter-energy is as a dream in universal mind.

In these terms, we are proposing that Western (and Western-influenced) societies are shifting from modern (based on an M–1 metaphysic) to postmodern (based on an M–3 metaphysic). At first thought, this may seem as outrageous a proposition as the heliocentric universe did to many in early seventeenth-century Europe. M–3 seems quite foreign to the Western mind, or certainly would have a generation ago. (It is not nearly as alien as it was one-quarter century ago if we may judge from the kinds of books purchased, motion picture themes and innuendos, participation in meditation and yoga workships, etc.)

Although Descartes postulated a dualistic universe, by the twentieth century, science was rather firmly committed to an M–1 metaphysic. Recently, as we have seen, a few scientists have felt the need of some sort of quasi-dualist view (M–2). Quietly, however, a growing number of scientists seem to have been finding that when they take their total experience into account, the M–3 metaphysic fits best.[5] As we have noted, the M–3 orientation is by no means new in human history. Throughout Western (and Eastern) cultural history there has long been an esoteric tradition of the potentiality for the individual to "awaken"—to become "dehypnotized" or "enlightened."

For myself, I find in my own experience that the longer I live with the M–3 metaphysic the better it seems to fit. It is in accord with the deepest wisdom of human experience down through the ages; at the same time, it does not contradict scientific knowledge in any irreconcilable way. It feels intuitively right; it does not conflict with personal subjective experiences of conscious awareness, inner freedom, and subjective sense of purpose and meaning, in the ways that positivistic science does. It leads to wholesome attitudes and inner peacefulness.

Furthermore, I encounter what seems to be a rapidly increasing number of other people who have come to a similar conclusion. To appreciate how much and how rapidly the cultural premises are changing, one has only to listen carefully to what is being said (about karma and reincarnation, power of holding a vision, meaning of near-death experiences, altered states of consciousness, transcendental meditation, and no end of other topics that simply were not on the agenda one-quarter century ago).

The crisis in science is increasingly recognized. The crisis to which the Western industrial paradigm has led us is far more widely recognized. The M–3 metaphysic is increasingly evident as a guiding factor in people's lives. The "new heresy" is alive and well.

The postmodern world is closer than we may have thought.

NOTES

1. Roger Sperry, "Changing Priorities," *Annual Review of Neuroscience* 4 (1981), 1–10; emphasis added. See also Roger Sperry, "Structure and Significance of the Consciousness Revolution," *Journal of Mind and Behavior* 8/1 (1987), 37–66.

2. Morris Berman, *The Reenchantment of the World* (Ithaca, N. Y.: Cornell University Press, 1984).

3. Joseph Wood Krutch, *The Measure of Man: On Freedom, Human Values, Survival and the Modern Temper* (1953; New York: Grosset & Dunlap, 1968), 177.

4. These three metaphysical assumptions are actually classes of assumptions; each has numerous possible variations. The M–3 metaphysics as I have used it here is meant to represent the assumption, inherent in the esoteric "perennial wisdom" of the world's spiritual traditions, of a single, underlying "ground of being" or "consciousness." Most of the other papers in this volume assume a pluralistic panpsychism, which is similar in regarding the world as we perceive it to be largely a construction of our minds. Like the version of the M–3 metaphysic that I have adumbrated, it rejects the two metaphysics of modernity, dualism, and materialism. It finds mind everywhere, and refutes the idea of insentient matter. But it stops short of the creative role of mind found in the mystical traditions and the "perennial wisdom." The two types of M–3 metaphysics should not be confused.

5. Some find the concept of a hierarchical arrangement of sciences as proposed by Karl Popper (Karl R. Popper and John C. Eccles, *The Self and its Brain* [Heidelberg: Springer International, 1977], 20) more congenial than an all-out M–3 based science. We might think of an ascending hierarchical arrangement of (1) physical sciences, (2) life sciences, (3) human sciences, and (4) spiritual sciences. The life sciences employ concepts more holistic than those of the physical sciences (e.g., organism, behavior pattern); the human sciences introduce conscious awareness and choice, etc. The possibility of "downward causation" (e.g., teleological causation)

as well as "upward causation" (reductionistic) is admitted. Level-1 science in this arrangement (physical sciences) implies the M-1 assumption; level-4 science (when we have one) implies the M-3 assumption; and the two views are complementary rather than mutually contradictory.

9

PARAPSYCHOLOGY AND POSTMODERN SCIENCE

Stanley Krippner

> Today the balance is strongly shifting
> toward a revival of mysticism . . . ,
> especially among cosmologists. It has even
> been suggested by certain physicists and
> popularizers of science that mysterious
> relationships exist between parapsychology
> and quantum physics.
>
> —Ilya Prigogine and Isabelle Stengers[1]

What is referred to as the "modern" worldview emerged in Europe during the seventeenth century; it is responsible for impressive advances in technology, industry, and scientific discovery. However, it has not prevented (and may even have been partially responsible for) unprecedented fragmentation, nihilism, and destruction. As Morris Berman states, "Western life seems to be drifting toward increasing entropy, economic and technological chaos, ecological disaster, and ultimately, psychic dismemberment and disintegration."[2] As a corrective to this situation, "postmodern" thought hopes to preserve the virtues of the "modern" worldview while replacing its mechanistic and reductionistic assumptions with those that are more organic and holistic in nature.

I. THE MYTHIC NATURE OF WORLDVIEWS

Worldviews arise from epistemologies which, in turn, are generated by the motivations that control them. In the seventeenth century, Europe adopted the epistemology of empiricism (i.e., the modern scientific method) that led to scientific principles that were repeatable and dependable. To a significant degree, science was able to control nature, predict behavior, and explain a multitude of phenomena.

The modern worldview claims to have replaced mythology as an explanatory structure. Indeed, it equates the term *myth* with the notion of falsehood. However, in its more traditional meaning, a *myth* is a story or organizing belief that embodies certain basic, guiding principles. In former times, cultural mythologies evolved for the purpose of helping members of a social group cope with their surroundings, guiding them through life's stages and crises.

The old cultural mythologies performed four functions. They helped people comprehend and explain the natural environment in an understandable way. They provided a pathway for carrying people through the succeeding epochs of their lives. They established social roles that facilitated congenial personal relationships and fulfilling work patterns. They enabled people to feel that they were participating in the vast wonder and perplexity of the cosmos.[3] Mythologies varied during the classical and medieval eras but still encompassed all four of these functions.

Modern scientists rarely comprehend that they are fulfilling a mythic function by providing explanations of the natural environment. Ancient observers believed that lightning was produced by Zeus, Jupiter, or Thor throwing bolts to earth from the heavens. The modern observer believes that lightning is an electrical discharge in the atmosphere caused by the electric-charge separation produced in thunderstorm clouds. The latter has replaced the former because of its parsimony and applicability, but both concepts can be seen as mythic in nature.

Primitive or totemic thought conceptualized people as an integral part of nature; knowledge was mediated through tribal shamans who heard "voices," saw "visions," and dreamed of "other realities." Later, for Greek and other people in the classical era, knowledge was obtained through rationally constructed metaphysical systems. In medieval times, knowledge was "scholastic," i.e., it was to be found in the correct interpretation of sacred revealed scripture.

The modern approach to knowledge—proper application of the scientific method—regarded the previous approaches as sheer superstition. However, each of these epistemologies can be seen as mythic in nature, as positing an "absolute truth," much like the Holy Grail or the Golden Fleece, a "truth" that could be obtained through a heroic journey that would penetrate the changing flux of experience and disclose a universal, underlying essence.

Modern science has fulfilled one mythic quest quite well insofar as it has provided explanations for observable phenomena. In addition, it has accelerated the abandonment of ancient and medieval beliefs that produced suffering for certain individuals and social groups. No longer are young people sacrificed to ensure the sun's reappearance following an eclipse. Only occasionally are women burned with the corpses of their husbands during funeral ceremonies. With increasing rarity do rigid caste systems and institutionalized slavery negate or warp the expression of affiliation and talent. And it is uncommon today for people to be maimed, tortured, or killed to satisfy the perceived needs of a bloodthirsty deity.

Some modern totalitarian states, perhaps unwittingly, have attempted to produce all-embracing mythologies using science and technology for this purpose. Entry into the state-approved political party is seen as a rite of passage. Work and family are given heroic status through awards heralding a worker's surpassing of production goals or the mother's production of an approved number of children. The founders of the state or the authors of the political philosophy underlying the social structure of that state become God-like in nature.

Aldous Huxley satirized this trend in his novel *Brave New World*.[4] In Huxley's counter-Utopia, science and technology had produced a society that fervently believed in its motto: "Community, Identity, Stability." Individuality was a thing of the past. Human beings were manufactured through mass production methods and conditioned to enjoy their social states. From infancy, "Beta" workers were taught to repeat, "I'm glad I'm a Beta," and the other social classes, from the Alpha Plus Intellectuals to the Epsilon Minus Morons, were similarly conditioned. Henry Ford, who was thought to have used the name "Freud" when he wrote about psychosexual matters, was the God-figure of the Brave New World.

With these exceptions in both fantasy and reality, modern science has not created new rituals to mark life's developmental stages; it has not found ways to fulfill people's needs for interpersonal intimacy or meaningful work, or their hunger for spiritual fulfillment through unity with a schema greater than themselves. Modern science, then, can be conceptualized as an incomplete mythology—one that has impressive explanatory power but that is better at demolishing older mythic constructs than establishing new concepts to replace them. In other words, science fulfills humankind's needs for understanding natural phenomena, but rarely addresses itself to the developmental, social, and spiritual needs that traditionally were fulfilled by cultural myths.

II. PARAPSYCHOLOGY AND
ANOMALOUS REPORTS

Modern science, by and large, has been extremely hostile regarding parapsychology since its establishment in the 1880s. The Society for Psychical Research, founded in England in 1882, was the first major organization to attempt the scientific assessment of what are now called *psi phenomena*. Psi phenomena are usually defined as organism-environment interactions in which it appears that information or influence has occurred that can not be explained through science's understanding of sensory-motor channels. In other words, these reports are *anomalous* because they appear to stand outside of modern science's concepts of time, space, and energy.

Psychology is the scientific study of behavior and experience; *parapsychology* studies apparent anomalies of behavior and experience, those existing apart from currently accepted explanatory mechanisms that account for organism-environment information and influence flow. Psi phenomena are usually grouped under the headings of *extrasensory perception* (ESP), *psi gamma*, or *receptive psi*, in which anomalous information flow is reported, and *psychokinesis* (PK), *psi kappa*, or *expressive psi*, in which anomalous influence flow is reported.[5] A dream about an unusual event that is actually occurring in a remote location at the same time as the dream is a possible example of receptive psi, while a possible example of expressive psi is the reported movement of a physical object at the same time someone claims to be thinking about that object, "willing" it to move.

The Parapsychological Association, founded in 1957 and an affiliate of the American Association for the Advancement of Science since 1969, consists of about 300 members in some 30 different countries. This group tends to exclude from its membership people who make dogmatic statements about anomalies; indeed, it has gone on record as stating that labeling an event as a *psi phenomenon* does not constitute an explanation for that event, but only indicates an event for which a scientific explanation needs to be sought.[6]

The Parapsychological Association also has emphasized that "a commitment to the study of psi phenomena does not require assuming the reality of 'nonordinary' factors or processes."[7] Despite these disclaimers and cautionary statements, parapsychology has been referred to by scholarly critics as a *pseudoscience,*[8] a *deviant science,*[9] or a *spiritual science*[10] which is incompatible with the modern scientific worldview. Indeed, parapsychologists have been accused of harboring a hidden agenda in their work:

> The anomalies are for most parapsychologists only the means to an end; ultimately, they hope, these specimens will demonstrate once and for all that science as we know it is badly mistaken in its materialistic orientation and that human existence involves an ineffable, nonmaterial aspect that may very well survive the death and decay of the

physical body. As long as the need exists to find meaning in life beyond that which is forthcoming from a materialistic philosophy, the search for the paranormal will go on. [11]

III. PARAPSYCHOLOGY AND THE POSTMODERN WORLDVIEW

Although all members of the Parapsychological Association ascribe to high standards and rigorous investigative methods, there is some diversity in regard to the interpretations they make of the results. Many parapsychologists conduct and interpret their work within the framework of the modern scientific worldview, and assume that anomalous phenomena eventually will be understood within the context of that worldview, albeit one that is somewhat expanded. However, another group of parapsychologists takes the view that psi phenomena mark the boundary limits of the modern scientific worldview. For them, psi "becomes a vindication of the essentially spiritual nature of man which must forever defy strict scientific analysis." [12] Members of this second group appear to be more in accord with the holistic vision of the postmodern worldview than with the fragmented mythology of the modern worldview to which the Parapsychological Association implicitly subscribes.

For example, the modern worldview is mechanistic, insisting that nature is a machine, composed of machine-like parts. In contrast, E. H. Walker suggests that psi phenomena support the concept of the human "will." [13] The modern worldview is individualistic; people are seen as separate egos encapsulated by their skins. W. G. Roll notes that "today's society adopts the premise that people are separate" while parapsychological research indicates that people sometimes "experience the whole of which all may be part." [14]

The modern worldview is scientistic, with the scientific method challenging the concepts of religion. However, E. H. Walker claims that the current scientific paradigm is "inadequate" and must yield to "an interpretation that incorporates the concept of consciousness, encompasses paranormal processes, and resolves factually the problem posed by the concept of God." [15] The modern worldview is materialistic; all existence is composed of measurable material entities. But C. T. Tart states that psi research data supports the notion that "a partial-to-complete separation of body and mind" is possible. [16]

The modern worldview is reductionistic; wholes are explainable in terms of their parts. Michael Grosso, on the other hand, thinks that "the parapsychology of religion would reunite these distinctive strands into one discipline and begin to forge a powerful science of the human spirit." [17] The modern worldview is anthropocentric, with humans mastering and controlling nature for their own ends. Yet Lawrence LeShan believes that parapsychology stresses humanity's "oneness" with nature, and predicts that the field will help people "move towards full humanity." [18]

The modern worldview is Eurocentric, patriarchal, and militaristic. However, most of the mediums and "psychic sensitives" investigated by the founders of the field were women. Moreover, Charles Honorton has pointed out an apparent convergence between many psi-conducive states of consciousness and Eastern methods of consciousness-alteration. [19] W. G. Roll observes that psi research may "contribute to man's survival and well-being in this world." [20]

The text *Foundations of Parapsychology* concludes by describing a society based on a new paradigm toward which parapsychology may contribute:

> Such a society promises much: a societal organization in which there will be less competition and more cooperation, and the feelings of the unity of society being greater than the assertions of the individual; less of a work ethic and more of a merging of work and play and learning; a greater tolerance of difference and experimentation; a greater respect for the potentials of consciousness; and institutions which will support these goals. [21]

However, parapsychology by itself will not produce a panacea; [22] even with the help of allies, there is no guarantee that the "postmodern world" will arrive soon or that its appearance is even imminent.

IV. A CRITIQUE OF PARAPSYCHOLOGICAL RESEARCH

These statements and the parapsychological research data upon which they are based are not taken seriously by most other scientists. One reason for this disregard is that they could be interpreted in support of the postmodern worldview and would hasten the abandonment of the modern paradigm most other scientists presuppose. James Alcock, for example, refers to this line of thought as "the new millennialism."

> Although the idea that the human condition will be greatly improved once psychic forces are understood has been held throughout the history of parapsychology, it seems that in recent years, perhaps because of growing disillusionment with the ability of science and technology to alleviate human social problems and suffering, there has been a growing tendency in some parapsychological quarters to look to the flowering of psychic abilities to save the world. [23]

One could make the case that many parapsychological phenomena are not suited for adequate exploration *via* the most commonly used methods of modern science. ESP and PK may be the results of so many interacting forces that a systems model rather than a simple cause-effect model should be used to do them justice. The role (and belief-system) of the experimenter may play such a crucial role in psi research that replicability depends upon finding another experimenter with a comparable attitude toward the experiment. Perhaps a postmodern science will be better able to encompass the subtle flow of information and influence that appears to defy modern science's constraints of time, space, and energy. Already there are many psi researchers who advocate moving from "proof-oriented research" to "process-oriented research," expecting that uncovering the correlates of psi will help to produce psi phenomena more reliably and to develop empirically based theories of psi.[24]

James McClenon, a member of the Parapsychological Association, surveyed Council Members of the American Association for the Advancement of Science as well as AAAS section committee members. Only 29 percent of the 339 scientists who responded were favorably disposed toward "extrasensory perception" (ESP), considering it "an established fact" or "a likely possibility." ESP was considered to be only a remote possibility or an impossibility by 50 percent. He concluded, "The population of elite scientists surveyed in this study demonstrated the highest level of skepticism over ESP of any major group surveyed within the last 20 years."[25] McClenon conjectured that elite scientists can be expected to defend the "scientistic" worldview more vigorously than other scientists "because part of their roles as an elite is to define the nature of science."[26]

Douglas Stokes, a member of the Parapsychological Association who has conducted critical analyses of the experimental studies, has arrived at a conclusion that comes close to representing a consensus of his colleagues:

> A fair and objective examination of spontaneous case material raises at least a reasonable suspicion that psi phenomena exist. There are hints from the experimental literature that it may be possible to bring such phenomena under experimental control. Because the reported effects are not as yet repeatable by the majority of investigators, it cannot be claimed that psi phenomena have been scientifically demonstrated to exist. It would however be premature to close the book on the issue; psi phenomena are worthy of further study.[27]

The leading text in the field, *Foundations in Parapsychology*, frankly states, "The bottom line is that the apparent ESP demonstrated so far in controlled environments is simply not strong enough or reliable enough to *compel* acceptance of ESP as a fact of nature."[28]

Of course, it should be observed that methodological problems, including those of repeatability, occur in all the social sciences. Anthony Stigliano has concluded, "If prediction is the mark of an empirical science, certainly the social sciences are not empirical sciences. If a unified theoretical and methodological point-of-view is the mark of a "mature" science, then the social sciences can not be called mature."[29]

Because of parapsychology's roots in the social sciences, the field may be reflecting a problem inherent in its subject matter and in the ways that modern science has studied it. The consensus of the field appears to be that parapsychology cannot be expected to be the leading influence in shifting scientific paradigms, if such a shift is warranted. Thomas Kuhn has observed that at any time in science facts are found that cannot be easily explained and observations that do not fit in fully with what is known. A paradigm shift often results from this accumulation of anomalous data once they reach a critical mass.[30] I take the position that parapsychological data *per se* have not attained the potency to justify a paradigm shift. However, parapsychology is one of several data sources that indicate that the modern worldview is incomplete at best and flawed at worst.

V. PARAPSYCHOLOGY AND THE EMERGENCE OF A POSTMODERN WORLDVIEW

Parapsychology clearly is not accepted and respected by modern science. Parapsychologists face a difficult choice. On the one hand, they could attempt to accommodate themselves to the dictates of the modern natural, behavioral, and social sciences, striving for tighter experimental research procedures, and focusing on lines of investigation that appear to hold promise for repeatable results. On the other hand, they could abandon the experimental paradigms used in contemporary science, switching to the research methods of so-called human science. These methods emphasize existential-phenomenological methods of inquiry, hermeneutics, and participant/observation research.[31] In my opinion, neither of these routes is viable; the first approach has led to frequent experimenter "burnout" with only occasional success in devising tests that are partially replicable. The second approach appears to hold considerable promise but could be interpreted to give up the hope that parapsychology will ever be accepted by mainstream science. Fortunately, a third alternative exists, one in which parapsychology can retain the best of the current scientific paradigm, supplement it with "human science" methods, and join with other models of disciplined inquiry whose data imply the need for a new worldview.

One of the most eloquent arguments for the postmodern worldview has been put forward by the philosopher Huston Smith who has described four aspects of the stress and distress apparent in the modern worldview.[32]

1. Distress Stemming from Reductionism. In a worldview reduced to factual information, institutions have lost a coherent sense of values. Facts, especially those gleaned from the study and control of nature, are given a higher priority than wisdom. But it is wisdom rather than facts that helps people fulfill the mythic needs of guidance, meaning, and enspiritedness.

Therefore, distress results from value uncertainties and science is helpless to afford relief.

2. Distress Occasioned by Reason. In the modern worldview, nothing is granted the credentials of "truth" unless it has been arrived at through reason. Reasoning may take the form of logic, observation, or experimentation, just as long as the process is objective, separate from nature, and mechanistic.

3. Stress in Evolutionary Theory. As a *description* of life's journey on the planet, evolution is a noble scientific achievement. But the modern worldview, perhaps unwittingly, has attempted an *explanation* of that journey through evolution. For example, it claims that natural selection working on "chance mutations" accounts for life forms. But the term *chance mutations* points to something inexplicable; its use as explanation demonstrates the mythic incompleteness of the current paradigm.

4. Stress in Quantum Physics. The reference points for the modern worldview are matter and motion—the materialistic, mechanical paradigm. Developments in quantum mechanics have thrown this paradigm into question, but they have not made a significant dent in this mode of constructing reality.

Smith's examples point to places where breakthroughs may occur because the modern worldview is vulnerable at those points. As mentioned, modern science is the predominant mythic construction of the age, but it is an incomplete myth. Its proponents have applied it successfully to humankind's need for explanation, but not to the need to cope successfully with social and personal change, or to the need for spiritual understanding. Parapsychologists, for the most part, have been wise to avoid filling these mythic gaps with spinoffs from psi research data. However, this is not to say that parapsychology lacks a role in the possible emergence of the postmodern worldview.

In 1986, the McDonnell Foundation of St. Louis, Missouri, gave a multimillion grant to Princeton University for an interdisciplinary study of human communication. Parapsychology was one of the fields brought into this consortium and its contributions to the problems investigated by the researchers will help determine the future role of psi research in similar undertakings. For example, a common ground exists between parapsychology and quantum mechanical theory.[33] Not only does quantum theory point out the impossibility of distinguishing between an "observer" and an "observed," but it can be interpreted in a way as to bring consciousness fully into the mainstream of scientific investigation. Another area directly relevant to parapsychology is the "holonomic" models of reality, ranging from the empirically based work of Karl Pribram[34] to the more speculative theorizing of Rupert Sheldrake.[35]

Applications to postmodern thought of biological synergy,[36] ecological research,[37] general systems theory,[38] and human science[39] have been proposed. Each of these movements indicates the potential value of a new paradigm, one that would herald important revisions of current myths as well as the construction of new mythic conceptualizations of the world and our place in it.

Perhaps parapsychology can play its role most productively if it attempts to forge alliances with some of these movements that are suggestive of an emerging paradigm. For example, many physicists do not see psi phenomena as inconsistent with quantum theory. Holonomic theory suggests that psi phenomena simply reflect the presence (to some extent) of all information at all levels of reality. General systems theory could subsume psi at one or more levels of a living system. In biological synergy and ecological research, psi may play an important role in mediating mind/body and organism/environment interactions. In fact, I propose that the role available to parapsychology is unique. Parapsychology has developed methods and techniques of investigating anomalous events that, by and large, are more sophisticated than those found in any other field. These approaches were derived from modern science but in combination with the forthcoming contributions of postmodern science could yield disciplined, rigorous means of research eminently suitable for the tasks ahead.

In the postmodern worldview, the conceptions and applications of psi might take on forms radically different from those that characterize it at the present time. This is not surprising because the current models of psi are the results of the modern worldview. Psi in the postmodern age might be simpler, more elegant, and more parsimonious than can be imagined today. The current dichotomies between "brain" and "mind," between "body" and "psyche," and between "matter" and "spirit" may be resolved in favor of a systems-oriented interactionist model of consciousness. What today is considered "extrasensory" may tomorrow be conceptualized as "supersensory"; current conceptions of "psychokinesis" may be subsumed by discoveries of the organism's "biological fields" and their distant influences.

If the postmodern age is to represent a substantive advance over the modern age, the world's antagonistic superpowers and sects will need to be reconciled; the earth's ecology will need to be restored; the dispossessed peoples of the globe will need to be empowered; the planet's dwindling food and energy resources will need to be augmented and carefully allocated; effective treatments for old and new diseases will need to be discovered. Psi research data, whatever their ultimate explanation, suggest forms of information and influence flow that are unitive in nature. The connective pattern characterizing psi phenomena may provide clues, models, metaphors, and even applications for assisting in solving some of the critical problems that must be faced both in our own time and in whatever postmodern world is able to emerge in the future.

NOTES

1. Ilya Prigogine and Isabelle Stengers, *Order out of Chaos* (New York: Bantam Books, 1984), 34.

2. Morris Berman, *The Reenchantment of the World* (New York: Bantam Books, 1984), 1.

3. Joseph Campbell, *The Hero with a Thousand Faces*, 2nd ed. (New York: Bantam Books, 1984), 34.

4. Aldous Huxley, *Brave New World* (New York: Doubleday, Doran, 1932).

5. Stanley Krippner, ed., *Advances in Parapsychological Research*, Vol. 5 (Jefferson, N. C.: McFarland Publishers, 1987); C. B. Nash, *Parapsychology: The Science of Psiology* (Springfield, Ill.: Charles Thomas, 1986), 76.

6. Parapsychological Association, *Report I: Terms and Methods in Parapsychological Research* (Alexandria, Va.: Parapsychological Association, 1985).

7. *Ibid.*, 2.

8. Keith Stanovich, *How to Think Straight about Psychology* (Glenview, Ill.: Scott, Foresman, 1985), 159–62.

9. Nathan Ben-Yehuda, *Deviance and Moral Boundaries: Witchcraft, the Occult, Science Fiction, Deviant Sciences and Scientists* (Chicago: University of Chicago Press, 1985).

10. James Alcock, "Parapsychology as a 'Spiritual' Science," Paul Kurtz, ed., *A Skeptic's Handbook of Parapsychology* (Buffalo, N. Y.: Prometheus Books, 1985), 537–65.

11. *Ibid.*, 563.

12. John Beloff, "Historical Overview," B. B. Wolman, ed., *Handbook of Parapsychology* (New York: Van Nostrand Reinhold, 1977), 3–24, esp. 21.

13. Evan Harris Walker, "Consciousness and Quantum Theory," John White & Edgar D. Mitchell, eds., *Psychic Exploration: a Challenge for Science* (New York: G. P. Putnam's Sons, 1974), 544–68, esp. 566.

14. William G. Roll, "Survival Research: Problems and Possibilities," White and Mitchell, eds., *Psychic Exploration,* 397–424, esp. 422.

15. Evan Harris Walker, "Consciousness and Quantum Theory," 545.

16. Charles T. Tart, "Out-of-Body Experiences," White & Mitchell, eds., *Psychic Exploration,* 349–73, esp. 371.

17. Michael Grosso, "The Parapsychology of Religion," *Journal of the American Society for Psychical Research* 77 (1983), 327–45, exp. 344.

18. Lawrence L. LeShan, *From Newton to ESP: Parapsychology and the Challenge of Modern Science* (Wellingborough, Eng.: Turnstone Press, 1984), 179.

19. Charles Honorton, "Psi and Internal Attention States," Wolman, ed., *Handbook of Parapsychology,* 435–72, esp. 437–38.

20. William G. Roll, "Survival Research," 422.

21. Hoyt L. Edge, Robert L. Morris, John Palmer, and Joseph H. Rush, *Foundations of Parapsychology: Exploring the Boundaries of Human Capability* (Boston: Routledge & Kegan Paul, 1986), 377.

22. *Idem.*

23. James Alcock, "Parapsychology as a 'Spiritual' Science," 560.

24. Hoyt L. Edge, *et al.*, *Foundations of Parapsychology*, 185.

25. James McClenon, *Deviant Science: The Case of Parapsychology* (Philadelphia: University of Pennsylvania Press, 1984), 162.

26. *Ibid.*, 163.

27. Douglas Stokes, "Parapsychology and its Critics," Paul Kurtz, ed., *A Skeptic's Handbook of Parapsychology*, 379–423, esp. 418.

28. Hoyt L. Edge, *et al.*, *Foundations of Parapsychology*, 182.

29. Anthony Stigliano, "An Ontology for the Human Sciences," *Saybrook Review* 6 (1986), 33–63, esp. 39.

30. Thomas Kuhn, *The Structure of Scientific Revolutions*, rev. ed. (Chicago: University of Chicago Press, 1970).

31. Don Polkinghorne, "Changing Conversations about Human Science," *Saybrook Review* 6 (1986), 1–32.

32. Huston Smith, *Beyond the Post-Modern Mind* (New York: Crossroad, 1982), 162–76.

33. David Bohm, *Wholeness and the Implicate Order* (London: Routledge & Kegan Paul, 1980).

34. Karl H. Pribram, "Behaviorism, Phenomenology and Holism in Psychology: A Scientific Analysis," *Journal of Social and Biological Structure* 2 (1986), 65–72.

35. Rupert Sheldrake, *A New Science of Life* (London: Blond & Briggs, 1981).

36. Gregory Bateson, *Mind and Nature: A Necessary Unity* (New York: E. P. Dutton, 1979); John N. Bleibtreu, *The Parable of the Beast* (New York: Collier Books, 1969).

37. Willis W. Harman, "The Social Implications of Psychic Research," White and Mitchell, eds., *Psychic Exploration*, 640–69.

38. Stanley Krippner, James A. Ruttenber, Suzanne R. Engelman, and Dennis Granger, "Toward the Application of General Systems Theory in Humanistic Psychology," *Systems Research* 2 (1985), 105–15.

39. Don Polkinghorne, *Methodology for the Human Sciences: Systems of Inquiry* (Albany: State University of New York Press, 1983).

10

OF MINDS AND MOLECULES: POSTMODERN MEDICINE IN A PSYCHOSOMATIC UNIVERSE

David Ray Griffin

I. THE POWER OF PARADIGMS

The evidence that the state of the mind or psyche[1] affects the health of the body, sometimes dramatically, is impressive, both in quantity and quality.[2] An author highly respected for his wisdom has written two immensely popular books on the subject, with support from members of the medical establishment.[3] And yet the psychosomatic approach has not essentially changed the nature of medical education and treatment in the West. An advocate reports that the evidence "is largely ignored in the education of physicians."[4] A critic says, "psychosomatic medicine is on the way out,"[5] portraying it as a passing fad.

If the evidence for the mind's influence upon the body's illness and healing is indeed impressive—which I believe and am assuming without argument here—why has it not been incorporated into mainline medical education and practice? In fact, why has psychosomatic or "holistic" medicine not become the inclusive framework within which the practices aimed only at the patient's body are incorporated?[6]

The answer seems to be that the dominant model or paradigm presupposed in our culture and educational institutions in general, and within the medical profession in particular, does not allow the evidence for psychosomatic interaction in matters of health to be genuinely regarded as "evidence." No plausible well-known theory exists by which to organize the various bits of data that medical people have read or heard. So these accounts are dismissed as probably errors, fabrications, exaggerations, or at best as "anomalies"—phenomena that cannot now be seen to fit into the formal framework but that can be safely set aside until they do. And, because most of us prefer to focus on evidence that supports our present framework—especially if this framework works reasonably well for most purposes in which we are interested—rather than on evidence against it, most people in the field probably do not seriously explore the abundant evidence available in the literature.

That is how a paradigm works. It is like a filter, not only coloring the data which enter (i.e., giving it a particular interpretation), but even determining which kinds of data enter. A paradigm helps us see certain things, and make sense of them; it also largely blinds us to other things—those things that would not make sense within that interpretive framework.

But if this is the case—if scientists are not pure empiricists, constantly altering their theories in the light of fresh data, and if the dominant paradigm of our culture omits evidence for psychosomatic illness and healing—how can we account for the abundant evidence in the literature? There are two answers.

First, the prevailing paradigm is dominant but not unchallenged. Other views of the mind-body relationship, for example, those from China, India, and Hermeticism, view bodily health as mind-dependent. Some researchers have been influenced by one or more of these traditions.

Second, people differ. Although we all have "paradigmatic minds" to some extent, we seem to be on a spectrum with regard to the relative importance of empirical and *a priori* considerations. Some people operate from a strongly *a priori* or dogmatic basis, being unable to accept the validity of "evidence" that does not fit within their present model or paradigm. Others are at the empirical end of the spectrum; they wear their interpretive frameworks loosely and can fairly easily adjust or discard them in the face of disconfirming evidence. A few people at this latter end of the spectrum might even approximate Karl Popper's austere ideal of the true scientist: one who actively seeks evidence to refute his or her pet theory! These people are undogmatic enough to accept and publish evidence that runs counter to the viewpoint they had inherited.

Most people are somewhere in between the pure dogmatist and the pure empiricist, staying with their theories in the face of considerable contrary evidence, but not being totally incapable of admitting the validity of such evidence. However, in most of us, the power of the paradigm is quite strong. It is only when we see the possibility of a new model, which will keep most of what we treasure in the old one while allowing for the new data, that we begin to incorporate these new data systematically into our consciousness and practice.

If this analysis is correct, the idea that people's bodily health is inextricably and importantly tied up with the state of their souls will not become part of the general lore in our culture unless a generally accepted framework makes this idea seem natural. Only a new paradigm, a generally accepted model of the human person—and, in fact, of reality as a whole, because the human person incorporates all levels from subatomic particles to self-conscious mind—will allow psychosomatic medicine to become the new orthodoxy and orthopraxis instead of a fading fad.

In the next two sections, I describe the two paradigms that have dominated the modern world since the late seventeenth century, *dualism* and *materialism*, showing both why they discourage the incorporation of psychosomatic evidence and why their difficulties should lead us to reject their common premise. In the following sections, I describe a postmodern organismic alternative, based primarily on the philosophies of Alfred North Whitehead[7] and Charles Hartshorne,[8] with special attention to the psychosomatic issue.

II. The Modern Paradigms

The distinctively "modern" view of the world, which through successful propaganda became virtually equated with the "scientific" worldview, had at its basis the rejection of "animism." Included under animism were all doctrines that saw the basic constituents of nature as having *perception* or experience of any sort and/or as having some capacity for *self-movement*. The "modern" view was a mechanistic molecular hypothesis. It combined a recursion to ancient materialistic views of nature (derived from Democritus and Lucretius) with a supernaturalistic theism (derived from Augustinian, Nominalistic, and Calvinistic theologians), which saw the "laws of nature" as totally imposed by an omnipotent lawgiver. It portrayed the basic molecules as totally inert bits of matter which moved only by being moved by other things—preferably by contact. Any suggestion of "action at a distance," even in interpreting gravitation, was suspect. The first version of this modern paradigm allowed these materialistic molecules to be moved not only by other molecules but also by minds—creaturely and divine. But the second version rejected this dualism in favor—at least apparently—of total materialism. The main reason was the impossibility of understanding the way nonmaterial minds could affect material molecules, and vice versa.

These two paradigms shared most points in common. Aside from the question about God, they differed only about the nature and status of the minds of humans—or more generously, of animals with central nervous systems. With regard to the rest of nature they agreed. This agreement can be summarized under six points:

1. Objectivism. The basic elements of nature—the subatomic particles, the atoms, the molecules, even the living cells—are purely objective in character. That is, they have no subjectivity—no experiences, no perceptions, no feelings, no purposes, no aims. They are "objects" not only in the sense of being objects of our experiences; they are, *in themselves*, nothing but objects.

2. Externalism. Objectivism could also be called *externalism*, for it says that the external side of things is their *only* side—it exhausts their reality. They have no internal nature that is inaccessible to our sensory perception and the instruments to magnify it. Modern thought has been committed from the beginning to the denial that there is anything hidden (occult) in matter. It has said that the appearance *is* the reality—as long as we get beneath ordinary sensory appearances to the appearances of the most elementary particles. Behaviorism, which restricts science to statements about the outer behavior of things, is thereby sanctioned.

3. Locomotionism. Because elementary objects have no hidden internal reality, the only kind of motion they can have is *loco*motion, motion through space from one location to another. There can be no internal motion, such as internal becoming, which would involve the movement from a state of facing alternative possibilities to a state of having decided among them. The only movement is the external, apparent movement. Nothing hidden to the objectifying eye (or measuring apparatus) is going on beneath the surface.

4. Mechanistic determinism. The causal interaction among these objects is purely mechanistic. That is, because no element of internal *self*-causation is found, all causation comes from external sources. This implies causal determinism, the idea that the present state of affairs is totally determined by the previous state of affairs, which was, in turn, totally determined by an earlier state of affairs, etc.

5. Reductionism. It follows from the previous points that all apparent "wholes" are in principle reducible to their parts. The behavior of all larger things is totally a function of their smallest parts, and their causal power in relation to other things is totally a function of the causal power of their smallest parts. So the state of an animal body is determined by the state of its cells; the state of each cell is determined by the state of its molecules;

the state of each molecule is in turn determined by the state of its atomic and subatomic parts. This reductive viewpoint means that all the apparently purposeful behavior of "organisms," such as cells, is really reducible to mechanical interactions. All apparent movements from potential to actual states are reducible to the movements of elementary particles through space. The rearrangement of elementary particles determines all the functions of the animal organism, including such highly complex processes as vision.

6. Sensationism. The epistemology supported by and supporting the modern ontology holds that all experience is rooted in perception, and that all perception is *sensory* perception. Accordingly, the only experience in the world is enjoyed by animals with sensory organs. This epistemology both presupposes and supports the idea that the elementary particles of the world have no sort of experience and hence no internal reality. Experience is, hence, a very limited feature of reality, occurring only where there is a central nervous system and sensory organs.

On all these points, the dualist and the materialist agree. They disagree only on the status of experience or "mind" in the world.

Dualism holds that the "mind" is something different in kind from the objects making up the body. This dualism seems obvious. Objects have no subjectivity, my mind does. Descartes was right: the mind's own subjective experience is what it knows most directly, even more directly than the objects of sensory perception. I obviously have an internal reality which is different in kind from my external appearance to others. I constantly exercise a kind of movement, from potentiality to actuality, every time I make a decision, that is different in kind from the movement of objects through space. My decisions are influenced but not totally determined by the causes acting upon me; I engage partly in free self-determination based upon goals I want to attain. Although reductionism is true in the physical world, my mental experience cannot be reduced to the deterministic locomotion of subatomic particles. The purely objective, quantitative world of the physical is converted by my mind into a subjective, qualitative experience. Mind is not just a complex arrangement of matter in motion. Mind is another kind of entity, totally different in kind from matter. So dualism states its case. But then it falters.

How can two such totally different kinds of things be thought to interact? Mind and matter are said to have different types of extension. The extensiveness of matter is purely spatial, that of mind purely temporal (duration). They are also said to be composed of different types of stuff. The stuff of mind is feelings—emotions, aims, thoughts; it is moved by attractive ideas, possibilities for the future. The stuff of matter is said to be none of these things; it is moved not by unactualized possibilities but by brute facts. If mind is nonspatial, durational experience and molecules are spatial, nondurational things devoid of experience, how can mind influence molecules, or molecules influence mind? The answer must be: We have no idea.

Much of the philosophy of the modern period has revolved around this question. Descartes said mind and matter did interact. But he saw the problem: he had defined them as so unlike that direct interaction seemed impossible. So he called on the pineal gland to serve as mediator, conceiving it as halfway between mind and matter. This gland was material, so it could interact with other matter; but it was such *subtle* matter that it could interact with mind. This suggestion was obviously desperate: nothing can be halfway between infinitely different things. Malebranche admitted that mind and matter could not interact. They *appear* to interact, he said, because God causes constant correlation: when my hand is on the hot stove, God causes my mind to feel pain; I then decide my hand should be moved, and God obliges. Leibniz found this demeaning to God's wisdom and omnipotence. He said that the constant correlations had been established from the creation of the world: it was preestablished that, when I decide my hand should rise, the various molecules in my hand and arm (which had come variously from carrots, apples, and cabbages I had eaten at different times and places) would spontaneously and simultaneously elevate themselves. Mind and matter do not really interact; they only run along parallel with each other. The point of this quick review is not to ridicule some of the brightest minds of the early modern period, but to show by illustration the absurdities to which the seemingly commonsense position of dualism can lead if one is honest enough to face the difficulties.

Other modernists (i.e., thinkers who accept the above six points) assume that this *reductio ad absurdum* of dualism constitutes an argument for complete *materialism*, because another alternative is not apparent. Materialism says that there is nothing other than matter. Dualism is replaced by *identism*, the doctrine that the mind is identical with the brain.[9] Accordingly, mechanistic determinism, locomotionism, and reductionism apply to the whole animal, the whole human being—not just to the physiological structure. Let us just admit that all of nature is made of one sort of thing, says the materialist. Then there is no problem of understanding interaction between unlikes. If the mind is just the brain and the brain is composed of the same kind of matter as the rest of the body and the rest of the universe, there is no difficulty in understanding the interaction of "mind" and matter—it is merely one more example of physical interaction. Materialism thus states its case against dualism. But then it falters.

Its problem is how to claim plausibly that objectivism, externalism, and locomotionism apply to the whole human being. If I am nothing but matter, how can I maintain that there is no experience, no perception, no inner reality to matter which is not apparent to external observation? I obviously have perception and other experiences which are not identical with any data that are available to your gaze or to your instruments hooked up to electrodes in my brain. And how can I plausibly claim that my decision (e.g., to accept materialism) is "really" identical with the locomotion of molecules within and between cells in my brain, a movement that can be described in purely externalistic, quantitative terms? Yet, this is what materialistic identists are compelled to do. Because they do not believe that matter in general has any internal movement or experience, [10] they hold that these mysterious properties called *perceptions, volitions, feelings* and sometimes *conscious thoughts* arise only when matter is arranged in the complex form of an animal brain. This is not dualism, they say, because no non-material kind of substance is posited. These emergent properties are said to be, *really*, identical with the brain, or certain of its aspects or functions.

And yet, objectivism and externalism are clearly violated. This identism is dualism in all but name. For the materialist is implicitly admitting that in this one part of the universe, some "properties" that are different in kind from other properties of matter arise. Of course, the materialist does not explicitly admit this.

Materialists, in referring to perceptions, feelings, volitions, and conscious thoughts as *emergent properties*, claim that these inner properties are simply further examples of a long line of new properties which have emerged throughout the evolutionary process, such as bones, scales, and feathers. But this claim obscures the difference in kind involved. All those other characteristics are *externalistic* properties, knowable to sensory experience. But *experience itself* does not belong in this category. It is what an organism is *for itself*, not something that is observed through the eyes, ears, or hands of another organism. We know what we *mean* by *experience* and hence can attribute it meaningfully to others only because of our own immediate experience. To put experience itself in the same class as those properties that are the *objects* of experience is a *category mistake* of the most egregious kind. It is only through this confusion that the materialist can claim to be different from the dualist.

Some would-be materialists have proposed a more desperate strategy, known as *eliminative materialism*. Recognizing that all subjective categories, such as those referring to sensations, purposes, emotions, and other private facts, are different in kind from the purely objective, externalistic categories used in physics and chemistry, they would devise a new language in which all subjective terms would be eliminated. [11] Rather than saying, "I'm hungry," I might say "K-14 is firing." When feeling jealous, I would simply say something like, "Dear, my G-3 is activated." To which my lover would presumably reply, "Dear, that really makes my G-7 go off!" The reader can infer that I do not expect eliminative materialism to catch on. (The program to replace subjectivist by purely objectivist language had already been attempted by the behaviorist movement in psychology, mentioned below.)

Modernity's two options, dualism and materialism, refute each other. Dualism rightly shows that materialism cannot handle the facts of experience—especially the experience of experience itself—without covertly introducing dualism. Materialism rightly maintains that if mind and body are understood to be different kinds of things, their relation is unintelligible.

Accordingly, modernity has devised a couple of compromise positions. One of these positions is *epiphenomenalism*. This is the doctrine that the mind, or stream of experience, is simply a by-product of the brain. This view agrees with dualism that the mind is a nonphysical entity distinct from the brain. Epiphenomenalism may even allow this quasireal thing to make decisions that partly determine its own experience. But this view agrees with materialism that a nonphysical entity *cannot affect the physical world*. Hence, whatever self-creative decisions the mind may make do not feed back into the body and alter its course. The body runs along, purely mechanically. There is no *inter*action; the action is all one way, from the body to the mind. The machine produces a ghost, but the ghost does not affect the machine.

The other compromise is *parallelism*: There is a ghost in the machine, but it neither affects nor is affected by the machine. Leibniz and Malebranche both held a form of parallelism. Of course, they appealed to God's omnipotent wisdom at creation to explain how the mind and the body became associated. More recent parallelists, however, have assumed a noncreationist, evolutionary perspective. They can give no explanation as to how the body came to have a mind in it or how the two just happen to be "in sync." For example, they cannot explain the origin and evolution of mind in terms of its survival value, for the mind is said to have no effect upon the body whatsoever.

The popularity of these two compromise doctrines, in spite of their difficulties, reveals a deep-seated motive of modernity. They both allow the scientist to admit what is obvious to anyone—that he or she has experiences—and yet to maintain that these experiences do not affect the material world. Accordingly, the material world can be regarded as a self-enclosed mechanism operating without any interference from the mind, which cannot be measured objectively and quantitatively and seems to act capriciously. If the mind could affect the body, then the body's processes could not, in principle, be predicted and controlled. This would mean, for one thing, that a scientific medicine would not be possible, if *scientific* is taken to mean, as it is by modernists, that the repetition of certain physical procedures can be guaranteed always to lead to the same results.

In any case, the effect of the various doctrines of modernity about mind and body has been to say that mind as a self-determining reality does not affect body, at least not medically. Materialism allows "mind" to affect the body, but denies to "mind" the power of self-determination. Epiphenomenalism and parallelism may allow the mind to be somewhat self-determining, but they do not allow it to affect the body. Dualistic interaction says that the nonmaterial mind does affect the body, but the practical implications of dualism, especially within scientific circles, are usually not greatly different from those of other positions. Some dualists are determinists, holding that the mind's contents are totally determined by the body; hence, the mind is just one more reliable link in the deterministic chain. Other dualists hold that the mind has *some* freedom to determine its own contents, but that it is *much more* determined by the body than the body is by anything novel showing up in the mind; this dualism is close to epiphenomenalism. Furthermore, the kind of influence the mind could have on the body has been understood to be severely limited, mainly to its effects on and through the voluntary nervous system. Hence, the mind might make a decision that would *indirectly* lead to illness, injury, or death, e.g., by taking poison or driving recklessly, but the mind's attitudes could not *directly* induce cancer, a heart attack, or even allergies.

In general, the effect of dualism from the beginning has been to separate mind and body into two autonomous realms. Science, including physiology and medicine, could therefore deal with the body without interference from theology, philosophy and introspective psychology.

In summary: the main purpose of this section has been to show how the two modern paradigms, with their compromise positions, have had the effect of predisposing scientifically informed people, and the culture at large, to assume that one's state of mind could have no, or at least very little, direct effect upon the state of one's bodily health. Dualism denies or minimizes the influence of psyche on soma; materialism denies there is any psyche to influence soma. Within this context, claims to the contrary always must be causes for surprise or skepticism; they are "anomalies" or simply false. Accordingly, it is no wonder that the psychosomatic literature is largely ignored in medical schools and that leaders of the orthodox establishment expect the "holistic" movement to fade away.

This section has also had a second purpose—to demonstrate how inherently problematic the modern vision of reality is by showing the impasse between the two absurd positions to which it leads. This demonstration is especially necessary because the position advocated in the remainder of this paper is one most modern Westerners assume they know to be absurd. (That was my own reaction when I first encountered it.) Given this expected reaction, I insert here a reminder of the distinction between a genuinely absurd position, which either contradicts itself or certain facts that cannot consistently be denied, and a position that only appears to be absurd because it contradicts some of the prejudices we have inherited from our culture.

III. QUESTIONING THE BASIC ASSUMPTION: VACUOUS ACTUALITY

The basic assumption of the modern worldview, which both dualism and materialism have in common, is that the elementary constituents of the world are "vacuous actualities," [12] wholly devoid of all inner reality, all perception or experience, all subjectivity, all aim or purpose, all internal becoming. This objectivist and externalist hypothesis is closely aligned with sensationism, which holds that perception or experience, and hence some internal reality, arises only in those exceptional entities having sensory organs.

Given objectivism, externalism, and sensationism, the other doctrines and the impasse between dualism and materialism follow.

But there is no good reason to hold that the elementary constituents of nature are wholly vacuous. In fact, several reasons exist for thinking otherwise.

One reason is that the origins of the modern paradigm show its contingency. The founders of this paradigm had theological and sociological motives for this idea which were more decisive than any empirical considerations. The idea of vacuous actuality was certainly not necessary for the empirical-mathematical study of nature to emerge, because this study had been emerging for some time in the context of a mixture of Neopythagorean, Neoplatonic, and Hermetic animistic frameworks. [13]

A second reason is that developments in natural science have overcome the empirical reasons that had existed earlier for considering the elementary constituents of the world to be inert. I can mention only a few examples: (1) Commonsense dualism is based upon the obvious difference between animate, apparently self-moving things, such as ourselves and other animals, and inanimate things, such as rocks, which only move if moved from without. But modern science has revealed that all such inert things are *composed* of smaller entities which are highly active. (2) Modern physics, with its famous formula $E = mc^2$, suggests (even though m stands for *mass* rather than *matter*) that matter and energy are convertible. What we call matter is simply energy in "frozen" form. (3) Transformations from one form of matter to another, and from matter to free energy, are in fact occurring all the time. (4) Quantum physics is consistent with the view that the elementary forms of matter and energy are not totally determined by the forces acting upon them but have some element of self-determining power. (5) Researchers have evidence that something similar to memory and decision occurs in bacteria. [14] (6) Studies on the DNA and RNA macromolecules suggest that they have something similar to memory. And the mutations, sometimes called *mistakes*, could be interpreted as evidence of a margin of freedom.

The proponents of the mechanistic philosophy in the seventeenth century, such as Descartes, Boyle, and Newton, connected the idea that nature was composed of "vacuous actualities," devoid of all experience, with the idea of inert matter. We now think of matter as active and energetic; physicists speak of the "cosmic dance." Does it make sense to retain the idea of vacuous actuality, so that the energetic activity is purely external locomotion through space? If the basic units of nature are *time-space events*, they have some duration. How can we give the idea of *duration* any content without thinking of it as analogous to our own experiential process?

A third reason for questioning modernity's purely objectivist and externalist interpretation of nature's elementary constituents is precisely the impasse between dualism and materialism to which it leads. Problematic conclusions suggest a problematic premise.

In the remainder of this essay, I sketch the alternative suggestion made by Whitehead and Hartshorne with special attention to the question of psychosomatic health and illness. They can in fact be said to speak of a "psychosomatic universe," because they portray the mind-body relation not as the great exception to normal causal relations but as a paradigmatic example of what is going on everywhere.

IV. PANEXPERIENTIALISM: BASIS FOR A POSTMODERN PARADIGM

The dualist has assumed the question, "How can mind relate to molecules?" to be identical with the question, "How can an experiencing entity relate to nonexperiencing ones?" The answer, as the materialist saw, could only be: "In no way." This mind-matter problem was especially obvious when experiencing mind was regarded as temporal but nonspatial while nonexperiencing matter was regarded as spatial but nontemporal. Like an unhappy couple with nothing in common, mind and body could not relate to each other. While the mind-body union hardly seemed a marriage made in heaven, it actually was a marriage that could *only* be made in heaven: only an omnipotent God, not thwarted by mere impossibilities, could join together what metaphysics would keep asunder.

But what if enduring material objects such as molecules are made of momentary events, each irreducibly temporal in the sense of taking (or constituting) a duration of time? And what if the enduring mind is not an unbroken *stream* of experience but a *series* of momentary experiential events, each of which occupies (or constitutes) a region that is spatial as well as temporal? Then the chasm between mind and molecules is partially closed. All that remains is the dichotomy between experiencing and nonexperiencing.

This dichotomy can be approached in terms of the notion of a *category mistake*,[15] introduced in Section II. When we think of a molecule as a nonexperiencing thing, we are thinking of it as experienced *by us*. Actually, we usually experience a large aggregation of molecules, as in a rock, and then try to imagine what an individual molecule would be like. In any case, we do not experience what it is to be a molecule. We only know it, insofar as we know it at all, from without.

But when we think of mind as an experiencing thing, we are thinking of it from within. We know what a mind is by identity, by being one.

This raises an intriguing possibility: Perhaps the whole contrast between *mind* and *matter* is the result of a category mistake: trying to compare one thing as known from within, or by identity, with another type of thing known only from without, by nonidentity.

The confusion would be between *physical* and *metaphysical* categories. As I am using these terms here, *physical* categories seek to describe a thing's appearances as known from without, through sensory perception and the apparatus to magnify it. *Physical categories* are ones such as size, shape, color, mass, and velocity. *Metaphysical categories* seek to describe what something is in and for itself. Categories that we humans use to describe ourselves as known from within include emotion, perception, purpose, satisfaction, and thought. Perhaps the problem of how "nonexperiencing molecules can relate to experiencing minds" arises only because a purely *physical* description of molecules has been treated as if it were a *metaphysical* description. To assume that some things without any experience exist would hence be a category mistake.

This suggestion becomes clearer and more plausible when we consider the strictly behaviorist approach in psychology. The behaviorists insisted that psychology could only become a genuine science when it adopted the methods and categories of the natural sciences. This program meant that the description of human beings would be limited to that which was objectively observable, from without. A "consistent and rigorous objectivism" [16] implied that the psychologist would drop "from his scientific vocabulary all subjective terms such as *sensation, perception, image, desire, purpose,* and even *thinking* and *emotion* as they were subjectively defined." [17] But we know that this behaviorist, strictly objectivist account leaves out half of the reality. It is true that part of what we are is the way we appear to others. But part of what we are is what we are in ourselves, and this we know by identity. (We do not consciously know *all* that we are in ourselves, because much of our experience is unconscious; but we do consciously know at least part of our experience, and hence what "experience" is, by identity with it.) Most philosophers and psychologists now agree that the behaviorist's externalist-objectivist approach can never be adequate. Our knowledge of human nature and action must be based in part on categories that are derived only from introspection. And most of us agree that these internalist or subjectivist categories must be used (analogically) to understand other animals. [18] But why should we assume that there is some line below which these subjectivist categories are totally inapplicable? Should not the results of applying only the externalist approach to ourselves suggest that this approach when applied to cells, molecules, and electrons also misses half of *their* reality? This line of reasoning leads to what has often been called *panpsychism*, which I prefer to call *panexperientialism*.

Three ideas make Whiteheadian-Hartshornean panexperientialism less counterintuitive than it otherwise would be. First, a clear distinction is made between *aggregates* and *genuine individuals*, with the insistence that only the latter have (or *are*) experiences. Accordingly, sticks and stones and stars are not thought to have an experience as wholes. The *pan* in *panexperientialism* thereby means that all actual things either *are* experiences or *are composed* of individuals that are experiences. This point distinguishes this position from most other "animistic" positions.

Second, great differences are allowed between levels of experience. It is not thought, for example, that molecules have anything approaching the kind of self-conscious experience we have (in which we are conscious that we are conscious), or even the conscious experience enjoyed by a mouse (in which the distinction between what is and is not present can be made). To say that a molecule has experience means only that it has some vague feeling-response to its environment. Nothing remotely approaching the clear and distinct impressions of conscious sense-perception is implied.

Third, this position rejects the assumption of the modern paradigm that perception is essentially sense-perception. Panexperientialism says that *sensory organs add precision and reliability* to perception but are *not the basis* of the most primitive form of perception.

Much of Whitehead's writing is devoted to a rejection of the "sensationist" doctrine of perception, according to which the most primitive aspects of our perception involve clear and distinct sensory images. According to that sensationist doctrine, all emotional and purposive experiences would be reactions to sensory impressions. If that were the case, then it would not make sense to generalize "perception" or "experience" to entities having no sensory organs. But Whitehead suggests that sensationism is a topsy-turvy view. The sensory impressions may be the features of our experience of which we are *most conscious*, but this fact does not mean that they are *fundamental*. After all, we now have good reason to believe that consciousness arises out of unconscious experience. Does this not suggest that sensory impressions arise out of a more basic level of perception, a level of which we are mainly unconscious and which is not sensory? Whitehead suggests that the most primitive level of human perception is a vague, emotional-purposive response to our primal contact with other things. We refine our emotions and purposes under the light of consciousness, which shines with particular brightness upon certain sensory percepts (because this clarity is needed for physical survival). But these refined emotional-purposive responses arise out of more primitive ones. On this basis, it is not absurd to attribute a vague kind of emotional-purposive perceptivity to those lower organisms that are devoid of sensory organs. Whitehead calls this more primitive type of perception *prehension* to make clear that it need not involve sensory-like impressions. To say that all individual events *prehend* the things in their environments is to say that they take influences from them into themselves and have some sort of emotional-appetitive response to them.

Of course, panexperientialism is an unprovable hypothesis; but so is the idea that low-grade entities do *not* have any form of experience. Each hypothesis can only be tested by examining the conclusions to which it leads. If panexperientialism can be more adequate and self-consistent than either dualism or materialism, should we not adopt this hypothesis?

Although several philosophers have suggested a panexperientialist position, Whitehead's philosophy is unique, at least in the West (Buddhism has had something like it), in making a *temporal* distinction between inner and outer (not a *spatial* one), and rethinking the *very nature of causation* in the light of this distinction. Through this unique analysis he demonstrates the way minds and molecules can be causally related.

To review and to introduce some terminology: each actual entity is an *actual occasion*. This term is used to stress that each entity is a happening, an event, with spatial extension and temporal duration. Each actual occasion is also called an *occasion of experience* to point out that what occurs in the time-space region occupied by the event is the becoming of a brief experience.

An occasion of experience has two sides: the experience *for itself* is the event *as subject*. As subject, the event is engaged in a brief process of becoming. This process involves two phases. The event begins by receiving influences from prior experiences. For example, I now receive influences from my previous experiences and also from the cells comprising my body. This receptive phase is called the *physical pole* of the occasion. But there is then a second phase in the becoming of an experience. I do not simply receive influences from the past passively; rather, I actively determine just how to respond to them, and thereby just which kind of experience to have right now. Experience is thus partially self-creative. This self-determining phase is called the *mental pole*, and the term is used in a strict sense. It does not necessarily mean consciousness: most experiences are not conscious. And, of course, *mental* does not here mean *experiencing*, because the whole event is an "occasion of experience." It is experiential through and through, the physical pole as well as the mental. Rather, to speak of the "mental" pole of the occasion is simply to refer to its aspect of self-creation. This aspect is called *mental* because it involves not simply a response to *actual* things (as does the physical pole), but a response to *ideals* or *possibilities*. To say that a moment of experience is not totally determined by its past, by the actual world, implies that it has alternative possibilities open to it. Its choice of one of these possibilities is what is meant by its "mentality." This choice can be quite blind, not at all enlightened by consciousness. The fact that the laws of modern physics apply not to individuals but to statistical averages suggests that some element of mentality in this sense occurs all the way down. The occasion of experience *as subject* hence combines receptivity (physicality) and self-determination (mentality).

When this process of subjective becoming is completed, the event then has another kind of existence. It now is a *superject* or *object*. It no longer engages in self-causation; it is what it has become. But now it exerts causation on subsequent occasions of experience. It no longer has experience, it is experienced by others. What had been a subject for itself is now an object for others. As stated earlier, the distinction between inner and outer is a *temporal* distinction: the moment of inner reality is completed before the event is an object for others.

To say that the event is now an object for others means that it is a *cause* on them. The term *object* is misleading insofar as it suggests something that just lies there, passively. The term *superject* is better. The occasion of experience is still exerting power, only now it is not the teleological power of self-causation but the *transitive* power of *other-causation*, the power to exert causal influence upon others.

On the basis of this analysis of *subjects* and *objects*, we can understand how objects can affect subjects. *Subjects and objects are not different in kind, merely different in time.* That is, an *object* is an event that had been, in itself, a subject. Accordingly, it *has the kind of stuff a subject can receive, i.e., feelings,* whether conscious or unconscious—feelings of derivation, feelings of desire, feelings of attraction and repulsion. The dualist could not understand how objects could influence subjects because of the assumption that an object had always been merely an object, that is, a vacuous actuality, devoid of all feelings, all emotions, all desires. It was assumed to have only objective qualities, such as size, shape, and mass. With such paltry, purely external features, it seemed to have nothing to contribute to a feeling subject. By conceiving of each event as *having been* a subject of feeling prior to being a felt object, we can understand how an object can influence a subject.

Accordingly, the cells in my brain can influence me, my soul, at this moment, because each cell is a rapidly occurring series of events, each of which is first a center of feeling for itself and then a source of objectified feelings for me. I feel the feelings that the cellular events "superject" into me. Likewise, my soul is a series of occasions of experience—enormously different in degree from the cellular occasions of experience, but not different in kind. After each of my moments of self-creation, I become an object or superject for the then-arising cellular occasions of experience. These cellular occasions of experience feel my objectified feelings, receiving as much from my complex feelings as their lowlier natures allow.

Under this analysis, the question "How can mind and molecules interact?" is no longer identical with the question "How can subjects and material objects interact?" It is not the case that the mind is simply and always a subject while the molecule is simply and always an object. Rather, the mind is a series of subjective-then-objective events, and the molecule is likewise a series of subjective-then-objective events. The difference between them is enormous, but it is only a difference in degree, not the absolute difference between having and not having experience.

One issue that has not yet been discussed is the relation between internal becoming and external locomotion. Locomotion is a characteristic of some enduring objects. But on the analysis given here, enduring things such as electrons, atoms, and molecules are not the fundamental individuals of nature. Each of these enduring things is a temporal "society" composed of a series of rapidly occurring events. The events are the most fundamental individuals. An event's "movement" is not locomotion but internal becoming. An occasion of experience does not move, relative to other events; it arises and reaches completion in one and the same region. Only the temporal society can be said to "move through space." This apparent movement is simply a reflection of the different regions occupied by successive members of the society.

Accordingly, locomotion is not the fundamental type of movement in the universe, to which experiential becoming must be causally related (for the dualist) or reduced (for the materialist). The reverse is true. Internal becoming is primary. Locomotion is derivative.

One other aspect of this analysis deserves mention: subjects not only can be influenced by objects, they *require* objects. The very nature of a subject, as a momentary experiencing event, is to prehend or receive feelings from previous events into itself as the basis for its own self-creation. Most philosophies have assumed that the basic individuals of the world were enduring individuals. (Dualists divided them into enduring subjects and enduring objects.) The relation of an enduring individual to its own past was then an absolutely different kind of relation from its relation to other things. The relation to its own past was a relation of total identity; the relation to other things was a causal relation. This idea fostered the notion that receiving causal influence from others was not really essential to an enduring individual, whether a subject or an object. Descartes could then give his famous definition: a *substance* is that which requires nothing but itself in order to be what it is. With this dictum, Descartes declared that the soul did not really need the body and that the bodily parts did not really need the soul (or each other, for that matter). What interaction occurred between them was strictly nonessential. This notion, combined with the idea that mind and body were totally different kinds of substance with nothing in common, strengthened the tendency to belittle psychosomatic interdependence.

Whitehead's view, on the other hand, says that an occasion of experience, to be what it is, requires *everything* in its environment. Of course, some things are much more important than others. My experience at the present moment could have been virtually the same in most respects, even if many other things had been different. But it would not have been *exactly* the same. Everything from the past streams into my present experience and helps, to some degree or another, constitute what it is. If my bodily experiences had been slightly different, my soul's present experience would be slightly different—at least at the unconscious level. And if my soul's past experience had been different, the experiences comprising my body right now would be at least slightly different.

A key difference from the view of primary individuals as enduring substances is that the *relation of my present experience to the past experiences of my soul* is a *causal* relation similar to my relation to my bodily cells. I, as the soul or experiential unification of my body, am a series of occasions of experience. My past experiences are now objects or superjects for my present experience, taken up in it and energizing within it, just as the previous events constituting my brain cells are now objects within my present experience, energizing within it. Each new experience is a unity arising out of many. [19] *E pluribus unum* is the ultimate nature of experience. It is, in fact, the ultimate principle of the universe. And the "many" out of which my present unity of experience arises includes my own previous experiences.

This principle states that actuality is social through and through. There is no enduring actuality that simply remains itself. There are only events and societies of events. Each event arises out of past events, which share their feelings with it. The new event then shares its feelings with subsequent events. A certain dominant line of inheritance can be maintained indefinitely, so that a human being exists for perhaps three score and ten years, a molecule perhaps for billions. But this endurance of minds and molecules is in each case a *social achievement*, based upon maintaining a dominant line of inheritance throughout a series of events in which each one constitutes itself out of its reception of feelings from its total environment, finally the entire past universe.

These three ideas, (1) that each moment in the life of a mind or a molecule is an essentially *social* event, (2) that each event arises out of *all* events of the past, and (3) that each event influences *all* future events, would lead us to expect the mind to be affected by all the events in the body, and for *all the events in the body to be affected by the mind*. This view hence leads to quite different expectations than do the modern paradigms, which have led us to assume that the mind would at most affect only some parts of the body through certain channels of influence ordained by God or Natural Selection.

V. Psychosomatic Universe

I turn now to the application of this panexperientalist position to the question of psychosomatic interaction.

As stated earlier, the mind-body relation is not a great exception in the scheme of things but paradigmatic for a type of relation pervading nature. Against dualism, the mind is not different in kind from the brain cells. Against materialism, *mind* is not just a term for the brain or some of its functions. The mind is a distinct series of occasions of experience, just as actual as cells, molecules, or electrons.

A similar nondualistic but nonreductionistic analysis can be given of a living cell. Against vitalism, the "life" of the cell is not some totally new substance or force, different in kind from the molecules making up the body of the cell. Against materialistic reductionism, the life of the cell is not simply identical with the arrangement and functioning of its molecules. Rather, there are "living occasions" in the cell. These occasions are greatly different in degree from the molecular occasions of experience. In particular, they have much more "mentality," more capacity for freedom from the shackles of the past. But there is no total difference in kind, no introduction here of some entirely new type of entity or power.

On this basis, the relations between the cell as a whole and the molecules within it can be understood. The cell as a whole has its own experiences, by virtue of the living occasions of experience. It can receive influences from its molecules, because they, too, have their even more lowly feelings to share. And for the same reason these molecules can be influenced by the cell as a whole because each molecule feels the cell's living occasions of experience.

(Because most readers probably still find it strange to speak of the cells of our bodies as having experiences, one should recall that an amoeba is a single-celled animal. Its behavior clearly suggests that it has feelings. If this single-celled organism has feelings, why should the cells in our bodies not?)

The same analysis can be extended to the relation between the macromolecule and its atoms. The molecule need not be thought of as simply an aggregate of atoms. Insofar as a molecule shows signs of responding to its environment with a unity of action, it can be thought to have a unity of experience. The idea that each atom can receive feelings from the molecular experiences explains how the whole molecule can act as a unity.

Finally, the relation between the atom and its subatomic constituents can be analyzed in the same manner. The atom is not just the sum of its parts and the relations between them; a series of "atomic occasions of experience" which gives the atom its unity also exists. Because each of the electrons, protons, and neutrons is a series of experiences, each of which feels the higher-level experiences of the atom (as well as those of its fellow electronic, protonic, and neutronic experiences), the atom's overall structure can be regulated. For example, the "Pauli principle" can be explained in this way.[20]

The human person is thus a nested hierarchy of experiences, with lesser experiences inside of more inclusive ones. The relation between the mind and the brain cells is repeated by the relation between each cell and its constituents, etc. In each case, the multitude of lesser experiences serves as the "body" for the superior experiences, while the series of superior experiences serves as the "mind" for that body. This point explains why Whitehead called his position the "philosophy of organism." Each level of individuality is a level of organism. Psychology and biology study the higher organisms, physics and chemistry the lower ones. The human being is hence a hierarchy of organisms: an organism of organisms of organisms.[21]

Given this hierarchy, the influence of the human mind upon every level of "matter" in the human body can be explained. The mind's experiences can affect the living occasions of the cells, which can in turn affect their molecular occasions, which can in turn affect their atomic occasions, which can in turn affect their subatomic events.

Furthermore, the influence of the mind upon the atomic and subatomic constituents of the body need not be transmitted only in this indirect way. The atomic experiences are not the only superior experiences an electron can feel; it can also directly feel the experiences of the molecule of which it is part, and also those of the cell of which it is a part. It can even directly feel the influence radiating out from the mind of the body as a whole.

Also—continuing the principle that each occasion of experience is affected by all the experiences in its past—the mind can be assumed to influence the subatomic events in its body through a variety of routes at the same time. The mind can directly influence protons; it can also influence them indirectly by influencing the atoms of which they are a part; it can influence then even more indirectly via the molecules and the cells that include them.

Even this analysis is simplified, for I have limited it to vertical relations from one level to another. But there are also webs of horizontal influences, e.g., from cell to cell, from molecule to molecule. There are also relations that are both horizontal and vertical, e.g., a molecule in one cell can be directly influenced by its reception of feelings from a neighboring cell. So the human mind could influence molecules through these ways as well. as well.

Whereas I have been concentrating upon the influence of the mind on the body, the same analysis reveals how, and the varied ways, the body can influence the mind. The mind is constituted to a great extent out of the feelings it receives from the bodily experiences. A distortion in the molecular structure of certain cells can result in distorted feelings being received on a regular basis by the mind. Somapsychotic as well as psychosomatic illness can occur.

In fact, because a constant interaction occurs between mind and body, one would expect mutually reinforcing effects, regardless of the source of the original cause. For example, assume that a person develops a chronic negative attitude due originally to relationships with other humans. This chronic attitude can produce molecular, i.e., chemical, changes in the bodily system. These chemical changes may then continue to support the negative frame of mind long after the human relationships had ceased to have much influence. In this situation, a purely chemical treatment might solve the problem. A reductionistic physician might then conclude (falsely) that the negative attitude had had purely chemical causes.

Contrariwise, a chronically negative frame of mind might have originally resulted from chemical causes. This frame of mind could then take on a life of its own, however, having become habitual. It could then continue to support a chemical imbalance long after the purely bodily cause of this imbalance had disappeared. In this situation, a purely psychosocial approach might overcome the psychological problem and thereby rectify the chemical problem. A mind-only therapist, such as a Christian Scientist, might (falsely) use this case as evidence that all apparent disease is due entirely to bad attitudes.

The two extreme positions have been called *epiphenomenalism* and *hypophenomenalism.* The epiphenomenalist sees all causation as going from the bottom upwards, from body to mind: mind is nothing but an effect of the body. The hypophenomenalist reverses this, seeing the mind as having all the power, with the body as nothing but an effect. Accordingly, all diseases, and all health, are due to the mind alone. No reason to fear nuclear radiation if your soul is harmonious.

Whiteheadian thought rejects both of these extremes in favor of a multiplicity of levels of power. Each level, from electron to mind, has power—the immanent power of self-determination and the transitive power to influence other things. The *higher* individuals have *more power* than the lower ones, i.e., the mind has enormously more power than does an individual cell, and the cell much more than the individual molecule. But each *lower level* has *more members* than does the level above it. For example, the human mind interacts with several billion brain cells; each cell in turn contains myriad molecules; macromolecules in turn contain vast numbers of atoms; and each atom contains several subatomic entities. So it might be that each level has approximately the same amount of power.

In any case, neither the epiphenomenalist's reductionism nor the hypophenomenalist's "elevationism" is supported: the source of all problems cannot be relegated *a priori* either to molecules or to mind. The source can be at any level, so an empirical approach is required. Cancer in a given person might be due to bad attitudes (at the conscious or the unconscious level), or to bad diet, or to bad environment, or to all three. So a lasting cure might need to deal with one, two, or three sources of the problem.

Two other implications of this position should be mentioned, both having to do with "precision." In the modern period, real "knowledge" has been virtually equated with "science," and science has been closely associated with "precision." The term *exact sciences* is almost redundant: something is usually not considered a "science" unless it is exact or precise. Aside from the inanimate aggregates on which Galilean-Newtonian science is based, we can be most precise about the simplest individuals in nature. They have very little freedom, being mainly creatures of habit. Their behavior is therefore much more predictable than that of higher individuals, which are not so bound by the past. Learning how they have behaved in one situation gives us a good basis for predicting how they will behave in similar situations.

The crucial question then becomes: when are two situations similar? Is a cell in a human being in an environment similar to that of the same kind of cell in the body of a laboratory rat? Or in the body of a different human being with a different attitude toward life? Or in the body of the same human being ten years later, after a significant change in worldview? From a reductionistic, epiphenomenalist point of view, the answer would be "yes." But from the psychosomatic point of view suggested here, according to which the human psyche is the most powerful agent on earth, the answer would be "definitely not." This answer, if true, means that the precision often assumed for a purely biochemical approach to medicine is illusory.

For the molecules in the cells are influenced not only by other habit-bound entities but also by that agent which is not only the most powerful on earth but also the most unpredictable, the human soul. A procedure that works quite well with 15 people might fail miserably with the next.

In summary: the transition from the modern to a postmodern paradigm will not only resolve the theoretical mind-body problem. It will also allow the evidence of psychosomatic interaction to be taken seriously in the science of medicine, leading to significant modifications in both research and practice. Postmodern medicine will not relinquish the precision in the search for localized causes which is the glory of modern medicine; but it will include this virtue within a larger perspective which brings personal causation back into science, a development that will encourage the full recognition of individual differences, even at the level of biochemistry. Besides being more adequate in this respect, postmodern medicine will overcome the alienating depersonalization that has been the bane of modern medicine.

NOTES

1. In some contexts it is useful to distinguish mind from psyche or soul, using "mind" for the more conscious and intellectual functions of the psyche. In this essay, however, I use the terms interchangeably.

2. See Kenneth R. Pelletier, *Mind as Healer, Mind as Slayer: A Holistic Approach to Preventing Stress Disorders* (New York: Dell Publishing Co., 1977), including its extensive bibliography, and Jerome Frank, "Mind-Body Relations in Illness and Healing," *Journal of International Academy of Preventive Medicine* II/3 (1975), 46–59. For some more recent items, see the bibliography in Norman Cousins, *The Healing Heart: Antidotes to Panic and Helplessness* (New York: W. W. Norton & Co., 1983).

3. Norman Cousins, *The Healing Heart* and *Anatomy of an Illness as Perceived by the Patient* (New York: W. W. Norton & Co., 1979).

4. George Engel, "The Need for a New Medical Model: A Challenge for Biomedicine," *Science* 196 (April 8, 1977), 29–36.

5. *R F Illustrated* 3 (1976), 5; quoted by George Engel, *ibid.*

6. A holistic approach also stands in contrast with psychological approaches aimed only at the mind. However, this tendency has not been a major problem; Christian Science and other purely spiritual and psychological approaches to healing have been on the fringe. The reductionistic bias of modern culture militates against purely spiritual or mental approaches, leading us to suspect a physiological source for psychological difficulties, while not leading us to suspect a psychological source for most physiological difficulties. Psychiatrists have degrees in physiological medicine, while medical doctors need not have a psychological degree. Even clinical psychologists, who need not have physiological knowledge, are trained to suspect an organic cause and to make referrals.

7. Whitehead's most readable writings relevant to this issue are *The Function of Reason* (Princeton, N. J.: Princeton University Press, 1929); chaps. II, VII and VIII of *Modes of Thought* (The Macmillan Co., 1933); and Part III of *Adventures of Ideas* (New York: The Macmillan Co., 1933). His most sustained treatments of the body-mind relation are in chaps. 5, 6, and 9 of *Science and the Modern World* (New York: The Macmillan Co., 1926); Part III of *Religion in the Making* (New York: The Macmillan Co., 1926); and the chapters entitled "The Order of Nature" and "Organisms and Environment" in *Process and Reality*, corrected ed. (New York: Free Press, 1978).

8. Hartshorne's writings are legion. One of his most important essays on this topic is the "The Compound Individual," Otis H. Lee, ed., *Philosophical Essays for Alfred North Whitehead* (New York: Longmans Green, 1936), the viewpoint of which I presuppose throughout this essay as an interpretation of Whitehead's views. See also *Beyond Humanism: Essays in the New Philosophy of Nature* (New York: Willett, Clark, & Co., 1937), especially chaps. 8, 9, 11, and 12; and *The Logic of Perfection and Other Essays in Neoclassical Metaphysics* (Lasalle, Ill.: Open Court, 1962), chaps. 3, 6, 7, and 8.

9. For several versions and discussions of identism, see C. V. Borst, ed., *The Mind-Brain Identity Theory* (London: Macmillan Ltd., 1979).

10. There are some thinkers who call themselves *materialistic identists* but who hold that all matter has an inner, psychical aspect. They are not materialists as I am using the term, but panpsychists. See, for example, Bernard Rensch, "Arguments for Panpsychistic Identism," in John B. Cobb, Jr., and David Ray Griffin, *Mind in Nature: Essays on the Interface of Science and Philosophy* (Washington, D. C.: University Press of America, 1977), 70–78. I develop a panpsychist position in this essay, but one that does not lead to the conclusion that brain and mind are identical.

11. See Richard Rorty, "Mind-Body Identity, Privacy and Categories," in Borst, ed., *The Mind-Brain Identity Theory,* 187–213, and his later reflections, "Persons without Minds," chap. 11 of *Philosophy and the Mirror of Nature* (Princeton, N. J.: Princeton University Press, 1979), 70–127.

12. The term is Whitehead's. He lists "the doctrine of vacuous actuality" as one of the "prevalent habits of thought" that his philosophy of organism repudiates (*Process and Reality*, xiii; see also 29 and 167.).

13. Several historians of science are adopting the point of view expressed in this paragraph. See, for example, J. R. Ravetz, "The Varieties of Scientific Experience," in Arthur Peacocke, ed., *The Sciences and Theology in the Twentieth Century* (Notre Dame, Ind.: University of Notre Dame Press, 1981), 197–206; Frances Yates, *The Rosicrucian Enlightenment* (1972; Boulder, Co.: Shambhala, 1978), 266; Hugh Kearney, *Science and Change 1500–1700* (New York: McGraw-Hill, 1971), 48; Hugh Trevor-Roper, *The European Witch Craze of the Sixteenth and Seventeenth Centuries and Other Essays* (1956; New York: Harper & Row, 1969), 132; Margaret C. Jacob, *The Newtonians and the English Revolution 1689–1720* (Ithaca, N. Y.: Cornell University Press, 1976), 126 and *passim*; Carolyn Merchant, *The Death of Nature: Women, Ecology, and the Scientific Revolution* (San Francisco: Harper & Row, 1980), *passim*; Eugene Klaaren, *Religious Origins of Modern Science* (1977; Lanham, Md.: University Press of America, 1985).

OF MINDS AND MOLECULES

14. See Julius Adler and Wing-Wai Tse, "Decision-Making in Bacteria," *Science* 184 (June 21, 1974), 1292–94, and A. Goldbeter and D. E. Koshland, Jr., "Simple Molecular Model for Sensing and Adaptation Based on Receptor Modification with Application to Bacterial Chemotaxis," *Journal of Molecular Biology* 161/3 (1982), 395–416.

15. I employ this term as did Gilbert Ryle in *The Concept of Mind* (London: Hutchinson's University Library, 1949), but to make a quite different point.

16. Clark Hull, *Principles of Behavior: An Introduction to Behavior Theory* (New York: Appleton-Century, 1943), 27–28; quoted in Floyd Matson, *The Broken Image: Man, Science and Society* (Garden City, N. Y.: Doubleday and Co., 1966), 48.

17. John B. Watson, *Behaviorism* (1924; Chicago: University of Chicago Press, 1958), 5–6, emphasis added; quoted in Matson, *op. cit.*, 39.

18. For a scientist who agrees, see Donald R. Griffin, *The Question of Animal Awareness: Evolutionary Continuity of Mental Experience* (New York: Rockefeller University Press, 1976).

19. While this position, like dualism and unlike identism, distinguishes the mind or soul from the body, it differs from dualism in two major ways. First, it does not make "mind-stuff" different in kind from "brain-stuff"; mind and brain cells are both composed of experience. Second, the mutual causal relation between the mind and its brain is not the mutually external relation usually connoted by the term *interaction*. Rather, each occasion of experience belonging to the mind is internally constituted by its appropriation of the brain-cell experiences in their objective or superjective mode. That is, the brain cells do not simply evoke our experience, they become part of it, they constitute it: the many (brain cells and other things) literally *become* one (our momentary partly self-determining experience). The same is true in reverse, as our experience becomes a superject partly constituting the experiences of our neurons.

20. Ian Barbour has made this suggestion; *Issues in Science and Religion* (Englewood Cliffs, N. J.: Prentice-Hall, 1966), 295–99, 333.

21. A. N. Whitehead, *Science and the Modern World* (The Macmillan Co., 1926), 115–16, 150, 161–62.

NOTES ON CONTRIBUTORS
AND CENTERS

DAVID BOHM is the author of *Causality and Chance in Modern Physics* and *Wholeness and the Implicate Order*. He is professor emeritus of theoretical physics at the Department of Physics, Birkbeck College, University of London, London WC1E 7HX, England.

CHARLES BIRCH is author of *Nature and God* and (with John B. Cobb, Jr.) *The Liberation of Life: From the Cell to the Community*. He is Challis Professor of Biology emeritus from the University of Sydney, and now receives mail at 5a/73 Yarranabbe Road, Darling Point, New South Wales 2027, Australia.

JOHN B. COBB, JR., is coauthor of *Process Theology, The Liberation of Life, Christian Identity and Theological Education* and coeditor of *Mind in Nature*. He teaches at the School of Theology at Claremont and Claremont Graduate School and is Director of the Center for Process Studies, 1325 North College, Claremont, California 91711.

FREDERICK FERRÉ is author of *Basic Modern Philosophy of Religion* and *Shaping the Future: Resources for the Postmodern World*. He is chairman of the Department of Philosophy, University of Georgia, Athens, Georgia 30602.

DAVID RAY GRIFFIN is the author of *God, Power, and Evil* and editor of *Physics and the Ultimate Significance of Time* and (with John B. Cobb, Jr.) *Mind in Nature*. He is professor of philosophy of religion at the School of Theology at Claremont and Claremont Graduate School, founding president of the Center for a Postmodern World in Santa Barbara, and executive director of the Center for Process Studies, 1325 North College, Claremont, California 91711.

WILLIS W. HARMAN is author of *An Incomplete Guide to the Future* and (with Herbert Rheingold) *Higher Creativity*. He is the founder of the Futures Research Group at Stanford University and president of the Institute of Noctic Scicnccs, 475 Gatc Fivc Road, Suitc 300, Sausalito, California 49465.

STANLEY KRIPPNER is editor of the series *Advances in Parapsychological Research*, and author of *Song of the Siren* and (with A. D. Feinstein) *The Psychology of Constructing Reality*. He is past president of the Association for Humanistic Psychology and the Parapsychological Association and is the director of the Center for Consciousness Studies, Saybrook Institute, 1772 Vallejo Street, San Francisco, California 94123.

RUPERT SHELDRAKE is author of *A New Science of Life* and *The Presence of the Past*. He has been director of studies in biochemistry and cell biology at Clare College, Cambridge, a research fellow of the Royal Society, and research scientist at an institute in India. He resides at 20 Willow Road, Hampstead, London NW3 1TJ, England.

BRIAN SWIMME is author of *The Universe is a Green Dragon*. Educated as a physicist, he teaches courses in cosmology at the Institute in Culture and Creation Spirituality, Holy Names College, Oakland, California 94619.

This series is published under the auspices of the Center for a Postmodern World and the Center for Process Studies.

The Center for a Postmodern World is an independent nonprofit organization in Santa Barbara, California, founded by David Ray Griffin. It promotes the awareness and exploration of the postmodern worldview and encourages reflection about a postmodern world, from postmodern art, spirituality, and education to a postmodern world order, with all this implies for economics, ecology, and security. One of its major projects is to produce a collaborative study that marshals the numerous facts supportive of a postmodern worldview and provides a portrayal of a postmodern world order toward which we can realistically move. It is located at 2060 Alameda Padre Serra, Suite 101, Santa Barbara, California 93103.

The Center for Process Studies is a research organization affiliated with the School of Theology at Claremont and Claremont University Center and Graduate School. It was founded by John B. Cobb, Jr., Director, and David Ray Griffin, Executive Director. It encourages research and reflection upon the process philosophy of Alfred North Whitehead, Charles Hartshorne, and related thinkers, and upon the application and testing of this viewpoint in all areas of thought and practice. This center sponsors conferences, welcomes visiting scholars to use its library, and publishes a scholarly journal, *Process Studies*, and a quarterly *Newsletter*. It is located at 1325 North College, Claremont, California 19711.

Both centers gratefully accept (tax–deductible) contributions to support their work.

INDEX